W9-CQM-168

# NEW ORLEANS STYLE

*Cover photograph: Bill Russell about to interview Willie Parker for the Tulane Jazz Archives (photo courtesy of the Ford Foundation)*

*Opposite: The Imperial Orchestra (c.1905). Left to right: John MacMurray, George Filhe, Jimmy Palao, Big Eye Louis Nelson, René Baptiste, Manuel Perez and Jimmy Brown.*

*Back cover: Bill Russell with his research files (photo: Floyd Levin)*

# NEW ORLEANS STYLE

## by Bill Russell

Compiled and edited by

**Barry Martyn** & **Mike Hazeldine**

# *To Bill*

Jazzology Press
1206 Decatur Street, New Orleans, LA 70116, U.S.A.
© 1994 by Jazzology Press, New Orleans

All rights reserved.
First printing October 1994
Printed in the United States of America by Wendel Printing, New Orleans, Louisiana


Library of Congress Cataloging-in-Publication Data

New Orleans Style / Bill Russell / Barry Martyn / Mike Hazeldine

Biography: p.


1. Jazz musicians – United States

Russell, Bill. 1905-1992.
Martyn, Barry. 1941-    .
Hazeldine, Mike.  1940 -     .

Library of Congress No 94-079279

ISBN 0-9638890-1-X

# FOREWORD

I am pleased that the book on *New Orleans Style* which my brother, Bill Russell, had planned to write has come to fruition through the efforts of Barry Martyn and Mike Hazeldine. For several years when I visited Bill he talked about his goal to write four books: "Jelly Roll Morton's Scrapbook", "New Orleans Style", "Bunk Johnson", and "Manetta". In a fifty-four page "Letter of Last Instruction" to me, Bill listed all four of the books and detailed plans for writing them. I urged him to concentrate on his writings but he could not bring himself to turn away anyone who came to seek information or talk about New Orleans music. I believe that he realized that he would not live long enough to finish the four books and I tried to get him to tell me who he thought could take the material and do justice in writing it. Probably not wishing to acknowledge that he would not complete the books, he did not suggest anyone to do the job – possibly since he had never felt any book he had seen on jazz met his standards or expectations.

After thirty years, shortly before his death, he finally completed his book on Jelly Roll. Within a week he started on the *New Orleans Style* book. I helped him sort out the interviews and tapes that he planned to use in the book and typed the chapter on "Chinee" Foster for him. After Bill's death, in going through his material on the *New Orleans Style* book I found not only the outline of the book but a copy of his introduction. I was so moved by the introduction and the outline, that I knew that the book had to be written

After much thought and discussions with others, I approached Barry Martyn, because I knew Bill had full confidence in him and my contacts were all favorable. I also knew that Bill thought highly of Mike Hazeldine when I observed them during my visits to New Orleans. The thing that has impressed me most is the diligence Barry and Mike devoted to the project. When they said they would complete it in two years, I was convinced they were totally unrealistic, so now I am resigned to "eat crow" and congratulate them for producing a book that I feel is faithful to Bill's intentions.

William Wagner
Lexington, Kentucky.
January 1994

# Editor's Preface

I had been aware that Bill Russell had been working on a book on *New Orleans Style* for many years. It took second place to his book on Jelly, of this there was no doubt. About four months before he died he asked me to look over his finished chapter on Abby "Chinee" Foster. Prior to this I had read through his Baby Dodds chapters, but that was in 1961. The pages on "Chinee" were wonderful and I told him so. He showed me his outline for the book (reproduced here on page 10) and I imagine he knew he would never complete the work. Since I had been working with him on the presentation of his American Music recordings for the past few years I guess I was the natural choice to complete the "Style" book.

After Bill's death, his brother William asked me if I would finish the "Style" book and naturally I agreed. It was an important document and I couldn't wait to get to work on it. It would be grand to listen to the likes of Roy Palmer, Lawrence Duhé, Omer Simeon and so many more, pour out their life stories. "Brother Bill" had already sorted out most of the tapes from which I worked, but I realized that there was a monumental task ahead. Possibly too much for one man. I made a call to my life-long friend, Mike Hazeldine, in England to ask if he would work on it with me. He readily agreed and we set six weeks aside of that year to get it together.

When Mike arrived that October we reviewed the project and the decision was made to present the work in the exact format that Bill had intended. There seemed no need to deviate from his plan. Some years earlier Bill had written the first draft of the introduction, which was about the most concise description of the "style" of New Orleans jazz that I had ever read. (An extract from this was included in Bill Carter's *Preservation Hall* book). We reproduce it here overleaf in its entirety.

The rest was just a matter of working odd hours to get it done. Since we had only one typewriter I worked from five a.m. to noon and Mike from then till dark, but we got the project finished in two years and you have it now.

While we have remained faithful to Bill's intentions, we left out Jelly from the plan because Bill had his own book coming out on Morton. We saw no need for duplication. We did, however, add short chapters on Louis Keppard and Lawrence Duhé from material in Bill's files. Elsewhere in the book, 'Tudi' Garland and Roy Palmer had discussed the show they appeared in with Mamie E. Lane. We felt that the opportunity to add these additional recollections was too good to miss.

Most of the introductions on each musician had already been written. He had also selected most of the photographs, but we added a few that seemed pertinent. I did the short piece on the seating of New Orleans bands because I knew what Bill was trying to say. We had discussed this many times.

All in all, this is Bill Russell's book, not ours, and speaking for myself, it was a pleasure to bring to publication.

Barry Martyn
New Orleans, Louisiana. 1994

# EDITOR'S PREFACE

During the time I was compiling the book, *Bill Russell's American Music*, Bill often spoke of his plans for the *New Orleans Style* book. One afternoon we examined the boxes of tapes, photographs and other material he had collected. Although most of the tapes had been recorded over thirty years earlier, his enthusiasm for the project was undiminished. He was determined that the thoughts and values of the musicians who pioneered the music should be passed on to future generations. There seemed no doubt in his mind that he would soon begin work on the book, although he was aware that his failing health might mean that he would never finish it.

When, in January 1992, he finally completed his *Jelly Roll Morton Scrapbook*, he earnestly began concentrating his energies on this new project. As I was due to return to New Orleans in October, it was agreed that I should assist him in exchange for the time spent correcting my *American Music* book. Sadly, Bill died before this reciprocation could be realised. I was therefore delighted when Barry asked me to work with him on the completion of this book.

The opportunity to listen to so many legendary musicians was too good to miss. It quickly became apparent, however, while listening to these tapes, that the musicians sometimes had differing recollections of their career details, when compared to previously published sources. There is consistency, however, in the pride in their origins, the high regard they felt towards many fellow-musicians, and the quality of the music that was uniquely of New Orleans. While we must be grateful for the wonderful music that has been recorded, there are sadly too few records which give any real indication of the sounds and musical standards to which these musicians refer. It was Bill's hope that their recollections would give us a better insight into New Orleans music – that "New Orleans style." We have, therefore, remained faithful to the original material as it was recorded, despite certain seeming contradictions and inconsistencies.

In compiling the chapters, we have drawn only from material that Bill had collected for the project. Most of these were taped interviews which he had specifically made for the book in the late 1950s and early 1960s. In a couple of cases we also supplemented the interviews from other material that Bill had collected or transcribed.

It has been a privilege to work on this book and the time spent listening to, transcribing and editing the tapes produced some of the most rewarding hours I have ever spent. Barry and I have worked on many projects since the early 1960s, but this book has been our most satisfying collaboration. We are grateful to the Hogan Jazz Archives at Tulane University, and especially The Historic New Orleans Collection for permission to reproduce photographs from the William Russell Collection, Chas Hudson for proof reading the final draft and to Peter Horsfield for compiling the index. We are indebited to Bill Wagner for his faith in us to complete his brother's work, but most of all to Bill Russell, for initiating it.

Mike Hazeldine
Manchester, England. 1994

# New Orleans Style

## by Bill Russell

At the dawn of this century a new music was born in New Orleans. It was a "good time" music, to make the people happy. Its appeal was so immediate that the music soon swept the whole country and then circled the globe. It was not so much a kind of music as a style of playing. Essentially it was simply a way of "playing a melody with a beat." New Orleans musicians learned to work together to produce the loose relaxed beat which is so irresistible that one cannot help but dance, or at least sway and pat one's foot to its swing. The easy going, almost hypnotic rhythm at times seems to run effortlessly by itself.

In this style of music, where all the musicians strive to help each other rather than grab the spotlight, it is natural for improvised ensemble choruses to be a feature. Working together harmoniously can generate a feeling of power. The ensembles often build with cumulative effect and surging momentum to thrilling climaxes.

New Orleans musicians seem by nature to be a friendly lot. It takes only a minute to get to know true New Orleans musicians. The friendly warmth and enthusiasm with which they work together is part of their life. Their audiences cannot help having a good time, because the band is having such a grand time.

In New Orleans style the melody is always to be clearly heard. The melody is never disguised but is sung by the various instruments with a beautiful vocal-like warmth. As one New Orleans trumpeter expressed it, the idea is to "play pretty for all the people." The tune is not obscured by harmonic padding and complicated arrangements, for these musicians know that the secret of true excellence in music, as in life itself, lies in simplicity. New Orleans style has never encouraged the hectic rushing and frantic, hysterical screaming that passes for jazz in many places. Instead, moderate, relaxed tempos to which people can dance or march, even in a hot climate, are chosen. New Orleans music has always been functional. To this day the business cards of most musicians read: "Music For All Occasions" – not just dances, parties and parades, but for everything from christenings and dedications, to funerals.

A New Orleans "band of music" can be of any size and instrumentation. Traditionally, the groups most favored have consisted of five to seven pieces with a more or less standard instrumentation. Each instrument has its own special role in building the final musical structure. Usually the trumpet (or cornet) is the musical, if not nominal, leader. He will call the tunes, except for requests; he stomps off the tempo to start the band; but mainly he plays or rather <u>sings</u> the melody (the "lead") in as beautiful and expressive manner as possible and helps drive along the rhythm of the band. The trombone, big brother of the trumpet, also can sing a melody or a countermelody. Often he punches out a bass-like rhythmic part and utilizes the unique sliding (glissando) feature of his instrument. The clarinet, most expressive of all the woodwind family, can sing voluptuously in the lower register or slash out dynamically in the upper register, but mostly the agile clarinet is used to "variate" and embellish the melodic line. Although all the "blowing instruments" of a New Orleans band are responsible for their share of the bouncy, pulsating drive, several other instruments are specifically charged with supplying the steady fundamental beat of the band.

The drummer, of course, is the "time keeper" as well as the rhythmic powerhouse of the group. He can also control the dynamics of the band and inspire its performance and spirit. Historically, the pianist of the New Orleans band has frequently been a girl. Capable of playing melodies as well as chording along in a harmonic accompaniment, the pianist can also double as a vocalist. The banjoist can play melodies with striking sonorities but is most useful in producing the regular rhythmic pulse and harmonic chordal foundation. The bass viol, (in modern times) mostly plucked and slapped rather than bowed, can help produce a terrific swing and bounce in a band.

The repertoire of a New Orleans traditional band is mightily varied. There are always a few old standards such as *High Society* and *Panama* which stem from the parade marches, cakewalks and rags of a bygone era, but there are also the popular songs of today and yesterday, the sentimental tunes the people love to sing and dance to, which are transformed by the New Orleans idiom. Usually they play a few hymns, including the ever present *Saints* and *Closer Walk.* Then there is often some folk-based music material such as the charming and lively Creole songs based on New Orleans' French and Spanish heritage, and there is always an assortment of blues, ranging from slow moaning chants to the fast stomp-like numbers or "joys."

Always the music speaks directly and simply – and at times even eloquently with heartfelt emotion – to its audience.

---

Old music is coming back today. In New Orleans "spiritual pieces" were used in brass bands as well as orchestras. The blues . . . that's the home of the blues, New Orleans and we knew nothing else but the blues sometimes.

Most of the New Orleans musicians, even if they don't see each other daily, or even if they've been away 15 to 20 years, you can still get them together and they can always play together. **Bunk Johnson**

# Contents

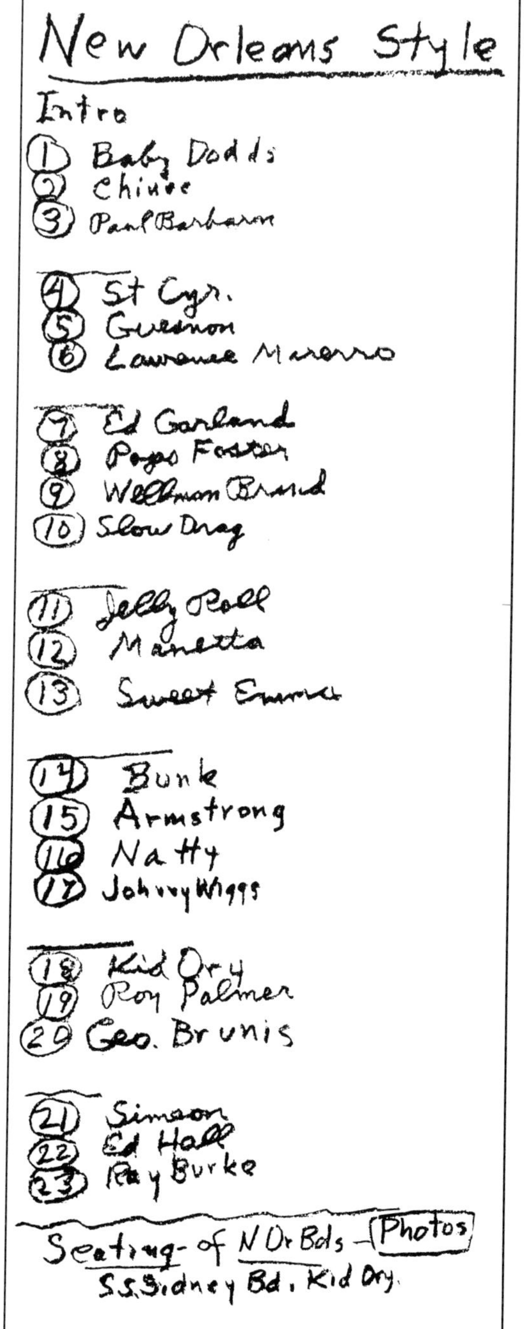

New Orleans Style

Intro
1. Baby Dodds
2. Chinee
3. Paul Barbarin

4. St Cyr.
5. Guesnon
6. Lawrence Marrero

7. Ed Garland
8. Pops Foster
9. Wellman Braud
10. Slow Drag

11. Jelly Roll
12. Manetta
13. Sweet Emma

14. Bunk
15. Armstrong
16. Natty
17. Johnny Wiggs

18. Kid Ory
19. Roy Palmer
20. Geo. Brunis

21. Simeon
22. Ed Hall
23. Ray Burke

Seating of N Or Bds — Photos
S.S. Sidney Bd. Kid Ory.

*Bill Russell's handwritten plan for the book.*

# New Orleans Style: Drums

# BABY DODDS

| | |
|---|---|
| Warren Dodds | Born: New Orleans, Louisiana, December 24, 1898 |
| drums | Died: Chicago, Illinois, February 14, 1959 |

*In 1912, Baby took drum lessons from Dave Perkins, then studied with Walter Brundy and Louis Cottrell. He played street parades with Bunk Johnson and Jack Carey, and dances with Willie Hightower, Frankie Duson, Manuel Manetta and Papa Celestin. In 1918 he joined Fate Marable on the S.S. Sidney, and in 1922 he joined King Oliver's band in San Francisco. He moved to Chicago with Oliver in 1923, and from 1924 worked with Freddie Keppard, Willie Hightower, Lil Armstrong and Charlie Elgar. He recorded a series of wonderful sides with King Oliver, Louis Armstrong, Jelly Roll Morton, and his brother, Johnny Dodds. From 1927 he mainly worked in small groups with Johnny Dodds, until his death in 1940. He recorded with Bunk Johnson in 1944/5, and appeared with the band in New York. Baby remained in New York, working with Art Hodes and appearing on the "This is Jazz" broadcasts. After a brief tour of Europe in 1948, the following year he suffered a stroke. In the early '50s he worked occasionally with Natty Dominique in Chicago, then at Jimmy Ryan's in New York, but was forced to quit playing in 1957. Baby Dodds is widely considered to be the greatest of all the New Orleans drummers. His autobiography, "The Baby Dodds Story" was published shortly after his death.*

## CHAPTER 1

Drums are essential, and before I will call you a drummer, you have got to drum as though they are essential. Now, there's more besides drumming than just beating. As a drummer, it's my job to know what that part is. I have got to find it.

I have the deepest study in mind – even a spirit study. I know that sounds very funny to some drummers to hear me say "spirit", but drumming is spirit. You have got to have that in your body, in your soul. And it can't be an evil spirit. It's got to be a good spirit, because music is no good if you're evil.

If you're evil, you are going to drum evil, and when you drum evil you're going to put evil in somebody else's mind, and the first thing you know, that somebody'll put the evil in somebody else's mind. Well, what kind of a band have you got? Nothing but an evil spirit band. Now, if a spirit is good, any good spirit will dwell with good spirits. And God help a bad spirit band!

When you are happy, you can pretty near wash the glumness out of someone else. If a group hasn't got harmony or brotherly love, laughter, and happiness of heart, well, you haven't got a good group.

If you hear a band play without drums, there's something lacking. In any organization I've played with, I felt that the drums were just as important as any other instrument. I feel that everybody that's working in a group is needed there. They should not feel like individuals, but always part of the group. No one can do anything by themselves.

Play for the benefit of the band. Oh, how I wish the young drummers today would feel that their part is to help the other fellow, not make him play himself to death or make him play something that he don't want to play. Their place is to help. Without help there is no band. Without a drummer that knows how to help, it's no band. Because, I know. I've heard some bands that's got some very good musicians sound bad. Why? One man, the drummer, started all the trouble.

Study a guy's human nature. Study his nature and just about what he will go for. You've got to study up something that will make the men work. When I sit down with a band, that's what I hunt for.

When a band is playing an ensemble, I find the kick to send them off with. I find something. Now, unless a drummer can find those things, well, he don't even talk to me as a drummer. Because I know he is not.

You see a band dead, a drummer can liven up everybody, make everybody have a different spirit. And a bad drummer can make everybody pretty angry, too. It's up to the drummer to keep everything lively. That's his job.

When I play in a band, I work with every man, feel them all out, because they all belong to me. I feel I'm the key man in that band and it's up to me to make them all feel like playing. Even if it's no more than joking with them. Joke along with a band, and you have somebody with a grin on their face, instead of a frown. Pass a word along and somebody will feel good. Well, all that helps their spirit.

So, that's the drummer's job, to keep the spirit up. He hasn't got anything in his mouth, so he can keep that spirit of chatter all the time in the band, not loud enough to ruin the music, but loud enough that somebody can hear. And it'll go around. His job is to keep everybody joyful, keep everybody playing, keep everybody's mind on what they're doing.

It's like a pitcher and a catcher. Now, you'd wonder why does a catcher go out to a pitcher and talk to him on the mound, and the pitcher never comes in and talks to the catcher. Because the catcher has got this pitcher in mind, to know exactly what to do for him to not get excited. Well, that's like my job.

In drumming, you've got to pay attention to each and every one. You must hear that person distinctly and hear what he goes for. You've got to give that beat to him. If he don't like that, if he doesn't get going, give him something else. In that way, you keep your band smooth, keep your band jumping and keep everybody lively.

When each man has a solo, I give him a different beat. It may sound to someone that's listening, even close by, like the same, but it's not. It has a different sound to it. At the end of each solo, I give some kind of indication that something new is coming.

In other words, if a guy is going to come in, I give him something to come in on, and it makes it different from the fellow that just got through. It's up to the drummer to make a distinction of some sort to indicate that a change is coming. Just like you would say, "What'll we do next?" And someone says, "Well, I'll tell you."

It's an indication that something different, someone else, is coming in with a solo. When I make the change, near the end of the chorus, it's got to be different because I've changed it. And you can feel the change. Even if you don't hear it, you can feel it. It's up to the drummer to make the changes.

If you go along, beat, beat, beat, right straight on, it don't give you anything to look forward to. But when you make something a little different in there, somebody says, "What's coming up now?" Then they hear the clarinet, or trombone, or some new soloist come in.

I don't make a finish exactly, but I make, abruptly, something different, so it makes the change very distinct.

When you're working with your companions, you got to be thinking all the time. It don't mean for you to beat louder than the solo. It means for you to keep down. If it's a clarinet or piano, you must keep lower.

Those things, some drummers don't think about. They beat the same way if it's a clarinet playing, or a piano playing. They beat just the same. Well, that don't make sense.

Nobody wants the same beat all the time. The band's got no pep that way.

So, that's my idea of changing like that – it's for the benefit of the band. Now, that's a study I had to pick up myself. No one told me that. No one showed me how. It was just what I had to do, for a band won't sound good if the drummer is just beating, and has no spirit.

That's why all guys are not drummers that's drumming.

But you've got to use diplomacy. I couldn't sit here and talk to you if it wasn't about something you would understand or be interested in. It's the same thing with a band. Always study the interests of the men and their nature, or you won't get any work out of them.

You can't holler at a man. You can't dog him. Not in music.

I try to work all the time with my fellow man. I want to see him happy, same as I. And then, when you work in harmony with your band, the people who are dancing or listening will have the same reaction.

# CHAPTER 2

Music has been my life, going back to the time when me and my brother John were two little mischievous kids running along with the second line at parades in New Orleans.

Back in those days we used to buy tin whistles from the bottle man who come around every other day for bottles which we would collect to trade him for the whistles and candy.

Whatever Johnny got into, well, it wouldn't be long 'til I'd be into it. And if I would start something, there he'd be. One time Johnny got a tin flute from the bottle man. It had six holes and he was blowing around, playing little things on it. Our Dad said if he wanted to play those things on a real instrument, what would it be? Johnny said, "Clarinet." Dad said he ought to have a real one, and he bought one for him.

That was about 1909 and I was just a little fellow, but I wanted to learn an instrument too. John was playing 'round, different places, getting paid ice cream and cake, and I would have to sit and look. Sometimes I didn't even get to go along. I said, "Oh, no! That don't go." I thought they should invite the baby.

Johnny was taking clarinet lessons. He studied with Luis "Papa" Tio and Charlie

McCurdy and he was an apt pupil.

I picked up that I wanted to drum. I got me some tin cans and cut rounds out of my mother's chair. I shaped them up like drum sticks. I commenced to beating with my heel on anything that was solid and would give tone. Then I got a lard can and put a lot of holes in it. I put some ten-a-penny nails in it. Not the large ten-a-penny nails – the small ten-a-penny nails. It sounded all right, so I beat on that lard can for a long time.

I was still beating on that lard can when we moved across Lake Ponchartrain to Waveland, Mississippi. I was in good then. I will say it the way it was. We had a "back house" there and the baseboard had a deep hollow sound. I would take my lard can out there and beat it and kick my heel on that baseboard. The tin can was the snare drum, baseboard was bass drum.

Sometimes Johnny would stand outside the door, playing his clarinet. I'd be inside and my tone would come out, big.

I started asking Dad to buy me a real drum set and he would say he thought I could make enough noise. The last time I ask' him, he said, "Daddy is sorry, Baby, but Christmas is coming and I have too many things to buy." I wanted him to buy my instrument so much because it hurt me to think he bought one for Johnny and not me.

Over the lake where I was, on the Gulf Coast, I couldn't get any work, so I had to come to New Orleans to get me a job at the Mentes bag factory. From then on, I worked and got my drums myself, piece by piece and stick by stick. They were second hand, from a pawn shop, but I loved them just as well as if they had been brand new.

Dave Perkins was my first music teacher. When I started with him, he ordered me, special, to work with the drum pad only. And, when he changed me off the drum pad, I taken just the snare drum – no bass drum. His advice to me was to never use the bass drum until he'd tell me. But, it was so long – I did a little dirty trick and used the bass drum when I got home by myself. I thought I got along real wonderful and Dave showed me how to do different things, like the rudiments. I stayed with him for a year.

There were two men I used to love to hear play drums in parades and other places around. They were Louis Cottrell and MacMurray. The man who first inspired me for drummin' was John MacMurray. I wish I could have drummed like him and then added my little bit. He was a very tall fellow, not too heavy. Kinda spare made man.

MacMurray used heavy ebony sticks. His roll was so perfect, I tried to pattern my roll after his. He used a single head snare drum like I started with. I tried to get everything like the man. He had a rope bass drum and so that's what I had. By that, you know I tried to get everything like him. And, I tried to play like him, but uh-uh. I wasn't versatile enough to do that. And, then I had to shift into my way. And "my way" is the way I'm playing today. Some people call it "old style," but, if nobody else can do it, I don't think it's "old style."

After I got a little further advanced, I left Dave Perkins and went to study with Louis Cottrell. He was a Creole fellow, and one of the nervous types. If you'd make one beat that he didn't tell you to make, oh! he'd frown at you and snatch your sticks out of your hand. That sort of thing. I felt that was almost a whipping for me.

Louis Cottrell would show you how to hold your sticks, how your hands must be level, and the holding up of your hands. That's why I'm light handed now. Cottrell was a very powerful, big fellow, but he was a light handed man. Oh, my, but he had some wrists!

He would never demonstrate anything on the drum or the pad. He'd demonstrate it sometime in his hand. He'd tell you and show you how his wrists was supple, show you how he worked his fingers, show you how he'd manipulate from one roll into another. Like that. But he never touched a drum pad. He left that to you.

I was a very poor reader of music when I went to Cottrell. About 1914, I had a chance to go to Chicago with Tig Chambers' band, but I was afraid to go after Cottrell told me, "Boy, don't go to Chicago. You've got to learn how to read music, got to play shows, and you've got to play everything. I don't think you're ready." So, I was afraid of Chicago and they took Tubby Hall's brother, Minor Hall.

I stayed in New Orleans and did a lot of street work with Bunk Johnson's Eagle Band, doing parades.

Our marching bands were only nine or ten men. When we had twelve men, we had a large band. Most of our brass bands consisted of nine men. Back then we never called them "marching bands", just "brass bands."

The usual band of nine men consisted of one trombone, tuba, baritone, alto, two cornets, E-flat clarinet, a snare drum and a bass drum. Sometimes the band would have only one trumpet. Sometimes we had two trombones.

Parade line-up of these bands was as thus: Trombone or trombones carried the front. Then came the tuba. Behind the tuba would come the baritone, then the alto and clarinet. Behind them came the cornets. Most of the time we used two cornets. Then came the snare drum and the bass drum. The men usually marched two abreast. The snare drum was to the left side, in order to carry a brighter tone to the outside.

The bass drum was opposite the snare drum to bring up the rear. That way you would have all your heavy blowing instruments, such as tuba and trombone, to carry the front. That balanced the whole thing.

The bass drummer had a cymbal attached, hand high, to the top of his drum. It was part of his job to hit this cymbal with a wire beater. He would have both hands going.

And the snare drummer – well! He really had work to do. He had to play what the band was playin'. Then, when the band would stop, he'd have to beat time for them to march to. And that meant that he kept going continuously. It was a pretty big job for one man. I got used to that like it was play. It was fun for me. I used to beat the snare drum in a way that was very lively. The guys would march by my snare drum just as good as with the whole band playing.

I'm sorry not all my friends heard me drum in the street. People got a kick out of it. I used to have my second line with the snare drum, just the same as the bunch did with the band. I used to like that. More guys would drop back by the snare drum after the band got through playing! And, I'd come on through. It was a lot of fun.

When those bands of only nine men began to play, you'd wonder how in the world a nine-piece brass band could play the music that those fellows played. And if we would have a larger band, why, somebody was going to loaf.

A lot of people ask about a funeral march. In the funeral marches, the snare drummer carries the whole responsibility. The simple reason is, he beats time for them to walk to when the band isn't playing. And he's got to break the time, because you don't walk as slow after you get through playing as when you're playing. Then, after you've walked at a certain little brisk pace, you break that time down to a very slow walk, and the bass drum comes in with a last, slow beat. And the band comes in and keeps that beat on through the funeral number that they are playing. After that very slow march, the snare drum picks up the marching time again – not too fast, but just fast enough for a guy not to burn himself out.

For a funeral, you would take the snares off. Or, if you couldn't get them off, you'd put a handkerchief in the snares, to muffle the drum. I've done that many a time. In ordinary parades, you have to have your snares on so you can hear the snare part. The weather you walk in could bring the snare drum up so high that the snares won't make the right sound. You have got to be adjusting them practically all day.

When it rained during a funeral march, if you'd happen to have a silk hand-kerchief, you'd spread it over the batter head and go right to work. A cotton hand-kerchief would soak up too much rain. It would get too heavy and would deaden the tone.

In the old days, we never used the rubber covers against rain. They are too heavy and the drum does not respond through them.

At a funeral, after they put the man in the ground, they say, "Ashes to ashes . . ." Well, that's the drummer's cue, right then, for him to get out of there. Alone, the snare drummer goes out in the middle of the street and starts a roll. He rolls loud enough that they can hear that roll within a block of where he is. Or, I'll say, half a block. When you're rolling loud, in the street, you can hear that drum on a clear day for about a block. That was my job – to get out and roll and call the band. Nobody called the band but the drummer. The snare drum alone.

And, you could see guys jumping over graves and jumping coming out of people's houses, or out of bar-rooms, and oh, just flying. It used to give me so much pleasure to see those guys that over-stayed themselves and came out running, some of them with a sandwich in their hand, their jaws all sticking out, some guys with an apple in their hand or a banana. They are peeling a banana, trying to chew fast and get it down. Some guys with some whiskey in their hand, and some guys might be kissing a woman, saying, "I'll see yuh, s'long, good-bye." And then, the door, "Slam! Bam!" See him running down the steps. Some guys with no hat on. They'd left their uniform caps behind. They had to go back and get it. Oh, it was a lot of fun.

Then, they all line up from the drum. Wherever I'm standing, they line up from me. The bass drummer'll get on the right. The lead trumpet gets on the right. Second trumpet will get on the left. And, they line up like that from the drums, to the front.

The minute the Grand Marshall put his hand up and the beat would come down – get walking! If you don't start on the right foot, you are out of step. Some fellows will hit off on the left foot. That's the wrong foot. You hit off with the right foot. That's your first step. Right, left, right, left, right, left. You see more guys skipping and hopping, trying to get in step. It's a very peculiar thing, and it's fun to see some guy out, tryin' to get in.

When you come out in the street to join the band, you'd better get to walking correct before you get in there. And, you can't play, off-step. If you are out of step when you hit your stride, you can't half play, because you are going to be off-beat. It's the stride that you walk in that puts you in the right beat. It's all taken from the snare drum. Not the bass drum, the snare drum. It's the snare drum keeps everybody in line. He can make them walk fast, or he can make them walk slow. He can beat so fast, he can practically make them run.

# CHAPTER 3

Walter Brundy was my last teacher. What a good teacher and what a man! Now, when I went to Walter, I was using the two drums. No more drum pad then. He showed me position and how to sit comfortable and how to hold my hands so they wouldn't drop. And, to sit erect. And to sit in a chair that you can have comfort.

And, that's got a lot to do with drummin'. Sittin' comfortable and knowing what you're goin' after. Now as far as your sitting at a set of drums, you must sit on a level with your drum. Mustn't sit perched up beyond or below. You must sit on a level with your drums, so you can have ever'thing in response, spontaneous, so you can go at them with ease. You don't raise the sticks 'way up over your head but hit nothing. You raise them, I'd say shoulder level, to reach those things.

When a drummer sits too high, he's got to peck down on the drums. But, when he's sitting level with his drums, he's just got to reach his arms out, that's all and pull 'em back. And, so, I think that's the most comfortable way to drum that I found.

The way the other drummers do today, sittin' way up high on snare drum cases and on sets made to prop themselves way up, it isn't likely that they can do a good job. Something is going to go lacking. A drummer's not supposed to be seen; he's supposed to be heard! I think they will accomplish a lot more if they are not sitting 'way up high, making a show. You haven't got to take my word. Try it yourself. Try sitting lower, if you have been sitting high. You'll get more results.

I had a little incident happened with Brundy, when I was on the steamboat, "St. Paul", with the Streckfus line. Walter came up the river playing on the "J.S.", which was a sister boat to the "St. Paul". When they got to St. Louis, the boss told him, "Well, you go on the other boat and hear a real drummer." Which was me.

And, when he came over, he's sittin' there, and we started to work. I didn't pay no attention to him, and then, I looked around and saw it was Walter Brundy, and I says, "What's the idea?" He says, "Well, the boss told me to sit over here and watch you. You was a real drummer, and that's why I had to drum like you."

Actually I was scared to death. I was just actually afraid. 'Cause I know, Brundy was my teacher. I told the boss, I say, "I can't drum with him." He said, "Well, never you mind that. You just go ahead and drum. And that is the way I want him to drum. Like you. Or else there's no place that he can drum on my boat."

So, from that, Walter quit the drummin' business. I think he sold his drums. And, he went back to New Orleans and picked up clarinet. You know he must have been a pretty finished musician to jump from drums to clarinet.

But he was a great drummer and a great teacher. I got my finishing touches from Walter Brundy, although, as I went along in years, I didn't follow all his teaching. I did things and worked things out the way I thought best. That's why I was even different from Walter, and he was my teacher. I was even different from he. I advise any drummer to go along with his teacher until he feels that he's qualified and then, follow a style of his own, be hisself, and no one else.

It was my teacher, Brundy, who first told me that the drummer's job is to make each man in the band feel the music and play his best. Brundy taught me to read music, but I wasn't a sight reader until I went on the boat, where they had rehearsals and hard music to play. If a piece of music is hard, it will make you think more.

All the Streckfus excursion boats had bands. When I first started working on the boats, late in 1918, they had two boats on the river. When I left, in September 1921, they had four steamers. Their names were: "St. Paul", "Sidney", "J.S.", and "Capitol."

Fate Marable was the leader of the band on the "St. Paul." He had been working on the boats for years, playing piano and calliope. Pops Foster, the bass player, was the one who got me the job. We got Louis Armstrong to leave Kid Ory's band and come on the boat with us.

When Louis first came on the boat, he used to wear jumpers, starched and ironed. That's the top part of coveralls. Louis had a double breasted one with buttons on both sides, way up to his neck. It had been washed so much and faded so bad that it wasn't blue anymore. And it was stiff with starch. He didn't care, but I told him he would have to stop wearing that. Louis wore a shirt without a collar, but bought a celluloid one to fasten on. We called them "hobo collars." The hobos wore them because they could wash them in the river or any place.

When Louis blew on his horn, on a high note, his neck puffed out, the collar button busted and one side of the collar flew out. Louis tried to fasten it down, but he couldn't, and, next thing the other side popped out. He just sat there looking like the end man in a minstrel show.

I talked to Louis and he said it looked like he would have to wear a regular starched collar, but we had a hard time breaking him of wearing those jackets. The low class hustlers, which was gamblers, wore those jumpers and that's what Louis wanted to be in those days.

I don't know if Louis gambles like he used to, but back at that time he was always broke from gambling.

But that was a wonderful band. The music sounded so pretty, especially on the water. Everybody was very congenial and everybody worked together. We had a lot of harmony in that band.

In the winter time we'd stay in New Orleans and work on the smaller steamboat, the "Sidney." There would be a moonlight excursion trip on the Mississippi River every night and before we would ship out, we'd play for about a half hour while the boat was tied up at the Canal Street wharf. That was to attract people and we had lots of people who would come down to listen to the band. Sometimes Fate would play the calliope, to draw a crowd.

*S.S. St. Paul*

Then in the spring, we would go up the river on the big side-wheeler, "St. Paul." It had a capacity of 3,500. Our destination was St. Louis, because we worked out of St. Louis all summer. But first, we went all the way up to St. Paul. We stopped at a lot of towns along the Mississippi for one-night excursions – Natchez, Cairo, Hannibal, Quincy, Keokuk and Davenport, La Crosse and Red Wing, were some of them. We also stopped at Vicksburg, Memphis, Cape Girardeau and Dubuque.

There was a beautiful, big, polished dance floor on the main deck and soda fountains. The quarters for the band were in the hold and we slept down there.

After we got to St. Louis, we played day and night all summer. In the daytime, from about two 'til six, we'd take an excursion trip out for mothers and children, with basket lunches. At night there was a moonlight excursion for grown people, which was from eight-thirty to about midnight.

Then in the fall, we'd start down the river to New Orleans, stopping at some of the towns we had missed on the way up.

The Streckfuses were all musicians and Captain Joe Streckfus of the "St. Paul" demanded that Fate have rehearsals every week.

The thing that happened to me many a time on the boat was, I would miss a passage. Everybody would know that I had missed it, and I would feel bad. After the rehearsal, Fate would say, "Don't you go, Babe. Something you missed and I want you to stay." Well, that hurt. You want to be so good that when you sit down, you can play your part like everybody else, and when the leader says, "Good, you can go for a rest or a smoke." But when a man tells you, "Uh, uh, you don't go anywhere," that hurts.

When I was on the steamboat, Captain Joe Streckfus used to put a metronome on me. Of course, I didn't see it. They would have it behind me or hidden somewhere, watching it to see if I was a steady keeper of time. And, of course, they found out I were. Captain Joe even used a stop-watch like they use for a race-horse and would see if we varied in the length of time it took us to play a number. But, in my own practice, I never did use a metronome.

When I was on the boat, in 1919, I started playing on cymbals with snare sticks. Now, everybody's doing it, but no one knows who it came from.

Some of the older people that would come on the boat couldn't dance to the fast two-beat time. So, Streckfus had a solution and introduced "toddle time." Four beats and not fast. Captain Joe worked out a certain tempo on his metronome, so then, the old people could just bounce around the floor, not doing anything – just bouncing. "Toddle time" would keep them going. If they got out of step, they had four beats to get in step with. Through Streckfus having the idea then, I was the one who first started using those four beats.

At that time, all drummers had a side cymbal attached on the bass drum. There was a little beater on the foot pedal that would hit this cymbal same time as the beater would hit the bass drum. It would make a "ping" sound. I took the little bass drum cymbal off, and then it was just a straight "boom, boom, boom." That little cymbal was just an interference but back then everybody was using it. Nobody uses it now.

But I am the guy that was supposed to have caused the "sock" cymbals to be made. That is sometimes called the "hi-hat" cymbals. One time at St. Louis, William Ludwig, that makes the drums, came on the boat to see me. It was in 1919. Maybe he just came on board for the ride. Anyway, he was very interested in my drumming and he asked me, "Do you think you can work your toe instead of the heel when you stomp your left foot in time to the music?" I used to always stomp my left foot – which all drummers do now. Only, I used to stomp my heel.

I told him, "I think so." For a fact, I thought nothing of it. So, he said, "Well, we'll try that." And, he measured my foot on a piece of paper and measured the space where I would have my foot. Then he made one of those things and brought it on for me to try. It was two cymbals, face to face, set up with a foot pedal. I didn't like it, never did use them, and don't until today.

That first one wouldn't work at all, so he brought one on the boat, raised up about nine inches, and well, I never did like any of them. The things are a great success today and I could have been in on that, but I didn't want any part in demonstrating them. I had just taken off the side cymbal on the bass drum. I was the first one to destroy that, and I didn't want to hear that tinny sound any more. So, that's one reason I never did get used to the sock cymbals.

Some drummers can't drum without the sock cymbals and I can't drum with them. Today the majority of drummers use them, but sock cymbals don't make the drummer. They feel that if they don't have them, they haven't got no tempo, or they've got no rhythm. But, sock cymbals don't make rhythm. Rhythm is from your two hands and feet. The rhythm do not come from sock cymbals. A lot of fellows use them just to get by, but they are not fooling anyone.

# CHAPTER 4

I'd like to talk about the blues that came from New Orleans. In the downtown district where the Creoles lived, they played blues with a Spanish accent. We fellows that lived Uptown, we didn't ever play the Creole numbers like the Frenchmen downtown did – such as *Eh, La Bas*. And just as we changed the Spanish accent of the Creole songs, we played the blues different from them. They lived in the French part of town and we lived uptown, in the Garden district. Our ideas for the blues were different from theirs. They had the French and Spanish style, blended together. We had but one kind. That's negro. We took our time and played the blues slow and draggy. When we used to play blues for a dance long ago, it was so draggy, sometimes people would say it sounded like a dead march.

Some of those people downtown didn't talk anything but Creole. Uptown, where I was, our people didn't talk like that. And, if someone moved in who did talk it, your mother kept you away from those people. Didn't want you to have any part of them. Now, my people, we were mixed with Indian, but we didn't want no parts of Creole talk. It was all backwards for us. It's a certain way you must hold your mouth to speak French words. If our mother would catch us trying to do that, she'd slap us in the mouth. Anytime we'd be caught playing with any Creole children, "Come in here!" That's the way it was. That's why we didn't ever learn it.

But in spite of that, I did have a little Creole friend they called "Guito." Name was Isaac . . . Isaac Antoine. He was very dark. Darker than I was, and he couldn't talk nothing but Creole. He was born around St. Ann Street, downtown. His people were very light, but he was very dark. That kid would follow me anywhere I went. We were about the same age. He was much taller than I. Both had such small heads, called us "bird heads."

When we got old enough, we used to go to Francs Amis Hall, but I couldn't get in until he would talk to those fellows on the door in Creole. Inside, the girls wouldn't dance with me until he'd tell them in Creole, "Dance with him," and would tell them I was from uptown and a nice boy. That's the way I'd get a dance, so I know what the life is.

Most dance bands of today play the old marches entirely too fast. The story on *The Saints Come Marching In* is as thus: that's a hymn, a sacred song, in the first place. Why, you know yourself, no one has any business playing a sacred song fast. But, you can play it in a nice tempo that it would seem very jazzy, but it also sounds sweet. And then, you're not rushing over your horn, you're not rushing over your instrument and everybody can hear it distinctly. Now, take *High Society*. I can tell you why the fellows play it too fast. That's for the benefit of these clarinets that can't blow. They have got to play it fast because they are faking. You should play every note of *High Society* distinctly.

*High Society* is a clarinet number. Originally, it was written for flute or piccolo. Do you know, a long time ago, there was a fellow in New Orleans by name of Charlie McCurdy, who used to play *High Society* together with Alphonse Picou as a clarinet duet? Beautiful! Beautiful! And it was never played as fast as it is now. When they play it they shouldn't pass over a note or half hit it. Every note is supposed to have its full value. These fellows today want you to think they are raising a breeze and they are not doing anything. If they don't know how to play it, they play it fast. That's why they play it fast.

Those fellows play *High Society* too fast, *Saints Come Marching In* too fast, *Tiger Rag* too fast. Those things are not to be played fast. Supposed to be played in a nice jump tempo, but not too fast.

Scott Joplin's *Maple Leaf Rag* is a number the guys won't tackle very much. It's too hard. Rags are not played fast and they're not played slow. You just can't play Scott Joplin's syncopations fast. That music is nothing if you don't give each note its full value.

In the New Orleans dance halls, members of the band were seated to bring about a natural balance. Facing the dance floor from the band-stand, there to the right would be me, drums. Next to me, on my left, would be the trombone. At the left of the trombone would be trumpet. If you had first and second trumpet, the second trumpet would be next to the trombone.

Next to the trumpet was clarinet, going left. And next to the clarinet would be piano and next to piano would be guitar or banjo, going left. When they used the violin, it would be between clarinet and piano. Bass was on the other end. Thus, by having drums on one end and bass on the other, you would have a heavy instrument on each end. You wouldn't imagine how different your music would sound if you would line up that way.

This seating line-up would go for recording, too. That way, you're balanced already, without wasting time. And you can hear every instrument distinctly. Now, if you jam them up or put this one behind that one and this one behind this one, it's not going to go good. When you go to a studio and they move a guy here and move him there and move him the other place, the recording will be bad. You have to let the men be natural when recording. Let them sit in their usual way and they'll feel natural. When you make recordings, you must be together and play together. And, whatever one guy does, the others have got to do. If one plays soft, the other guys play soft. And, if one plays loud, the other guys have got to play loud. That goes for any band, when you're recording or not.

For recording, I never did pad a drum. You have to learn to beat the bass drum with less pressure for recording. But you've got to do it with the same snap so that the tone'll go. But muffling drums – I don't believe in it. I like to hear a round tone. That's my idea on that.

As long as a bunch of men are together and want to cooperate with one another, I don't think it's necessary to have seven or eight pieces. Even four pieces are all right, which my brother and I had a long time. We used to put out some pretty good music I think and I have played with three pieces which sounded all right. I can vouch for that. To make a band of music sound full, you haven't got to have seven or eight pieces.

*Baby Dodds – 1935*

Lots of times in New Orleans, we used seven or eight pieces, and no piano. And, then when everybody was down soft, it sounded real good. For my particular share, I'd rather play soft than play a lot of loud music.

Back in New Orleans, when we used a violin, he played a straight lead, with the other instruments jazzing up the melody or going off on chords, or whatever they would do with the harmony. I think it helped a band, to have a violin to carry the straight melody at all times. A trumpet is supposed to be a lead instrument, but still, he has to take his horn down. He doesn't continue to go all the time. But a violin does.

The way we used to play a long time ago sounded awful sweet.

When we began to use a piano in a band, the piano player played his straight part with plenty of melody, because the guitar, drums and bass did enough chording.

When I played in a three- or four-piece band, I had to come in with more variety, to keep the band filled up. Not louder, though. You could play soft and just as well, but every little hole, or every little pause, you'd have to fill up with drums. But, you'd have to fill it up in a way that sounded in accord with the music. I think a band should blend together, if it's one, two, three or five men.

In the tradition of New Orleans, the leader always taught you, when you start a number, to hit the introduction. Hit it! Loud! After you play one chorus, then you drop down soft. That way, when some solos would come along, you're still soft.

When the band would come in to the ensemble, the leader would tell you, "Shu-sh," and you'd come in very soft and do about two or three choruses that way. When you did that, you got some feeling out of it.

Then, he would tell you to hit it. That would mean for you to come up loud and you would play one chorus that way. Next one would be "double forte" and you'd play that one out. When the band was playing like that, you'd know that meant "going out." You didn't have to have anyone to tell you, "This is the end." You'd know, "This means out."

It was all up to your leader, how he wanted you to play. Trumpet player, he would tell you, "Sh-sh-sh," for you to come down, mezzo forte, and then he would tell you, "Sh-sh-sh," meaning "come down a little lower." That's to piano, and so forth. Sometime I've seen them come down to actually a whisper. A room full of dancers would see them making the motions of playing, and they would be dancing. They'd think they were hearing the music, but it would be nothing but their own feet making the noise. A lot of times we used to leave them on the floor that way. It made a novelty.

The youngsters today don't do anything like that. They just don't know any better. A bunch playing loud all the way don't make much sense. That is why people will say, "This is a lot of noise." In some of the places in New York, that's the way they play all of the time. Loud. And they say that's the way you have to play or they won't hire you.

I believe if they'd get the real New Orleans style in there – if they would hear it once or twice and get the idea that you can make your intro very heavy, first chorus heavy, then come down very soft for the ensemble before you blast it out at the very last – then, that way, the people would get to jumping. They would feel it better. But, just loud, loud, loud! Oh, no!

You know, the effect of music is based on introductions and endings, anyway.

You make a good introduction and a good ending and the stuff you put in between, that will sound all right. But, people get sick and tired of a band that is loud all the time.

When we used to play, long time ago, people never got tired of our music. When it was time to go home the people would say, "Oh, no. We don't want to go home." It was because the music was so sweet. When I came along, the fellows could play music. That's all we had then – music. But now – sometimes, nothing but noise. When they say, "Go home," you are tired enough to walk right out of the place, you don't want any more of it. Not for that night anyway. I guess when a lot of the people get home, they still hear that noise in their ears. You know, that don't make sense.

# CHAPTER 5

There's just as much music in a drum as there is in a piano, trumpet, or any other instrument, and I believe it can be gotten out through a long, hard study. I believe, today if I hadn't been sick for five years starting in 1949, I would have come very close to mastering that instrument and to bring melody out of drums. It can be done, I feel, and I think it will be done some day. I would just like to be on earth to hear the guy that finds melody in drums.

It may not be a melody in a certain key, like a trumpet melody, but when the snare drum picks it up, you'll know it's the same tune the trumpet of the band just got through playing.

Once you like a melody and get it in your head, you never lose it. If you hear it beat out on tin pans, or anything that's got any tone to it, you'll know just what the tune is. It will even sound like it's in the right key. That's the way the mind works.

I've tried to play melody on the snare drum with the band. Any melody that the band would carry, I'd attempt to play it on the snare drum. I think I learned that from playing in street parades, because on parade, when the band stops playing, the snare drum has to carry on alone.

In playing along with a band, the drummer must follow the phrases. That's why I want to know, each time a band starts playing, what's the number they're going to play. If it's one I don't know, I follow it very closely and pay strict attention. If it's a number I know, I know where the phrases come in.

In a lot of bands, you say, "What are you going to play?" And, they say, "What do you want to know for? You're only the drummer." But they don't know it is very essential for the drummer to know what tempo the number's going to be in and to be able to follow the phrases of the melody.

The secret of good jazz music has always been to carry the melody at all times. The melody is supposed to be heard distinctly from some instrument – the trumpet, or trombone, or clarinet, or violin. At all times.

Until today, I feel that drums have as much music in them as any other instrument ever made. Quite natural, the guy that made them first knew what was supposed to be gotten out of them. But I doubt if anyone else knows. In my estimation, drums should play according to the melody and still keep time.

Some of the other instruments in the band may rest sometimes but the drum is supposed to go all the time.

The drummer's job is to keep strict tempo, the tempo he is given by the leader. The trumpet man can knock off the time for me, or the piano can knock off. The violin can knock off, clarinet, even the trombone, I wouldn't care. Anybody.

But that tempo, what he gives me, that's what he's going to finish with. I'm going to try my best to make him finish with it. That is my job, personally. To keep that tempo first given me by whosoever the leader is. The only way that it would be changed is for the leader himself to feel it should be changed. "That's too fast. Slow it down, Babe." He can't slow it down any other way. I got to slow it down, when he tells me. And, if it's too slow, he'd say, "Pick it up a little bit, Babe." If he don't, it won't go anyplace. He could pick up all he wanted, but it still won't go nowhere, if I don't want it to go.

Every man in the band has his own rhythm to keep. They didn't learn to keep time by a bass drum. When they learned, they kept their own beat. That's why I don't understand why people say, "The drum threw me off." Oh, no. That's too simple. And, sometimes you will hear a drummer say, "Well, he threw me off." That's too easy to say, and it's said too often.

Why would you have to take the time from somebody else? Why would you have to hear the time from the drummer, for you to know how to play your instrument in time? Some drummers of today feel if the piano player don't give them the beat, they haven't got the beat. That is not the way I learned. I learned the drummer is supposed to carry the time, regardless.

I must explain one thing about playing in a dance band. The drummer must be very careful not to confuse the blowing instruments, clarinet, trombone and trumpet. He must not only be careful in counting but must not use certain beats that will upset the breathing of the guys blowing instruments. A drummer can ruin a band. He can hurt it to its heart, because a bad beat goes into them and they can't throw that off.

But, the blowing instrument is carrying his own rhythm just like the drummer carries rhythm. A drummer is not alone responsible for rhythm. His job is to send the other guy – make him play.

In a band, the trumpet or clarinet will sometimes delay and fall what we would call "a step behind." Although they are "with it," they are just a little behind, say, one-eighth of a beat. Now, the drummer mustn't drop back there, because, if he does, the time is gone. He has to keep right on the beat. If the drummer drops back, that changes the whole complexion of the time. So, he just ignores that. He doesn't even hear it, because if he does listen to it, he's going to drop back, too.

So, you hear nothing but yourself, and keep steady, doing whatever you're doing. That's one time when you don't listen to the band. You listen to yourself. The blowing instrument has got his time all figured out. He's got to catch so much wind. He's got to hold that wind and do so many notes with it. If you slow back to catch his beat, then the whole band is off.

Lots of drummers don't know whether they are pulling back on time or not. However, once a beat is going, a drummer hardly ever pulls back time. If anything, he usually races it faster. Sometimes another musician will think the drummer is lagging and he will be the one pulling back. He doesn't realise it.

If the drummer is any kind of timekeeper, he will know whether he is pulling the time or not. The strain on his ankle will make him know that. If the tempo isn't steady, a drummer feels the strain on his ankle, same as a guy blowing ought to feel it with his breath. The muscles in his stomach have a load to carry.

When your leader knocks off a band and he gives you the tempo, that's your tempo. It's up to the others to get in there, and if they don't get in there, that is nothing to you. You have got your tempo. And, never you mind, the band will come up with the right tempo.

I had a lot of trouble with one leader I used to play with a lot. He'd knock off a tune a little fast and when he couldn't wind his lips around the mouthpiece enough to make all the notes, he'd pull down the time. I wasn't going to pull it down, and we had a lot of humbugs. When he give me the tempo, I'm gone with it. You should not make a practice of picking up the tempo or slowing it down. If you start that, you'll never be able to keep time. Your ankle gets very sensitive to those things.

I was classed as one of the best timepieces of drumming that there were, because I wouldn't vary. If I would speed up, my leg and my ankle would get tired. With a steady time, I could beat my foot four beats all night and all day and never get tired.

When I went to France, in 1948, I had a perfect ankle. I don't care how fast they played, I could beat it, how slow they played, I could beat it. And in between, it would never vary.

Right here, I will tell you one of the hardest things for a drummer to do. Put in some waltz rhythm when playing in four-four time, then to get back into four-four without messing up something. The way you do this, you stop the bass drum and roll on the snare drum. Then, you hit your bass drum back in your tempo, and you won't throw anybody. Your roll will put you right back in line. It will have to be a heavy one, though. Quite natural, a guy can't do it with brushes.

Music for drums is like arithmetic. Lots of times you have to add and, sometimes, you have to subtract. You must know arithmetic. That's the definition of music. You have to learn to say, "One and two, three and four," or say, "One and one is two and two is four and four is eight."

What I mean is, that's the way you've got to count. Sometimes, you can't count them, "One two, three, four." You have to count, "One _and_ two _and_ three." Like that. That's the way my teacher taught me. Put _and_ in for eighth notes.

So, you must learn to count. And, a drummer beating his drum mustn't let anything distract his counting. If you see a one-measure rest coming up, you know how many counts you have to give that. If it's two measures, you know it's twice as many. And, if it's sixteen measures, well, you know at the count of sixteen, there's half a chorus gone. You can't just sit. You must count it out. You can sing, if you want, so long as you get through at the right point.

In New Orleans, when we used to play after-beats in a number, we called that a "Boston." Say "Boston" in front of any musician from New Orleans and he knows exactly what it is. In other places, like New York, they might think you were talking about beans. And, many musicians can't play if you are playing on the after-beat. They don't understand because they don't count. With them, if you do a chorus with the Boston, I'll bet everybody will be right on the same beat with you when you finish.

In doing the Boston, you have got to learn also to get back in time on the beat. Just as you pulled it off to start, by dropping a beat, you've got to catch that beat up at the end of the chorus, by hitting it on the beat instead of waiting. That'll throw it right back on the beat.

When I first started, I used to try to listen to somebody else, listen to the melody, listen to the trumpet, or listen to someone that's carrying the melody. And, many a time, I found myself right out in hot water and couldn't get back. Now, the story is, I learnt this the hard way – count your own music. You hear everybody, but still you don't hear someone. The only one person you listen to is yourself.

Keep in time yourself, and, don't worry, everybody will be in time, too. Some fellows claim that you must follow them. You don't follow anybody but yourself. There's no way for a drummer to follow anybody. Because, he's got the time. That's what he's supposed to be – a timepiece in a band.

If somebody takes a solo break, you ain't supposed to touch nothing there. If you have to play, play so soft that you're not heard. The man that's making the solo, he'll feel you in there.

That's very difficult, because you have to play very soft. You'll hardly hear yourself. But, remember, the other fellow has the solo, not the drums. If the drums was heard, the other fellow hasn't got any solo.

Actually, a drummer could throw the whole gang out of time if he wanted to be that mean. And a drummer can put them back in time. Now, you wonder how that's done? Well, this is the way. If you find a band off, stop the bass drum, just make a roll, and everybody'll come along with that roll. You put the roll on the beat. Then, when you hit the bass drum, everybody is right. How many drummers know that? None, I bet you. It don't seem like a snare drum has no beat. But, snare drum can set everybody in time.

If you, the drummer, want to make a band play loud, you can make it play loud. You want to make a band play medium soft, you can make it play medium soft. You want to make a band play <u>piano</u>, very soft, you can do that. No band is going to play with the drums doing nothing. They are going to feel there is something wrong. They are going to come down, too. If the drummer's beatin' his head off, fellows say, "No matter what, we got to keep over the drums. Drums are going to drown us out." So they are going to blow louder. But, if they feel the drums are soft, they are going to come down, too.

The majority of drummers today don't know how to raise or lower the volume of the band. They don't know when to do it. Those fellows might as well leave that to some individual who knows how to do it. You can leave it up to the trumpet player, then. When he come out loud, that means – everybody! So, the trumpet can raise it up, or drums can raise it up, or they can lower it.

Play nice, soft drums and send the other guy and you'll be heard, too. And felt. Well, when I started, you better not beat no loud drum. You wouldn't have no job. You had to beat drums soft enough that the fellows should feel it. Not know it, but just feel that beat. And, they're gone.

When the Oliver band was playing at the Royal Gardens, we used to get so soft you could hardly hear it, but still you knew the music was going. It would be so soft you could hear just the people's feet. Now, today, the guys won't play like that. We played for the comfort of the people, no blasting, but so soothing, and with a little jump to it. You just had to dance or do something.

You must have relaxation to play music. You can't be a good musician unless you relax. You can't be tightened up, excited, angry or afraid that you're going to do wrong. Be relaxed in what you do. Then, you've got clear thoughts, and can keep your mind on your music and do your best.

A drummer ought to go to a teacher to be taught the rudiments of music, and what time means. He must know from whom to take the time and what to do with it after he gets it. Time is his job. You don't rush time. You don't pull time. You've got to keep it solid.

A lot of people today think that a drummer doesn't have to know music, but it's very important for him to know music. I even think this – if it's possible, he should learn another instrument, which is piano, or clarinet, or anything, even a jaw's harp. It would help his drumming.

On my first night with Charlie Elgar's Creole Band, at the Savoy Ballroom in Chicago, they picked out a number they tricked drummers with. I saw everybody look peculiar. I said, "Well, maybe they're just looking." The music was in manuscript. That's the worst music to try to read.

They hit off, and when they got down about twenty-four measures, there was a drum solo big as I am. It was on a cymbal and a snare drum, with syncopation on the bass drum. Well, I didn't pay much attention to it, because I had seen harder things than that, and I just went on and made it. Then, there was another part where the drummer was supposed to lay out for four measures. Their average drummer had been beating right on into the four measures, but when I made my part, I stopped. The band played it out and I picked it up again.

They were all surprised that I stopped playing right in the middle of the number, and, afterwards, they said to me, "Oh, where you been? What kind of drummer you been?" Or, "Where have you been? Man, I didn't know you could read music like that."

They had figured none of the King Oliver outfit could read music. What they didn't know was, I came from a hard school. I came from that boat. And, that boat was hard. If you didn't read, you'd better spell awful fast. On the Streckfus excursion boats, we had rehearsal every day. Nothing but music. Strictly music.

When Louis Armstrong came to Chicago to join Oliver's band, he could read music faster than average. Fast as Joe, or faster. When I joined Joe Oliver out in San Francisco, the first number that they put on me was *Canadian Capers*. I will never forget that. When I read that number down, the bunch was surprised, because, in some places, I had to make the same rhythms on the bass drum that the bass player had to make.

The bass player was very much surprised at me. On down the line, I had some parts that the cornet player made. Well, on the snare drum I made that. They all were very much surprised. I was keeping up and they knew if I wasn't reading I was faking awfully good. So, that's what happened out there.

It's pretty tough when you don't know how to read and try to play music. Those notes pass you so fast that you think they're laying down, 'stead of standing up. I got so good that I could just throw away the music and do my stuff in there and sound all right. I would just know what to do. To do it that way, you must have what the average drummer hasn't got – an ear. Then you will know what to do and when to do it. That's my say about that.

But, I just love drumming, anyway, whether it's done right or wrong. I love it.

# CHAPTER 6

Light hands, that's my secret of drumming. That's typical of Baby Dodds. By having light hands, I use heavy sticks. The technique I use, I hold the hands up as a balance and just touch the drums. It's just the stick that hits, not the weight of my hand. Just the stick hits. If I used light sticks, I would have to use the force of heavy hands to hit the drum.

I use the Ray Bauduc stick (Ludwig 4A). I like the balance of it. They gave me about six pair around 1938, and I've used them from then on, and I've found them to be very good for my work. The Ray Bauduc stick is not too big and it's got a little more body to it down at the lighter end, near the bead. The thicker body keeps the end of the stick from busting off when hitting cymbals, the rims, wood blocks, or cow bells, or something.

When I started out on drums, years ago, I used to use the real military sticks which are very heavy. They are very big and used for street work. They feel like broomsticks now, to me. That's heavy. Maybe that's the reason why I developed such light hands. Starting out with these big military sticks made me have to have a combination of light wrists and fast wrists and supple wrists, and pull up my arms – not let them down.

I never used metal practice sticks. I have used, long years ago, very heavy ebony sticks. I found the ebony sticks too heavy for me, but it helped me an awful lot, for development of my wrists and hands.

If a man uses very light sticks, it means he must have very heavy hands. He'll have no looseness or technique in his hands, and will have to come down heavy with his arms to make the sticks come down heavy.

Another thing about using the sticks, you can't raise the sticks above your head and pound down. You can't do that. You should raise them, say, not quite to shoulder level, and then go down. That way it sounds like you're hitting heavy, but you know you're hitting light.

If your hands are held too high you can burst the drum head that way. Sometimes you have seen drummers burst the head playing. I have never burst a head in playing. Maybe if I bust a bead on my stick and leave a sharp point, and I hit it not feeling the bead is off; but I never have sit right straight down in a chair drumming a dance or show and split a drum head. And you know why. It means I have light hands.

Now, when you pick out a pair of drumsticks, you roll them on a counter or something that's level. If they wobble on you, that's no good, because you can't keep a steady hand with a crooked stick. So pay particular attention in buying drum sticks that they're not warped. Some guys don't even look at that. They get the feel of the stick for the balance they want and the stick can be crooked as a ram's horn, but that don't make any difference to them. But to me it makes a difference.

I think a drum pad will help students a great deal before they start on a snare drum. The pad will help a student to get a snap to his wrists and to have a balance of the hands and arms.

The kind of drum set I had in the beginning! It was terrible. I hate to tell you. I had an old 26" drum in height and about 14" across. That made it high and narrow. And, it was a rope drum. What I mean by that, you had to tune it up by rope, like some military drums of today. I wouldn't advise that kind for anybody to start on. And, if I had been able to buy a better one at that time, I would have done it.

For a fact, the drums nowadays – snare drums and bass drums with the modern thumb screws – are very wonderful. Very few people remember this, but they used to have snare drums with little keys on each tuning rod. They were smaller than the keys on the bass drum, but you just used your fingers to tune it.

I think it's up to the individual about what set of drums he wants to use, or what he wants to do with them, because most modern drums are good.

But, first of all, I would advise, a lot of drummers of today are using a drum - a bass drum or a snare drum - and they don't know the tuning, or snare head, from the batter head. If they don't know, they should ask someone the difference between a batter head and a tuning head. I've had a little experience on that, from a fellow whom I saw in New York. He was going ahead and beating right on the tuning head of the bass drum. And, the same for the tom-toms. He didn't know any different.

Well, now, I think in a case of that sort, with a beginner, or a fellow that's young in the business – he should ask someone that he feels is capable enough to tell him. The batter head is heavier and has a different tone.

I got a bargain on the snare drum I have, which I love very well. A fellow brought it by the Lincoln Garden. I saw the little drum and I ask him do he want to sell it. "Well," he said, "Yass." And that's the one I use today, which I love very well, and I don't think I paid over $10.00 for it. And that's what I'm using today. I got that drum in 1923. It is a Ludwig, metal shell, 4$^1$/$_2$" x 14".

I like my shallow snare drum better than a deep one for small outfits of five or six people. A 4" shell gives me enough snap for the small combos of today. You don't want your drum sounding deep enough to drown out the whole band.

You aren't supposed to be heard as much as you are felt. That's something you've got to feel. The same as a car running. You know how the motor sounds when it's all right. Well, that's the way I feel about drums. They're supposed to be felt, and heard, but so lightly that you know everything is all right.

The drum that I did love best of all when I first started, not my first set but my second set, when I turned professional, was a Leedy, a wood shell, 6" x 14". And, I loved it very much.

Only thing, when I went to work on the boat, in 1918, and dampness would get in the wood, it quite naturally would affect the heads. When I got the metal drum, well, the dampness didn't penetrate the metal as the wood. That was my reason for changing.

I use a regulation bass drum, that is, a 14" x 28". I don't imagine that you can get a perfect tone – what I call a perfect tone – a nice, round tone, out of a little tiny bass drum. And, that means an awful lot, I think. Because, if a drummer's going to drum for tone, he's got to have his instruments the right size. I think the fellows that use small drums, they're only thinking of the point about carrying them.

Well, I want a nice, big, round tone out of a bass drum. That is the way I feel about it. And, if you don't have them tuned up right, you won't get that tone. That little, small drum has got a "biff", like hitting a sack of salt. That's what I don't like, because I was taught to hear, and listen and tune my drums for tone, and that's what I do yet. That's why I definitely don't believe you should use pads on a bass drum.

When you beat a bass drum, you're supposed to be heard, and after a band once have this tone in their ears, well, then, they're gone! But, if it's something they can't hear, they just have to imagine it's there. That's no good.

I don't care for putting a name on the drum. I think it's a little bit of neurotic.

Also, I don't like to see lights in drums for decoration. The only thing you use lights for in a drum is to dry the dampness out. Now, pretty pictures and names all over it, I don't like that because, you paint a drum head, you're going to lose tone. If you put paint on a tuning head, it's certainly going to deaden tone and you'll never get the tone back anymore.

And as for these guys that take a Turkish towel and split it all up and put it inside the bass drum! Well, I don't like that either because it's killing tone.

My bass drum beater, in the first place, was just a small size. I would say about 1¹/₂" diameter. And I would buy the lambswool covers, and when one would wear down, I'd put another on, until, now, it's normal size - about 3" in diameter. That's the way I built it. And I've never taken off a cover. I just put another on. Of course, that makes it heavier and heavier. But, I like it heavy, because that's why people think all the time that I hit a powerful lick on the bass drum. But I don't have accuracy in my ankle and I'm just touching it. And, it's hitting like I'm hitting a terrible lick. That's the reason of that.

I don't like the tone of the small wood beaters. It's the same way beating a bass drum in a parade. If you got a small mall, you know you can't hit as powerful a lick as you can with a large one. There you are. It's that same way with your foot. The whole thing in hitting a bass drum is in the accuracy of your ankle. If I just leave my foot lay, it's going to make a couple of these "Boom-Booms." See? But owing to the accuracy of my ankle, by raising my foot quickly, it just hits once. The weight of the heavy mall I use makes the pedal pull back. I just raise the foot. So, that's a definition of my bass drum power, it's all from the ankle.

That's not an easy part of your study. A student's ankle gets tired, but he still can't give down. He's got to keep it up. The majority of drummers go to slowing up when their ankle gets tired.

The foot pedal I use is the Ludwig Speed Pedal. It's pretty fast and the accuracy of it and my ankle blend just fine. A foot pedal is the same as the use of drum sticks. If you got a heavy foot, well, you use a stiff foot pedal. You got a light foot - you use a fast pedal and a heavy mall. Just like if you've got light hands, you use heavy sticks. So if you got a very accurate foot, from the ankle, you use a ball bearing pedal for speed and you don't have as much strain on the ankle.

If I have my drums right in the room with me, I can tell just about what the change in the weather is going to be. If it's a nice dry day and the drums commence to fall on you, you can bet for a fact it's going

to be sultry. They're a pretty good reminder for weather.

If it's warm, and you're going to have a change in the weather, you'll feel that with your drums. Your drum heads will go down. And when they start to cracking, you know it's going up or down. You have to be careful so it don't burst.

Sometimes the wire brushes that guys use make their drum heads black and hard, and lots of drummers think that the head is wore out, and will often get rid of them. But not an old guy like me that knows what it's all about. I don't get rid of no head. The only way I get rid of a head, is for it to burst on me. Then I have to get rid of it. I can't mend that.

But, if it gets hard, before it would crack, I take it off and wash it with soap and water, just like you wash your own skin. That's what it is. Skin. You wash it, it comes so firm and nice and pretty and clean, and you put it right back on the drum again, while it's wet. Have a beautiful tone to it again.

I've used a drum head as long as thirteen years. It was a good Angora batter head on my snare drum. Instead of calling 'em "mountain goat", they're called "Angoras." It's goat. A calf doesn't go up on the mountain. He stays down on earth. The altitude has a lot to do with the toughness of the skin. That's why you buy Angora heads. They can stand dampness and don't burst. They don't stretch too much.

Then, some people buy timpani (or kettle-drum) heads for bass drums. They are very good. They're sensitive and you can get a nice tone out of your drums. They're easy to tune up. But then, when you bust one of them, they cost more than the average drum head. The tuning of them will last longer – with the timpani heads.

But, after all, tuning a drum is no more than tuning. Still, I think that any drummer should learn this. I think a lot of drummers don't know this: you tune your bass drum in G and you tune your snare drum in E natural. That I have told lots of drummers and they don't see how it can be done. And they holler at me, "Oh, no, you can't tune a snare drum in E. It would burst it." But just go ahead and tune it up. You'll see. I know that sounds very high. And, sounds very high for a bass drum to be tuned in G. But, you know, it's not high G. It's your low G. You can sound it from the piano or bass viol and just make it low G. On your bass drum, all you tune is the tuning head up to G, then you bring your batter side not quite as high as your tuning head. Then, you hit the bass drum with the pedal, to hear if the tone is all right. You have to have a good ear for tone.

My tom-tom set, I only got acquainted with in 1945, just before I went to New York. Before that, I used a little Chinese tom-tom, one of those 6 or 7" things, and also the big barrel one. I loved that one. But, I wanted to be a little modernistic, and when I went to New York to play with Bunk, I got this set of tom-toms I have today. But, I used to love that big tom-tom very much. And it was an ugly thing. There wasn't no looks to it at all. Looked like a barrel. It was untunable, with stationary heads. These that I use now have independent heads, and I like them better, for my work.

A lot of fellows don't understand what I do with my tom-toms, and how I get the tone out of them. They don't understand there's one particular thing – they must be tuned. That's why they've got independent heads. Well, I like to tune them in fifths. I throw off the snares at the bottom of my snare drum, which makes it the same as a tom-tom. So, I used it along with my set of three tom-toms and the bass drum. I get my tonic from the snare drum. In other words, that's my lead.

About cymbals. I got two Zildjians, one large one. I guess it's about 16". And, I got a small one about 13", and I love them both. The tone is what I like about them. It isn't too sharp nor too heavy. When you get one too sharp, it's too light for some kinds of work and it rings too much.

These two that I have, they're kinda in a lower pitch. 'Course, some drummers don't like them that way, but I do. And, if you want them in a high pitch, you got to hit a little harder. As for the old Chinese cymbals what they used to use, I think there's only about one more fellow I know of today that's using it. That's Ray Bauduc. He uses it yet.

I used a Chinese cymbal in 1920 on the boat. I used it when I went to Joe Oliver in San Francisco. I didn't discard the Chinese crash until 1932, at the K-Nine Club. I was working there and a drummer who used to work there evenings before I came to work, had a small cymbal and asked me did I want it. And I had taken the sound of that

and I loved it. That's what I use today. Now, everybody of today don't like little cymbals, but I do. These what I have gives me the tone that I wish.

The big cymbal that I have, I've had since 1919. The Streckfus people, who owned the excursion boats, bought that for me in 1919. Cost me $75.00 then. And I could have got a pair of them for $150.00. I don't know why I didn't.

I use a little 3" tim-tim, like a cymbal, on top of my bass drum and I still use the quartet of cow-bells I bought at Grunewald's store in New Orleans in 1916. And my old wood block. That's my pet.

Some years ago after I came to King Oliver, I used to use a slap-stick, sometimes, in shows. Different shows call for those things. Slap-stick, steam-boat whistle, and in a picture show, I used the Canary. If some guy was doing a comedy act, I used a cyclone whistle. But, long in my coming, they had all those things marked on the music, and that way it wasn't out of place. You had to use them. Around Christmas time, I used sleigh-bells. I have the set yet. The last time I used those was over at the Beehive, Christmas of '48.

I used to use a triangle on waltzes, schottisches, and some parts of quadrilles. Also, at times, I've used a tambourine. So, I have used a lot of traps.

I picked up a ratchet in 1920. I used to use it for different breaks I would make. I'd go on 'round the cow-bells and the cymbals and then turn the ratchet on the last beat, and it made a pretty nice impression. The one I have I have practically worn out.

I have worn out a couple of the things because I used to put my cigarettes in them. They made very wonderful ash trays, but the wood in them would get burned. I stopped using a ratchet when I went to New York in 1945, because it was so awkward for me to put in the drum case. I've had a lot of fun with a ratchet. Loads of fun. I'd just give it a slight yank and I was gone with it.

That's why I didn't like to sit up high. I would sit down low, so I could catch these things like the ratchet and go right to them without missing that break. If you sit up high, you are going to miss sometimes.

A ratchet comes in very handy for show work, like when a guy is sliding across the floor. You turn the ratchet at the same time. You can also blow a cyclone whistle. It comes out very nice.

# CHAPTER 7

When I started on drums, my drum method that I used very successfully was "Excelsior." It gave you from the beginning on to beyond – to professional. But I doubt if you can find that book now. I bought the book and didn't know what I was doing.

When I went to Dave Perkins, my first teacher, I asked him how about the method and he said it would be wonderful. The "Excelsior" book had pictures drawn to show how to hold the sticks in each hand. When it told you how to do things, it was so plain it was almost like a guy talking to you.

That method I carried along with me through the years until 1946 and I had it in New York. I left it in my car and put the car in a garage. When I came back there wasn't no more book. And that hurt me to my heart, to feel I had the book all those years and waited until 1946 to lose it.

People ask when is the proper age to start drum lessons. I would suggest you get the student's sentiment on that. When would he like to start? And mostly all kids like a drum. But, for the sentiment of the child – have him know that you're not talking about a play toy. It's a working instrument. That some day he'll make a living with it. And I think if you give him that knowledge and let him know what it's all about, he'll go to it in a correct way.

From an hour to hour-and-a-half of practice each day is plenty, at first. Now, any more than that, and what happens is that the kid would get tired and disgusted. Then it would be nothing. But in that length of time he'd be anxious and he'd be very ambitious to study for that hour-and-half.

I think that if a student has his instrument at heart, he'll learn much faster, and his teacher won't have so much pounding to do. He'll just give him a lesson and tell him, "You have that lesson when you come back," and the kid'll have that lesson.

You can take one long lesson a week, say, one to two hours, and you'll have enough to last you all week. Going to your lesson once a week gives you time to think and settle your brains on what you're going to do. That's more important than running to take lessons two or three times a week. I don't see that. Nobody wants to keep running to lessons to do the same thing over and over. He wants something new each time.

Of course, with music or anything else, too much at one lesson is no good. But, just enough makes you think like this, "Well, that's what I got to do, so no need foolin' myself." Just enough. That's the teacher's business. He should be versatile enough in mind and spirit to know how much to give a child to encourage him. Not to overload him, but give him enough.

My first teachers never used drums to demonstrate what I should do. First they would tell me what to do and say, "Son, do you understand?" I would say, "Yes." "Well, all right son, I want to see you do it." Then, I would go to it. And if I would do one thing wrong, they'd stop me right there. Right there in the middle of a phrase. Teacher would say, "Now, that ain't the way I told you. I told you how. Now, let me see you do it."

And I would start all over from the beginning. When that happens to you, you know, you are going to be thinking about that place where you were stopped. You put your thinking cap to working. I never did have to go over a lesson twice. Not I. Because I wanted to learn and paid strict attention, and tried my best to do just what I was told, adding nothing and taking away nothing.

I don't think it's an easy job to learn to drum. If a thing comes hard, that's the way you have to do it.

I never took any special exercises for development of my left hand. If I had to do something pretty hard with my left hand, I just concentrated on it and forced it to do what it had to do. I kept on practising until the left hand came natural.

But, I think a lot of people favor their left hands too much. Say, "Oh, I can't do it with my left hand." But, you can. Each hand is for you to be natural with. If something happens to your right hand and you can't use it, you soon learn to do the same things with your left hand you used to do with your right. You can do the same thing when nothing is wrong with your right hand. It's all in concentration.

I'm not left-handed, but I do a lot of things with my left hand in drumming. I've concentrated so much on that, until now, if I carry anything heavy, I pick it up with my left hand. I very seldom pick anything heavy up with my right hand. That's from practice. If your right hand can do it, your left can do it.

I think it's alright if music students want to pat their feet when they are learning to keep time. But it isn't necessary. It's not compulsory. I can sit and listen to music all night and never want to pat my foot.

Those things are all in the individual. Like, you would walk down the street and you see a girl. Well, maybe you would look around the second time, where maybe I wouldn't even look around once. It's the same thing. If patting your foot makes you feel good, well, it's all right for you. Some people feel good over something and they'll pat their foot or they'll sing, they'll clap, they'll rock. It's just that music does different things to people.

In 1923, I was using the very big, heavy sticks, and Joe Oliver said, "I want to try to get you to beat light." So he bought me some wire brushes. I beat so heavy with the wire brushes, Joe said to me, "Well, listen, you'd beat heavy with two wet mops. Gimme those things. Take your sticks back."

I couldn't get anything out of wire brushes. It seemed lazy to me. Then I started getting very technical with sticks. That's why I can beat so light now with sticks. In those days, if you didn't do what the leader told you, well, they were just through with you.

Now, wire brushes are no good for anyone to get used to, because, if you do, you've got heavy hands. If you've got a pair of sticks in your hand, you're not going to throw the sticks down just anyway at all. You are going to lighten them up to express what you're trying to do. You don't give in to them. You use technique in holding them up, for expression. With wire brushes, there's no expression you can get out of them. They will do only one thing – make a sweeping noise – "sss-ppp". Well, that's nothing much. You can't bring a band up with that. You can't let it down with it. Using two sticks, you are able to raise a band and you can lower a band.

Brushes is only for some guy who don't know how to drum. They may feel as though they're getting a rhythm with them. But, brushes don't make rhythm. They may try, but they'll find they won't do anything with brushes. And, not only that – they'll stick some holes in the snare drum, I betcha'.

When you go to a teacher, he doesn't teach you with wire brushes. He teaches you with sticks. It takes a lot of work to learn to handle sticks. I use heavy sticks because that makes my hands lighter. You have to get used to raising up the heavy stick. You have to use your arms and hands to work the sticks. Brushes will cause heavy hands. I would never advise any drummer, even professional, to use brushes unless he particularly has to do it, on things like in a song, or to make a noise like a train. You can do that very nice with brushes.

A fellow can play very soft with sticks. I play very soft with sticks, and that is for the simple reason because I use my arms as my technique and my wrists for rebound. That's the way you can get a real soft rhythm with sticks. But, remember, no one is going to play soft, with their brains feeling they must hit hard.

Some of the drummers today just can't use a pair of sticks. Some young drummers don't know how to roll a snare drum. Brushes don't let you bring a roll out. If you practise with brushes, you'll never use a stick. Brushes are no sticks. They aren't big enough for you to control with your fingers. You can never grip them enough for you to do anything with them.

Some fellows, they call theirselves wonderful, using two brushes, fanning you. Nobody's hot enough to fan. Anyway, use the two sticks first and then you can fan with the brushes if you want. But, before that, you have something to learn. You have something to do. When you get to where you can fan with sticks, that's when you are really going some.

Now, these things I take up in drumming is why a lot of fellows call me old-fashioned. But they don't know what I'm doing. If they was good drummers, they wouldn't say I was old-fashioned. They would say I was more up-to-date than what they are doing today. Because they would know that I had to study what I'm doing to make things sound like I do. I don't say that I'm so fine a drummer, but I bet you that I'm not a "nineteenth-century drummer," as these guys call it. I'm not that kind. That I know. I will even say this. I will do a lot of things that these "modern" drummers don't do, and can't do. Even if they say I'm a nineteenth-century drummer.

I don't care anything about that, because I know what I can do. I don't like bop and I won't try to play it. But I could play bop if I had to. It's just things that I know. Bop is nothing but biff notes, syncopation, and off-beats – and no beat at all. Well, bop is like a man who sits down to write a letter and never finishes a sentence.

You never get through learning, though. Every time you drum today and drum tomorrow night, there's something else for you to learn. I got about four different rhythms that I have worked nightly. I wouldn't know the name of them, because I don't go around patenting names, but I've got about four of them. And, that's what I worked with different bands. Worked with different fellows. What they liked. And, any time I find a beat to push a band with, I use that beat. If I find a beat that don't make anybody happy, I don't use it. I don't use it just because I know it.

Every day you drum, you can find some new beat. You never get through learning. You'll see some guy who'll say, "I been drummin' ten years." Why, he hasn't drummed any. When he has drummed for thirty years, he can find some beat he didn't know.

Don't think, Mr. Drummer, that you're so smart, you're such a swell drummer there's nothing you can learn. There's always something for a drummer to learn.

# CHAPTER 8

When a drummer with a band takes a solo, he's got to stay completely within the melody and count out all the measures.

If a drummer's going to take his solo, the band stops at the ending of a phrase or chorus, and he picks up there. But, he mustn't pick up just anywhere, because it's no good that way. He must keep the melody in mind. He's got to know the melody he's playing, know the bridge and all parts of the melody. He must keep his solo as near to the melody as possible.

That means the drummer's got to count. He has got to know when he finishes a thirty-two measure chorus. The band has to count it too, so they know when to come in.

Naturally, I would never play the same solo in two different numbers, for each number is different and it's the melody we're playing. I wouldn't go that far from the melody. A drum has melody in it just the same as any other instrument, but you have to know the drums thoroughly to get the melody out of them.

To the drummers that now call me "old style" I would like to say, "You get that melody and I will call you 'up to date'." That's my way of thinking.

After the drummer hears the melody played by the trumpet of the band, he must remember it when he takes his drum solo. If the drummer doesn't follow exactly the phrasing of the original melody, his solo won't sound like anything.

With my solos, you can sing the tune along with the drum and it will sound like the melody the band just played. This is the way I made the drum solo of *Maryland My Maryland* [Folkways Album FP30]. It was also the same thing I did with *Dinah* as a drum solo. I followed the melody of *Dinah*.

When I do solo work on drums, I keep in mind the bridges and endings. I must have all that in mind before I start to play a solo. Then, in order to make it sound like melody, the drums must do the phrasing at all times. That's where the press rolls and little biff notes come in – at the exact place, so you can tell it's a phrase.

*Dinah* was the very first solo I ever did as special number, with all of my drums. It was at a jam session Bob Crosby gave for Joe Sullivan, in April, 1937. I did sixty-four measures of it, with my brother's band making an eight-bar introduction.

The first thirty-two measures were slow and the next were fast. Then, the band came back in and finished it up with the same eight measures they started me off with.

During my solo I had to keep the melody going in my head. You have got to concentrate to do that. You must have in mind how many measures in a chorus, whether it's a sixteen or thirty-two bar chorus and make your repetitions just like you do if you are playing with the band.

I first played my tom-tom solo, *Tea for Two*, in about the year 1940. Little Harry Lim was in Chicago giving jam sessions at the Sherman Hotel. I wanted to do something different. I was thinking about it, but I never tried it before. Somebody gave me a bottle and it gave me nerve.

Brunis had done a solo and Lonnie Johnson had done a solo and all the guys around had done something. I said, "I'm not going to sit here and beat two drums. That's a cinch." Then I made an announcement that I was going to try something that I don't know if anybody ever saw or not, and they could tell me what they think of it. So, I stood up and taken this tom-tom. And it was my barrel tom-tom. The skins were put on with nails all around.

I had kind of dampened the tom-tom head so it would be loose. And, then I stood up and put my right foot on it and beat it with the snare drum sticks in my hands. I moved my foot different places to make different tones. It was very effective and made a nice novelty number.

I got rid of that tom-tom in '44, to get the set of tom-toms I have today. That cut out the foot solo, because I couldn't put my foot over the rims and move it about. Now, if anybody asks you, that's the way I come about that.

Today, the majority of bands play the "tag" ending. The drummer alone makes the tag for four or eight measures, before the band comes in for the finish.

The tag originated in New York City. That's the first place I ever heard it, but it's gotten to be a fad now and they all do it. And, it's a right pretty good little stunt if the guys do it right, but the drummers of today sometimes just keep beating right on through and try to do a whole lot of fancy stuff. Well, they just throw everybody off, because the band listens to the drummer and when the time's out, they still have got their horns down.

When I go to play a tag, I make a distinction in starting off. I still play the melody of the number that we're playing and in the last measure of the tag, I make a great ending of that – distinctly, a complete finish, in a way. Then, the band knows when to pick up the next beat right after the cymbal.

The average drummer don't do that, because he's not counting. You've got to count the measures. But the guys that come in with the horns have got to count too. If they're not counting, well, they are lost.

About 1939, when I was playing with Lonnie Johnson at the Three Deuces, I put out what I called the "nerve beat." With just guitar and drums, I had to play very soft, so I picked up the nerve beat because it was spicy and it was a change. Instead of beating on the shell, I would use this beat. It was soft enough so the guitar strings would go right through it.

Nervebeats

How you do it is this: you put the two sticks loosely in your right hand. Then, let your hand shake just like it shivers when you are cold and the two sticks will hit each other. To make that beat, they have to hit with a certain touch. If you hold the sticks too loose, they drop out of your hand. Have them too tight and you won't get any shake out of them. They got to click. They hit each other's body, and that makes the noise. You can make it as keen as you want, or you can make it as heavy as you want. It's all in your fingers, your hands, how you loosen up, how you tighten up. The looser you have them, the louder you can shake them and the more tone you get.

This part is easy enough, to make the arm quiver. But, to make a quick change from having a stick in each hand to two sticks in your right hand, and then back again without losing a beat, makes it not such an easy job after all. There is no short cut to anything you do on drums.

When I made the press roll in my moving picture, I'm only sorry I didn't do my shimmy part. I didn't do that. I haven't done it in about five years. I think I've lost it.

I started using the shimmy beat with my press roll in 1918, and I went all that time shaking up my insides. That was part of my drumming and I loved to do it. Every muscle in my body moved. A lot of people didn't know how I did it.

And now I have to let the shimmy go.

Now, on a press roll you must have very light hands, because if you haven't, you can't do it. If I had heavy hands, I couldn't make a roll like I do.

I think a drummer should be versatile. You can't go along with a one-track mind and be a good drummer. I don't think a drummer is qualified unless he has experience of playing all the different types of music and in different types of bands.

It doesn't puzzle me to work in a theater pit. There you come in contact with all kinds of music.

And, I don't shun working in a band or orchestra that plays classical music.

But if you don't know all those different types of music when you see them, well, you are just out there. In a show, most of the dances depend on the drummer for the different times. On some numbers, the drummer has to pick up or slow the time down. On others, the drummer may have to go into a different rhythm. If you make a mistake, the fellows know just what you are. You ain't nothing.

Now, catch some drummers of today. They don't know what to do next. Don't know what hand to put down first. They don't know when to hit the cymbal. They hit it anywhere. It ain't like that. All these things have to be studied and looked after.

With a singer – I can make a singer sing. You wonder how? I got a way of doing it with my drumming. A fellow dancing – I can give him certain beats and make him dance much better.

A drummer has to watch the singers with a band, to know what they are singing and the phrases that they use. He can't just go ahead and beat, not knowing what he is beating, not listening to anybody.

My first suggestion on playing for dancers in a show is to pay strict attention to the dancer. Some dancers won't want you to make different effects, but the majority of dancers want you to play a variety of things. Like – if they're doing a step, you accompany it on a shell. Or, if they do another step, you use the cymbal lightly. Do another step – you do that rhythm lightly on a cow-bell. Or, at different times you hit the cymbal on the jumps and make a roll on the turns.

Today, in dance halls, most people like to dance in a medium tempo, about the same as the dance step called the "toddle time" when I played on the river boats. It was just a walk with a little bounce in it and was good for settled people that can't skip and run all around the place.

Through the orders of Captain Streckfus, I put that beat out, and now all drummers use it. Of course, I don't imagine some guys would give me the credit. They don't know where it came from. They don't know who originated it.

This toddle time had four beats to the measure. Well, now, a lot of people don't realise that's where the four beats in dance music came from. It was a strange thing to hear a piano playing in 2/2 and the bass drum beating four to the measure.

It reminds me – in playing a waltz, you keep your bass drum always in three-four time, but with your snare drum, you can pick up and make four beats or three. Also, you can vary the rhythm with rolls.

When I first began playing, in certain halls in New Orleans, the bands all had to play waltzes, quadrilles, "mazookas", polkas, and schottisches.

In quadrilles, they have a little introduction that's two beats to the measure. It may be eight or twelve measures long and you stop. The introduction is for giving dancers notice to get their partners. Then, you've got another part you play, while they get lined up. And, you play another part and they start dancing.

In a quadrille, which is a reel, they got about twelve parts to it. There is a waltz and also a mazooka. A mazooka is in three-four time. But, there is one little catch to this three-four. Always, at the end of every measure, it's got a little accented "boomp-boomp" – two-eighth notes. And, then, you pick up three-four time again.

There was a time that we used to play in "slow drag." If you play a slow drag now, you know what they call it? A funeral march. And, if you play a funeral march, they wouldn't know what to say, because a funeral march is actually so slow that you can hardly walk by it. And if you don't look smart, you can't walk by it.

You play the blues or something like that and – "Please! Oh, man. Can't you play something lively?"

They don't know what they're talking about. Blues is supposed to be played slow, but not as slow as a funeral march. As I was just explaining to you, you can hardly walk a funeral march. You get off balance. But, anybody can walk the blues. So, it shows you right there that one is faster than the other.

It's a different feeling to be recording than what it is playing for a dance. You are more careful than when you're not recording. If you make a bad note, or if a guy's playing a horn and his lip slips, it's just too bad.

When you're playing for a dance, your lip can slip and you wipe it with a handkerchief and go right on. A drum can go after something and miss it, and mess up the time. In recording, there's no correcting. You can get very unnerved. Nobody wants to make a mistake, recording. But, they make plenty of them not recording.

When I first began to record, I was with the Oliver band. That was a crew that was really together. It was then I began to use wood blocks, the shell of the bass drum and cymbals more in recording than I usually did, because they would come through. Bass drum and snare drum wouldn't record very well in those days and it was my part to be heard.

The idea of hitting the rims of the bass drum, which I worked out myself personally, I often use. I started to beat on the rims for the toddle on the boat, after I removed the tinny sounding cymbal from the side of the drum. A lot of people think I use the wood blocks, but it's the rims.

The wood block was so loud and so sharp and piercing to the ear, I used the rims and shell on the bass drum instead. And, it sounded so pretty and soothing and soft.

Now, about playing different rhythms at the same time – I map the whole situation out in my mind. I do triplets with the right hand and two strokes with the left hand and four on the bass drum. I think the easiest way for me to do that is to start off with the right hand and come in with the left hand to compete with the right hand. Then, the foot combines with that.

I can use different rhythms in each hand when I beat on the rims, and for a fact, I think it sounds more effective than it does on the snare drum, because a snare head is too bouncy. The wood has stability. And then, the tonation of the wood is better than the snare drum, to me. To my ear. That's why I do it with the wood. I don't map that out until I get to playing, until I hear a number. If I feel that it will fit in a number, I'll do it.

Lots of things that I have in mind to do, won't fit the melody, won't fit the tune. Then, I don't do them. But each time I do any work like that in a number, I've studied it out and fixed it all out in my head; routine. Then, if the number isn't a fit number for that, I don't do it. I never throw a band with these things. The way I do different rhythms, it keeps the band going, keeps the band playing all right, because I'm right even with the melody.

Some of those beats that I make are pretty complicated even to listen to. Sometimes, when I do rim work, I do it in triplets – fast. Or, it may just be a straight beat, but I'm doing it so fast, it sounds like triplets.

Anything I make, even on tom-toms, I arrange out for the melody. I don't just go along and make those things anywhere in the number.

The way you vary the tone on the rims, for the light, soft parts you use the keen part of the sticks. If you want a heavy tone, move your hands in closer to the rims and use the heavy part of the sticks. Then when the clarinet or something soft comes in, pull your hands out and use the keen end of the sticks.

If the piano comes in with a solo, I play on the shell of the bass drum, with a press roll. That's on the shell, not the edge of the rims. Modern drums that have the pearl finish shells don't have the tone of the old time drums with solid wood shells.

It's the same with the rims. If three-quarters of the rim is cut out to put in pearl, that cuts out some of the tone and makes it lighter, so you have got to hit heavier.

When the band comes in, all together – the ensemble – move the sticks in closer and use the heavy part, and if you think they're going to play loud, you take the butt end of the stick to beat the rim, and it makes a contrast.

I use all these things in a band, and, quite natural, it makes the band sound different and better. There's nothing harsh about rims and shells – no loud beating. You can soften the band down by jumping to the rims, and all those sounds come out when you make them play soft, so it sounds good.

You have to be thinking all the time to do something different – to make the band sound different. You can't drum just sitting there beating. You got to think. That's why you have a head on your shoulders.

# CHAPTER 9

When I was a little fellow in New Orleans, I wanted to be a doctor.  My mother said she was gong to send me to Tuskegee, but she didn't live.  So I turned out to be a doctor of skin – beating drum.

But I enjoyed every minute of my life drumming.  My enjoyment, that I was getting out of music, I was sending through to others.  I know that some of my drumming touched a lot of people's hearts.  If someone who was angry, even with domestic troubles, came in where I was drumming – drumming with my heart – they'd just forget their troubles and be happy.  Even if I'd been a doctor, I couldn't have done any more than that.

I've always loved to drum.  It's really my life.  I started to drumming when I's about 16, and I put everything into it.  I've had a lot of fun playing music.  To play real music, you must have a happy heart, a happy mind.  A bad temperament doesn't go with music.

Anytime you are angry or displeased about something, you can't play good music.  You have to be pleased, satisfied, with a good heart, and you must have a sense of humor.

Yes, I've had a lot of fun in my work. I loved it.  I didn't just drum to make a dollar here or a dollar there, to make a living.  I drummed because I loved it, and I drummed in a way to make everybody else love it.  I didn't just drum for myself, but so everybody would enjoy it as I enjoyed it myself.

I do believe when I get back to drumming every day, if God says the same, I'll be a different and better drummer from what I used to be.  I haven't got the spirit of liveliness that I used to have, because I'm getting older, but I still have a little bit left.

There's lots of things I've learned the last few years, even sitting down doing nothing.  Just thinking.  A lot of things.  I will drum better because I will drum so that everybody will feel relaxed.

I have been thinking today that I wish I could get any drummer – I wouldn't care, I'm not partial – could be white or black – could be Indian or Chinese – any nationality – I wish I could get him to take up my chores and think like I think about it, like whatever he do, do with all his might.  That is the way to drum.  He should not drum just to be sitting up there beating drums.

Sometimes I think musicians are born, not made.  Most all good musicians have a talent you can't learn.  They have got it and you can't take it away from them.

Individuality cannot be duplicated. Someone may say, "Oh, you sound just like Louis." Or, "You sound just like Baby." But Louis is an individualist. Baby Dodds is an individualist. Who has the originality? It's got to be the one who was copied.

I never copied behind anybody. I played different even from my teacher, which caused him to lose his job on the boat. It wasn't my fault. I just was an individualist, that's all. I didn't go away from his teaching, I just added a little bit more. I taken his teaching and made something bigger out of it.

Before I close my eyes for the last time, I would love to have a group of drummers working together. There could be six or seven drummers. I figure an odd number of seven would be best.

Each drummer would have a full set of drums, a regular set-up, same as I use. The leader could sit in the middle, on a raised platform with the other drummers around him. Each set of drums would be tuned a little different, some lower, some a little higher so there would be a contrast in tone.

You know there are no two drummers that drum or phrase alike. I want each one to follow his own way of phrasing, but yet, it blend. The other drummers could follow the leader. They would all be in the same tempo, but each could be doing a little different beat.

They would have to be versatile and pay a lot of attention to make a contrast to the leader. They could raise the volume and lower it and come down softly just like a regular orchestra, and I think it would be a grand thing. It could be like a conversation with each drummer talking to the others.

I've got a piece of paper written out in my head. It has been in my mind a long time. Once I knew about six guys in Chicago I'd like to get together, like Tubby Hall, "Snags", Johnny Wells, Wally Bishop. Now I doubt whether I could ever find those kind of drummers today, unless I would bring up a lot of school kids and teach them myself.

I think it could be done by a bunch of kids that want to learn and do something different to get recognition. A group like that could go on indefinitely, and it would be such a novelty people would love it.

Not too loud. I wouldn't want it blasty. I'd want the drums to rise and fall. After working on a very low level, they could raise out of that almost to a blast then go back in to that low part again. And you'd have those different tones coming out of each set of drums so you would be able to distinguish them one from another.

The tempo could increase, then drop back to slow. Some parts could be in waltz time, and you could have abrupt stops sometimes. Just constant beating and beating on drums would run you crazy, but with a lot of contrast from tuning each drum set different – and if each drummer would do the opposite of what some other fellow was doing and still blend, it would come out very pretty.

I've done this with Dave Tough, and I've done it with George Wettling. If two drummers can do it, four can do it. If four can do it, six can do it. That's the story. Hindu and other oriental drummers do it, so it's a cinch American drummers could.

Somebody is going to say this sounds foolish, but I would say again, "It's music." Even though it's out of drums, it's still music. My intention has always been to bring melody out of drums. I think it can be done and I think I shall do it one day.

# ABBY "CHINEE" FOSTER

Abby Foster
drums

Born: New Orleans, Louisiana, March 19, 1900
Died: New Orleans, Louisiana, September 8, 1962

*"Chinee" Foster for decades was one of those fabulous, legendary New Orleans drummers, along with Black Benny, Jean (John) Vigne and others about whom little was really known. Chinee started playing drums when very young and was the only musician mentioned in the newspaper accounts of the 1913 Easter shooting at the Tuxedo Cafe in the District. Evidently he retired from playing during the Great Depression of the 1930s. He made a comeback, and recorded in the early 1960s.*

I was born on St Joseph's day, March 19th, 1900. I first started on drums when I was a little boy. Musicians wasn't like they are today, they were very scarce. They didn't have juke boxes then. Well, when I was a little boy I used to play with colored and white bands. Some of them thought I was Mexican, Puerto Rican or Spanish. When I got to playing a lot around the French Market with different bands they didn't know whether I was colored or white. Some of them used to suspect that I were Indian, or Mexican, just like Lorenzo Tio, that great clarinet player. One time I went on a show and done a Chinese act, so from then on, white and colored started calling me "Chinee." A lot of people would say, "Why do you call him Chinee, because a Chinaman is not dark like that." They say, "Well, he do that chinee act so good, we just call him Chinee." And from that time on, they've been calling me Chinee, and very few people know my right name.

I lived on St. Philip Street, near Burgundy. When I was eight years old I started playing at the Ivy Theater, at Annette and Villere with a white band. Clarinet and piano. Nobody taught me drums whatsoever. Nobody in my family was musical. I was so small, I had a special stool made so I could reach the pedal. I had a 14" x 26" bass drum which they used to tighten up with a rope. My bass drum used a cymbal on the side which I would beat together with the bass drum pedal. I also used a Chinese crash cymbal, suspended. At that time we didn't have a Turkish cymbal, but there was a small cymbal on the bass drum. My snare drum was 3" x 15" double-head with gut snares. I'm not bragging on myself, but I could take the old style of drums, with that cymbal on the side and I would make the same style that they play today with all the new style tom toms. I had to do it all with the bass drum, with snare sticks, as what they make today with three or four tom-toms. I did have one small Chinese tom-tom, double-headed, with all the nails around the heads. Also, I had woodblocks. At the time when we started recording, in order to hear the other instruments, we used nothing but tom tom and the woodblock.

You can hear when I played the woodblocks and whistled on the Celestin records [Okeh 1925]. The slide whistle was a Ludwig, all metal, 11" long. There wasn't but three I know played those whistles – Louis Armstrong, "Red Happy" Bolton and myself.

I played with John Robichaux's band in 1910 at St. Katherine's Hall, near the church across from Charity Hospital on Tulane Avenue. I was making my first communion

then and they were raising funds for the school. I asked the fellows to let me play one number. They said I wasn't large enough to fit in a band, but Father Carter told them that if I broke anything on the drum that he would pay for it. So after I played one number it went so good they asked me to play another one and so from then on that started me out. Kimball was playing bass with Robichaux, a lady by the name of Miss Margaret was playing piano, Eddie Atkins, trombone and Charles McCurdy was playing clarinet.

The next band was the Imperial, with Manuel Perez, cornet; Buddy Johnson, trombone; Alphonse Picou was playing clarinet, René Baptiste, guitar and Jimmy Brown, bass. I played my first job with them at Lincoln Park.

When I was a boy, before my mother bought me any drums, I'd practise on a cheese box. I'd use sticks from a chair. Later I always used lightweight sticks because I could do more with them, could handle them better - 2A - Ludwig sticks. I used Leedy or Conn snare drums. Conn's had drums in those days. They were the first to put out nickel plated drums: Leedy were wood. I tune my snare drum up to F and my bass drum to D. I also used four cow bells and four china blocks; their real name is temple blocks. They look like a coconut. When I used those, I'd watch myself. That's one important thing drummers do not watch. When I'd use them in the chorus of a number the band was playing, I'd make sure not to hit those blocks unless I'm in tune with the chords of the blowing instruments. I always make a style of my own, especially if a drummer's around me trying to catch on to it. If he thinks I'd make one thing, I'd make something else in the opposite way. Just like right now. I have some breaks that I haven't heard anybody make since 1926, that I could mix in.

You see, in making breaks and drum solos you must be in time and not rush the tempo or slow it down, or you're going to throw the band off. Never let your hands interfere with your feet. Your feet is time; your hands are what you make your foolishness with. See, in other words, I can play a 3/4 waltz time or a two-beat 2/4 time on the bass drum with my foot, yet I'm playing in groups of four with my hands. The hands, that's what you make your monkey-shines with, but I'd keep time with the bass drum. You never stop the bass drum, because that's your time.

I was taught by John MacMurray. He sat down and gave me these instructions about keeping time. I liked him as an orchestral drummer. I also liked Louis Cottrell as a street drummer. MacMurray used a single head snare drum back around 1908. The snares were right up underneath the head and were made of gut, not steel. One day at Lincoln Park, MacMurray and I were talking and he took a nice liking to me because he saw that I was interested, and he say, "Some day you'll make a great drummer, but I want to tell you one thing, with all that you do, always watch your bass drum, because that's the time that can make or break a band. It's not what your hands do, it's what your feet do, so always bear that in mind." Well, I paid attention and I listened to what he was saying, and I come home and practise at it and find it to be natural, just like he told me. So I kept that up, up until today. Sometime I would take a drum solo chorus. Plenty of fellows they try to make it with their feet but with their hands they cannot do it. Because your hand is just for effect, and your feet is time. When I'd play a solo, I'd hum the melody to myself. That way you can't go wrong.

Now, you see the way I strike these sticks together? You have to strike 'em at various places to make the sticks change tone. If you notice, your sticks almost make notes. You've got to squeeze 'em to a certain extent to make 'em change the tone. See, when I play a blues, I'd make like that with the sticks and then I'd follow on the snare drum, going over different things, but my feet don't take effect. What most fellows make on the tom toms today, I'd make with my right hand with the butt end of the stick on the bass drum and keep the snare drum going with the left hand. Sometimes I'd change over and make what I want with the left hand.

I never did use any pads or muffle on my bass drum. Sometimes you can choke the bass drum by letting the beater strike the bass drum head and remain there a second. I never could see why they use the pads. You can't hear the bass drum. It has got to have a kind of humming sound to it. A pad will take the sound off the drum and make it sound out of tune. Plenty of drummers do not know how to tune a drum. Many drummers today, all they think about is that you just have to tighten a drum. You don't just tighten the drum, you've got to tune it. The outer head is always looser than the batter head. That's why they put rods with separate tensions on the drum. You tune your snare batter head up to F and you don't worry about the other one, you just keep it looser. I use kangaroo heads, but sometimes you just take anything you can get. But kangaroo don't take the dampness out as much as the calf head do.

Also, I played in brass bands, both pick-up and organized, such as the Onward, the Excelsior, Pickwick and Tuxedo. The Pickwick was Henry Allen and little Red Allen. I always played snare drum, because my hands were too fast for the bass drum. I'd forget I was playing bass drum and I'd go to making the beats that the snare drum is supposed to make. The bass drummer I liked was Ernest Trepagnier. Also Black Benny was a great bass drum player. He wasn't an orchestral player but he was a great bass drum player. In other words, he was the one that came out with the 4/4 beats out on the street. Trepagnier is the one who put me in the Tuxedo dance band. He turned his job over to me because he said he was getting too old, his feet was getting bad on him. Ridgely was the trombone player with Celestin's Tuxedo Band then. We played at the Louisiane Restaurant, Southern Yacht Club and the New Orleans Country Club. We used to play there at Carnival time, also the Boston Club. At the Louisiane every Saturday night they used to have a big supper dance and everybody would go there and have a good time. They had champagne after their suppers. They used two bands, Robichaux and the Tuxedo Band. Sometimes Joe Oliver too. I remember him, and played with him when he was playing with the Ory Band. They weren't working anywhere steady, just gigging, such as Pete Lala's and a little theater on Claiborne between Conti and St Louis. That was the year before Oliver left for Chicago, when Louis Armstrong took his place and started playing with Ory. Ory used "Red Happy" on drums and Henry Martin, a left-hand drum player. Now, as for "Red Happy," Happy Bolton was his real name. I'll tell you, he was a great drum player. Him and I used to fight all the time. It was a long time before they could find out who was the best, him or I. Quite naturally they had friends of mine, who would say I was the best; then they had friends of his that would say he was the best. So after I had come up they had a tell-tale showdown at the

Italian Hall on Esplanade between Burgundy and Rampart. Well, he were playing with Chris Kelly's band and I were playing with Celestin. So it came to a showdown and the musicians voted for me, and told him they were sorry, but I was the best. See, what I was the best at, I always had the sense to play like the band wanted. "Happy" wanted to play the way he liked. If the band wanted to play a way I didn't like, I'd play like they wanted it, then, every now and then I use my ideas in between. So it come to another showdown. They gave a concert and gave prizes, a loving cup, which I have at my house right now. I was voted 80 to 20 over him. "Happy" was about two years older than me.

A trumpet player told me, "That's the stuff, that's the real stuff that you play. Without that you can have everything you want in the front line and you simply cannot play." You see, it's all up to the drummer to make or break a band. A drummer can make a band or he can break a band, no matter how good the rest of them are. If a drummer's bad, the whole band is bad. It's all up to the drummer to give the band pep. If you got a lazy drummer you can have the best trumpet, trombone and clarinet in the world, but they can't make what they want to. It's got to be that drummer. Now you take this man up there, that photo of Bunk Johnson on the wall. Now him and Joe Oliver was on the same style. Now, take like Peter Bocage, he is a nice trumpet player. Manuel Perez, Arnold Metoyer, Andrew Kimball, those fellows, they were more of musical men but they couldn't get rid of that exercise book. When I was a boy, I don't know how it was with white bands, but I can tell you how it was with us. If you had a number one band, they wouldn't hire a drummer that could read. Now, don't that sound awkward? They wouldn't hire a reading drummer because he'd play too much of the music. If you're playing with a symphony orchestra, or something like that, well, it calls for a reading drummer, but you see a drummer playing in an orchestra for dances he's got so much faking to do in order to swing the band. He's got to use so much out of his own head, what he thinks ought to be played there. They've got to use so much of their own ideas because sometimes the music is so empty that it don't fill the band. The beats are there but still not enough to swing a band. Maybe you might have a real jazzy trombone player. The drummer got to know just how much beat to give that trombone player, or that trumpet player, to send him.

He can make that trombone player or that trumpet player make more than they can make, for the simple reason he's got the feeling. They don't have to tell the drummer, he's got the feeling where that man might fall at, where his weak spots are. The drummer has to know all that, to uphold a man. To cover his mistakes. The drummer's got to be so fast, and think so fast that if someone walks across the floor and falls, or makes a mistake by accident, the drummer's got to play something to take people's attention off the accident and make it look intentional, so they might come right back and play the same mistake like it was done on purpose. The drummer's got to be very smart. He's got to be thinking and on his toes all the time. Maybe in a show, or something, a comedian holding a glass of water or something in his hand is walking and he drops it. We know he didn't aim to do that. Well, the drummer's so fast and smart he makes a big explosion. The comedian may do the same thing over again and the drummer plays again like he meant to do it, so the audience never knows it was first done accidentally.

I learned about drumming by listening to other fellows talking and arguing and I'd ask questions. Like MacMurray, he was a good all-round drummer. In other words, he was a good street drummer, he was a good show drummer and he was a good dance drummer. Jean Vigne, he played mostly dance band. He played in the street too, but he wasn't much of a street drummer. The real street drummers were Louis Cottrell and Ernest Trepagnier; also, in later years Bebé Matthews, who is Bill Matthews brother. Bill was playing drums before he took up trombone. All four Matthews brothers played drums: Bill, Raymond, "Happy" and Bebé, who was the best. He played a while with Manuel Perez when they had the Imperial Band. Walter Brundy was a great show drummer, a great orchestra drummer too. He wasn't no explosive man, but he could balance a band nice. Henry Zeno was a good drummer, both street and dance band.

I never did hear Buddy Bolden that I could remember because I was quite a kid then. I have played with fellows that played with him, like Frankie Duson and Cornish. I heard a lot of talk of him though. All the old time musicians that's older than me say Bolden was the most powerful trumpet player they ever heard in their life. White or black will tell you that. I liked to hear Joe Oliver on the regular jazz barrelhouse music. For real smoothness, a musical trumpet player I liked was Manuel Perez. I played with Freddie Keppard, a nice blues player. He wasn't a real musical reader like Perez, he was a blues player. My favorite musical band was Celestin's. For a faking band, I always liked the Kid Ory band.

Cottrell, I think he was the best rolling drummer we had. He could make more different rolls than any man I heard in my life. He was very good in the street, like in the action between the band numbers, when the band would stop playing and march to the snare drum alone. Cottrell was good on that, and also when they'd send a a band off, roll off. He'd get the real natural tone out of a drum. Henry Martin was a sensational drummer, which I mean dance, street, show drummer and everything.

I tune my snare drum to F, a medium tension on the top batter head. The bottom snare head is tuned to a lower, lesser tension. That helps the bottom head to bounce and helps ring the snares. So your bass drum is in D and your snare drum is in F. I notice that the white brass bands on parade keep the bass drum going between band numbers, also the army and navy bands. None of the black boys do that

*Louis Cottrell Sr.*

at all. Never did do it. In marching bands, the bass drum is always on the left of the snare drummer, for either left hand or right hand drummers. You start off on a march with your left foot. You also count your time with the left foot on one.

All the drummers had different beats. Some would be lazy and didn't care how they played, and would be playing for their self. Another fellow, he'd be playing with his whole heart and soul because he wants to give everything he's got. I always try to get with the best, the better the fellow is, I try to get next to him. If you can do something, you can do it. The more professional a fellow is, the closer I try to get to make friends with him some kind of way, white or black. I'm going to talk to him and swap ideas.

*Showing how drummers sing across the snare drum*

In playing drums, it's what comes in my mind. Sometimes I can't tell you what I'm going to make. Just all of a sudden it comes to me and I'll knock it out in my head. Then I'll hit it all of a sudden; if it comes out good then I'll keep it up. If it sounds bad, then I'll stop using it. But a lot of those things, I couldn't tell you what I'm going to make my own self. When reading music, if I feel that the music don't have enough support for the band, I'm going to add something to it, or either take it away. That is going to make it convenient for the other men. If I feel the drum music is not enough support to swing a band, if it has too much empty space, I'll add something in there to correspond with what the blowing instruments are playing. See, you save the man that's playing the blowing instrument. The guitar player, or bass or piano player, all they're doing is beating just the same way as me, but you got to help the man that's blowing, because he's using his breath while you're using your hand and foot. I can add something in there – give that man that's blowing a chance to catch his wind. The drummer is supposed to work with those people and save them. If you play drum music straight, like it's written, there's no support to the band.

Plenty of time I get music that's written in one-two beat, but if I find it's not enough to support the band, I'll use a 4/4 beat. Or if it's written in 4/4 time and I find that it's crowding the men too much, I'll change it from 4/4 time to 2/2 time. You see music is just like arithmetic, you've got to add, subtract or divide.

Never copy behind another fellow, because I figure some people might like another fellow's style, but someone likes your style. Always make a style of your own. Like when I had my cards printed, I had printed, "I originate while others imitate."

# PAUL BARBARIN

Adolphe Paul Barbarin
drums

Born: New Orleans, Louisiana, May 5, 1901
Died: New Orleans, Louisiana, February 10, 1969

*Paul Barbarin was one of the best known New Orleans drummers. He came from a musical family, his father (Isidore Barbarin) being a pioneer alto horn player in brass bands. Three of his brothers became musicians, and he was also Danny Barker's uncle.*

*Paul's first important job was with Buddy Petit's band in 1915. He went to Chicago in 1917 and a year later began working at the Royal Garden with King Oliver and Jimmie Noone. He worked regularly with Oliver in the mid-1920s and also played a few dates with Jelly Roll Morton. In 1928 Barbarin joined Luis Russell's band in New York and also played and recorded with Jelly Roll. In the 1930s, for several years, he played and toured with Louis Armstrong. He returned to New Orleans in 1940 and formed his own band. Apart from a few residencies in New York, Chicago, Los Angeles and Toronto, he continued to lead one of the most popular bands in New Orleans. In 1960 he re-formed the Onward Brass Band, and died whilst leading the band on a dedication parade in 1969.*

I happen to come from a musical family. I was born May 5th 1901, right on the corner of Barracks and St Claude. My father's name was Isidore John Barbarin. He was a trumpet player, well, cornet in those days. Later on he picked up the mellophone. They called it alto horn then, but it's called a mellophone today. My mother's brother was a great clarinet player. He was my uncle and was named Louis Arthedeau. He played in the Onward Brass Band, and from what I am told by a lot of the old-time musicians, he was one of the finest clarinet players in New Orleans. Well, my mother, she liked to sing in the kitchen, liked to dance where there was music, you know. I mean just loved it. That's really how I came to start out in music. I used to take two forks, you know, and I'd whistle and sing, just playing the forks. Beating away while my mother and my sisters were all dancing in the kitchen. I broke up one of the chairs, probably from beating on it, and since it was broke, I took the two rungs and made points and then on used them for sticks. I would hang out on the corner with some other kids. I was always the main attraction. The others had like a comb and paper or just straight whistled. We used to play on the corner till the cops would chase us away for disturbing the peace. Someone would call for the cops and here they would come on horseback. Those horses didn't stand a chance. When we seen 'em we would be gone. Most of us was barefoot and we could run like rabbits.

Three of my brothers played music too. I have my brother Louis that's now playing with Papa Celestin's band, under the direction of Eddie Pierson. Then Lucien. He died about a year ago. I have another brother who plays trumpet. Pretty good too. His name is Willie, but he would rather work in the day than fool with the trumpet. I just don't understand him. We also have my sister Rose's son, Danny Barker, who plays good guitar. He is up in New York, trying to get his book together, which I hope he does, 'cause I'm tired of hearing about that book.

With
to Oli
F

I don't rightly remember the first music I heard, but I do remember hearing Buddy Bolden. His band was playing a banquet at Perseverance Hall. That's on Villere between Annette and St Bernard. I was living in the back street from the Hall and my mother, she said that was Buddy Bolden blowing over there. That man sure could blow.

They had a lot of music out at Milneberg. They had camps out there and picnics every day. I mean every day. Some of the bands was organized and some just get-together bands. But they had music galore out there. In fact I had a cousin that was killed on the Smoky Mary train going out there. It ran at about five miles an hour but this kid he just kept hopping on and hopping off and he fell on the wheels and got killed. His name was Rogers. But anyways, they had all kinds of bands. Colored bands and white bands. I heard a lot of white bands around then. They had the Christian's Band. I don't know if it was Emile Christian himself or his brother had the band, but they used to play at Elysian Fields and Dauphine a lot. They would play on the gallery out there before they would go inside, to let the people know they was there. This little gallery or what you call a porch was always one flight up. Just like the dance halls. They always had the musicians upstairs in a air-view bandstand, then all the dancers would be on the floor below you.

When I started in music I always did admire the clarinet players. Sat right by them always. In fact I started on clarinet but couldn't execute. I knew the fingering and everything but I just couldn't execute fast enough. I even took a lesson or two with my godfather Paul Chaligny, but I soon got disgusted and switched to drums.

I went to work at the St Charles Hotel. I was running the freight elevator there and I'd get paid every two weeks. So, my mother, she knew I wanted a set of drums and she said, "Well. Let's put the money aside. We'll soon have enough money to make a down payment." So we goes over to Grunewald, where my father dealt at, and decided to get me a set of drums. Anyway, the same evening I got my drums, a bass player named Johnny Predonce heard about it. He didn't have a drummer for a job he was fixing to play for a guy fixing to run for Alderman or something. So he hired me, and I made $1.25. That was good money back then. We only played for an hour or so. Ballyhooing, you know. From then on I was gone. Worked with all kinds of bands until I left for to go North.

In those days all the bands sat the same. In a straight line. Always on the band-stand in a straight line. You had the bass, then the guitar, clarinet, cornet, trombone and drums. Bass just on the one end and drums on the other. They had so many great bands in New Orleans then. The Golden Leaf Band, Maple Leaf Band, Superior Band, The Olympia, The Eagle Band. Oh, so many. For instance, the Imperial Band was Manuel Perez, trumpet; George Baquet, clarinet; Buddy Johnson, trombone; Willie Santiago, guitar; Jimmy Brown, bass and Bebé Matthews on drums. The Superior had Bunk, cornet; Big Eye Louis, clarinet; Eddie Atkins, trombone; René Baptiste, the guy always had a big cigar, on guitar; Billy Marrero played bass and John MacMurray on drums. Now he was a very sensational, very good drummer. The first time I seen him, and the last time too, he had a banjo head for a snare drum. I don't know how he got the snares on it , but he had it, that's what he had. MacMurray always carried lots of contraptions with him. Whistles and ratchets and all that for breaks. In one particular tune he had a chain, like on a horse and wagon. Well, he would take this chain and lift it up and in this rag, I can't recall what rag, but anyway he'd take this chain and drop it. It would come out perfect in time. He was a wonderful drummer and anyone living today that can recall will tell you that. The last time I saw him he was playing with a four-piece band on Rampart and Julia.

Most of the guys then used a bass drum with ropes on. You'd have to pull the ropes to tighten the drum you know. They all had the upright pedal for the bass drum. I mean, it came from the top with straps on and a spring down there with a wooden pedal. They sometimes used tom-toms, but the Chinese kind. No tuning. Some of us had a woodblock. I carved my own. But now, the first one I seen playing on the rim of the drum was Baby Dodds.

You see, drummers like MacMurray or Jean Vigne. Them fellows they never played no four beats. All those drummers then played two beats. Never played four. The first time I ever heard four beats played was King Oliver and Ory and them playing at the Economy Hall. They was playing the blues and "Red Happy" was their drummer. Happy was an older boy than Louis. His real name was Bolton, Happy Bolton. He did a whole lot of scat singing and he was a very sensational drummer. He was uncouth though. He'd come and pick up your sticks and say, "Give 'em here boy. You don't know what you're doing. Let me play something." Take the sticks right out of your hand. Bully you. I used to feel sorry the way he used to do poor little Mack Lacey. He'd borrow Lacey's drum or cymbal and never give it back to him. Lil' Mack never said anything. Daren't say anything. Red Happy was a tough man.

Mack Lacy was the drummer with a band that Buddy Petit played with. Jimmie Noone was on the clarinet, Yank Johnson, Buddy Johnson's brother, played trombone, John Marrero on guitar and Simon Marrero played bass. I still say he was one of the greatest, little Mack Lacey. Nobody ever mentioned him. He was a wonderful drummer, smooth, I mean clean too. Not a whole load of noise. No open spaces. He filled them in. I would say my kid brother, Louis, plays something on the order of Mack Lacey. Smooth, you know what I mean. Not rough at all, but Mack was a lot better drummer than my brother. I admired him out of all the old-time drummers the most but, like I said, nobody knows a thing about him. Maybe Baby Dodds mentioned him.

Anyhow, to get back to this four-beat thing. See, playing this kind of music, this dixieland music, a lot of people are going to dance. See, the older people they don't know where to start. They go out there to dance but can't get started. Too many beats. But see, with this kind of music that we play, they know where to come in and put their foot. The two beats is good for dancing. A good beat. If you've got a good bass man working with you and can play that two beats, you can really push a band and especially the dancing people.

All through we played for dances and I played in many bands. Around 1916 or 1917 I was working with Chris Kelly at a picnic held by his boss, who operated a lumber yard. Chris once saved my life. We was furnishing the music and a woman started flirtatiously winking at me. Her escort discovered this and got real hot. The woman blamed me. Said I was winking at her. I was too young to even be thinking about flirting.

The man threatened me and old Chris, he pulled out a gun. He told the man I had trouble with my eyes and had to blink. I had never blinked much till then, but I sure started. The incident was settled without any violence.

I worked with Walter Robertson's band for a good while. He played trumpet; Emile Barnes was the clarinetist; Ambrose Powers, trombone; "Tit" Rouchon was our bass player and Buddy Manaday, guitar. I worked at Tom Anderson's with a five piece band, with Fats Pichon on the steamer "President". In the real early days I never played in bands that had a piano. They all had guitar. The first time I played with a piano in the band, it felt funny to me. I had to get used to it. I didn't say anything but I thought, "That don't belong in a band." Later, of course I had piano in my own band.

Another thing I want to mention is the street drumming. Brass band stuff. Louis Cottrell was about the best snare drummer they ever had. No one like him. When he hit that snare drum you heard a snare drum. Boy, I'm the only guy trying to imitate him. A lot of these people don't hit a drum. Play in a whisper, like they want to keep it a secret. But not him. He played with the Excelsior Brass Band all the time. Clay Jiles was the bass drummer, but I didn't like the way Jiles played. He was good, especially on those marches and things. He didn't play a jazz beat. Just played straight. I mean for bass drum players, Ernest Trepagnier and Jean Vigne were the best. Everyone talks about Black Benny, but I wouldn't say Benny 'cause he was overrated. He was all right, but

Red Allen played as much bass drum as Black Benny. I never could see how he had a reputation like Jean Vigne or Ernest Trepagnier. I mean those two guys. Oh, Benny was good and he had a reputation all right. I used to watch him at the time I was at Tom Anderson's. He got that reputation from fighting all the time and hittin' someone in the mouth. He was always in jail for something or other. The warden would let him out to play a parade and he would just go right back in again after it ended. He would just like to fight. He never killed nobody or stole nothing, he was just mischievous, that's all. Like people would get too close to his drum in the street. He would take his beater and hit them in the head. Some girl eventually killed him up on Gravier and Franklin.

You know something about New Orleans? Everytime I get into a discussion with somebody they think that New Orleans is the only place in the world that had music. But, when I came up, in those days, I saw music and heard music all day. The peddlers in the street singing rhythm. People walkin' rhythm. You heard the pastors in the Baptist Churches. They were singing rhythm. More so than a jazz band. And some churches, when you passed, they were swinging like crazy. The peddlers, they're walking in the street, they're peddling. Everything they do is in rhythm. A one-legged man, a walking rhythm. I don't know, something about negroes. Everything they do is just in rhythm.

*Left: letter from Paul Barbarin
to Bill Russell*

I remember talking with an old circus trumpeter in New Orleans back in 1915 on a dance date, a fellow named Sam Rickey. He told me that they had been playing ragtime down there for 30 years. New Orleans, too, was the spot where the bands first started off a tune with two warning beats. **Jack Weber**

Dee Dee Chandler – I believe he was the first drummer that ever used cymbals in a band. He used to have a cymbal attached to his bass drum. **John Joseph**

I had a card here of Fischer's Band, where it had printed on there, "Fischer's Ragtime Military Jazz Band." Now that's when I first played, I was eight years old, that's the first job, the first parade I ever played. Now, if I was born in 1903, that was 1911, and the word "Jazz;" they used it on that card. **Monk Hazel**

There were so many bands in New Orleans. But most of the musicians had day jobs . . . They had to work at other trades 'cause there were so many musicians, so many bands. It was just about the most musical town in the country. Most of the kids took lessons of some kind, and I got my inspiration from my uncle, Willie Bontemps, who played bass and guitar in Jack Carey's band. I played my first jobs with Steve Lewis – house parties and such. **Zutty Singleton**

Baby Dodds was the drummer on the boat, you see, and Ray Bauduc, Leo Adde and myself, the three of us, we used to all go in there, and copy all of Baby's licks. So at that time, if you heard any one of us. you heard the same thing, because we all played the same licks.

But there was never any drum solos; you got two bars, or maybe four bars at the most. There was never anything more than four bars. That's why I can't stand drum solos today; we were taught that the drums were supposed to be felt, not supposed to be heard, and if you played loud, they called you "Mulefoot," you know. You wasn't supposed to play all that, just as loud as you could play; you were supposed to work for the band. You had to be even below the piano, so the piano could be heard. So long as you didn't interfere with anybody, everything was fine.

The word "Dixieland" now, the way they use it now, it disgusts me, because we never played those tunes. We played anything. Man, if a tune come out, take *The Old Spinning Wheel*, we play the tune, but we play it in the New Orleans way, and swing it. We used to have a sign on the piano: "No requests we can't fill." If we didn't know the tune, we'd get you to hum it for us, and if we got the first eight bars, that's all we needed. **Monk Hazel**

I played a date in Europe with Kid Ory. Ory said, "I can't hear the bass drum."
**Wallace Bishop**

# New Orleans Style: Guitar & Banjo

# Johnny St. Cyr

John Alexander St. Cyr.
guitar/banjo

Born: New Orleans, Louisiana, February 17, 1890
Died: Los Angeles, California, June 17, 1966

*St. Cyr became a leading guitarist in New Orleans at an early age and played with Piron, the Tuxedo band and Kid Ory before going on the Mississippi excursion boats in 1918. In 1923 he went to Chicago where he recorded with King Oliver's Creole Band, Jelly Roll Morton's Red Hot Peppers, and Louis Armstrong's most famous group, the Hot Five. He also worked with Freddy Keppard and Jimmie Noone in Doc Cook's big band before returning to New Orleans in 1930. There he resumed his trade as a plasterer and also played with Armand Piron and Paul Barbarin. He moved to Los Angeles in 1954 and led a New Orleans band at Disneyland from 1961 until his death.*

Although I was born and raised a Catholic, most of my friends were Baptists and I often went to Baptist services with them. That's when I first got interested in music. Those Baptist rhythms were similar to the jazz rhythms and the singing was very much on the blues side. You could dance as well as shout to those rhythms. Those Baptists really enjoyed themselves.

My mother never wanted me to go to the public school as she always taught me not to fight and she thought the other boys would pick on me. When I was 10 she thought I should have some education so she sent me to a Methodist private school nearby. Professor Nickerson had an uncle who ran a private school at St. James's Hall, right back of St. James's Methodist church. The school was on Derbigny, between Bienville and Iberville. Although I'd never attended school I used to play "school" at night with the other children. So I learnt the alphabet (both forward and backwards) and learnt to read. When I got to school I could read pretty well, so they put me in first grade. I also attended St. Katherine's School which was a Catholic school near Tulane, and attended one session there until I got my first communion. At weekends I used to line sugar barrels for 50 cents a hundred. At 14 I'd passed my fifth grade and I felt I was ready to work with my step-daddy. He was a plasterer and he let me carry mortar and water for him while he worked. I watched how he did it and he let me try it too. Pretty soon I was doing it as well as he was, so my mother said if I was doing okay and enjoying it I'd better learn it as a trade. So my step-daddy got me an apprenticeship with the man he worked for. After four months I was making 75 cents a day and at 14 I felt like I was a man. Pretty soon after, my step-daddy and I went into business for ourselves.

Jules Baptiste was the man who got me started on guitar when I was about 11. He used to play mainly fish fries, where there'd be only two instruments – trumpet and guitar or maybe violin or clarinet and guitar. To compensate for having no bass or drums, he used a lot of bass figures in his playing. I took lessons from him and adopted his style of playing. Many of the bands used just four pieces and most of the jobs I worked then with were bands with four pieces. This was considered the strongest instrumentation: violin, cornet, clarinet and guitar, and sometimes violin, cornet,

trombone and guitar. I played enough bass on the guitar to balance the band. I learned most of this from Jules Baptiste, but I also grabbed a few tips from Bud Scott as well. Frank Landry was another good guitar player. "Stalebread" used to work with him playing around the bars and on the street. Frank Landry was about 40 years ahead of his time. He played the sort of style that the boys are playing today. He had long fingers and played both mandolin and guitar. He had a technique of playing the chord with his fingers and playing his own accompaniment with his thumb. He used a pick when he played the mandolin. Frankie used to like my playing even though I was just a kid. He'd tell my mother to let me go out on jobs with him and he would make me a great guitar player. But she thought I was too young and she didn't want me mixing with all those liquor heads like Frankie. He drank himself to death in the end. He never worked with any bands; he was a hustler. If he was working with another guitar player, he would take his mandolin and go around all the bar rooms and pass the hat. He didn't do any singing, but most of the guitar players he used were good songsters.

Pretty soon, Lorenzo Staulz and I were considered the best guitar players uptown. Downtown, Joe Brooks and Willie Santiago were considered the best. Willie was really better than all of us and he was also a very good mandolin player too. Sometimes on a Sunday morning I would go to his house and we'd have a jam session. He'd play mandolin and he liked the way I accompanied him on the guitar.

I was working mainly with Armand Piron in four-piece bands when Papa Celestin and old man Francisco Valteau asked me to join George Jones's band near the lake. George Jones was a bass player who used number-8 thread for the hair on his bow and he would saw right through his G-string every night. Every day he would have to get a spool of number 8 thread to fix his bow and buy a new G-string! We used to call him "George the Rhymer." He would play for conventions and was very popular with the business people. They'd hire George and his band and someone would give him the low-down on some of the important guests that were present, and he'd remember all their names. Like you might be there, Bill, and they'd tell him that you were, say, chairman of the entertainment committee and a famous jazz researcher and record collector. He'd get a simple melody going and come up to your table and sing: "I'll sing this song and I ain't gonna hustle, but I know your name is Mr. Bill Russell." All the important guests thought this was wonderful. They didn't know how he knew their names. They thought he was a mind reader or something and would give him $5 or $10 tips. When he'd got around the tables he'd come back with $30 or $40. When he came back to split all the money, the guys would accuse him of cheating, and he'd pull out all his pockets and come out with about 60 cents of change.

He worked at the Bungalow for a while and at the West End. One night he got into a disagreement with the man at the Bungalow, he got into a fight, and they put them all in jail. So this guy at the Bungalow wouldn't have George anymore. So he went to Jim Thorn's Roadhouse about two blocks away. George hired me, Valteau and Papa Celestin. Valteau and Celestin opened with him and had worked two nights before he hired me. He asked them about guitar players and they mentioned me. He was all right until he started to put the money in his pocket. When I suggested a kitty he said, "Ain't been having no kitty." I said, "We're gonna have a kitty if I work here." So the floor manager, a Jewish fellow by the name of Levy, said, "What's the matter, George?" "That man want a kitty; we've been having no kitty here." Levy said, "What's wrong with a kitty, George? Why not?" Levy went into the bar room and got an empty cigar box and cut an oblong hole in the box. When George still objected, Levy offered a straight salary and he would take the kitty. We were getting $1.50 a night. Levy suggested $2.50 a night and he would take the kitty. We said no. The kitty would run about $4 and $5 on a dull night and on Saturdays and Sundays around $14 or $15 per man. We got the kitty. In the restaurant the band was lined up against the wall with two of the band on one side of a pillar and two on the other side. The kitty was next to George. We used to have turns to pass the hat and one night George went out and came back with some change. He dropped some money into the box except for two half-dollars. He left one half-dollar on top of the box and the other by the box. After the next number I said, "George, what is that half-dollar doing on top of the kitty?" "Just didn't drop in the box, that's all, just didn't drop in the box; never had nobody like you working with me before." "No, I'm sure you haven't," I said, "never worked with nobody like you before either." I took the half-dollar and put it in the kitty. Some time later George got up to go to the rest room. I noticed he was dragging his feet and he was trying to slide the other half-dollar into the rest room. He still used to steal, but we were up to all his tricks, so he didn't steal as much as he had before. He wanted to leave dividing the tips till the end of the week, but I said, "No, give me mine now." So the boys used to call me: "Gimme Me Mine Now." But George was an old-time hustler who didn't like sharing tips. Before I joined him, he'd go out to collect tips and always go to the rest room before he'd come back to the band, and there'd be a lot of money missing. He had secret pockets sewn into his coat sleeves and pants legs. If the musicians said, "Where's the rest of the money?" he'd get angry and say he'd only got some small change in tips.

Francisco Valteau was one of the solo violinists. Another was Paul Dominguez, he was very good. (He was a barber, and he taught Armand Piron to be a barber. Piron got to be a very good barber). Paul had a barber shop, and Piron used the shop as his headquarters. He and Paul used to practise from two French study books, first and second violin. They used to practise on slow days in the barber shop, which was about three doors from the Musicians' Union, on Claiborne, between Kerlerec and Columbus.

Paul never was popular as a dance orchestra violinist. He'd play now and then, they'd call him, but he was inclined more to be a classical violin player. He and Piron used to get out these books and start playing those heavy operas and boy, there'd be people crowding around the barber shop like the circus had come to town!

Johnny Lindsey's brother Herbert Lindsey played violin, everything he played he played with the double stops. His brother played bass and his father played guitar.

Peter Bocage and Piron were the violinists that stood out. Jimmy Palao was good but he wasn't in their class. I worked with Jimmy around 1918 or 1919. He was what we called at that time "business style" – good jazz orchestra violinist, but nothing flashy about him. He wasn't equipped to play any concert music but he was good for dance music. He didn't play any violin in Chicago. They had top-notch violinists a dime a

*Armand Piron – circa late1930s*

dozen. There was Darnell Howard, Clarence Lee, Clarence Black and Will Tyler. These were violinists and they could play. They were paying as high as $8 for lessons. They were still studying, but they'd run rings around you. But if you want to know the truth, Piron was the greatest violinist we had in New Orleans, but these Chicago boys could run rings around him!

Jimmy Palao died in Chicago in January or February 1935. It was about 14 degrees below zero and Jimmie Noone, Freddy Keppard and I went to his funeral in an open car. We almost froze to death! They had another funeral going out at the same time, out on Western Avenue. For some reason we got into the line of the other funeral, and when we pulled into the graveyard, we stopped behind all the other cars and we realised it was a white funeral. They were burying Jimmy about two miles further on, but it was so cold that we just turned back.

Henry Zeno was probably the best of the old-style drummers. I wish people today could have heard him. "Red Happy" Bolton was another good drummer we had in New Orleans. He was also a buckdancer. Henry Zeno, Happy and Black Benny were in about the same class. All of them were from Uptown. "Red Happy" came up to Chicago around the summer of 1925. He came down to the Dreamland where we were working. There was a band that was due to go and work in Canada. It wasn't a New Orleans band, and Joe Oliver recommended Happy. "Red" didn't have any drums, but he was told Andrew Hilaire had a spare set at home. Andrew told Joe, "I don't know anything about the man. If he's your friend and if you will stand responsible for the drums, I'll let him have them for Canada, but I will hold you responsible for them." Joe agreed. The drums were worth about $80. When Happy went up to Canada, he died from an overdose of drugs. The drums disappeared and Joe had to pay Andrew the $80.

Zue Robertson was a little younger than me, but he started playing before I did. He was a very good musician. He played both piano and trombone. He just had no scruples about telling a man he couldn't play. A guy would sit in with the band and play a number and when he would get through, Zue would complain, "You don't know how to play. If you're going to sit in with the band you should learn how to play." He was a little bitty old slim guy. When the circus came to town, Zue would be off. He loved to travel. Willie Humphrey's daddy was the same – didn't play much around New Orleans. When the circus would come and hire musicians, he would be off with them.

Sidney Bechet also liked to travel. When he was coming up he had trouble keeping time and I taught him how to count. His brother Joseph Bechet played guitar and he was also a plasterer; we were working for the same contractor. He was older than Sidney. One day we were working and talking about music and he told he how his little brother played the clarinet. So I went up near St. Bernard Circle, where they lived, to hear Sidney. He played me a little number he'd made up and a blues. He was a little fat kid, about 13 years old. He didn't know "A" from anything else, but he knew how to play. So I told him to come over to my house on Sunday and I'd play the guitar with him. He could play a terrific blues, but he had a tendency to jump time. He'd skip a beat. So I told him to come around maybe once a week and we would work together, and I would show him where he made a mistake. He came around and I showed him and he got it right, he got the concept of it.

Around the corner from me was the Artesian Hall and they used to run dances from 2 to 6 p.m. for teenagers. Big Eye Louis and Manuel Perez were playing in the band. I told Sidney to ask Louis Delisle to let him play the blues and that I would appreciate it very much if he would give him a few lessons. So he played the blues and took the house down. Louis gave him a few lessons and then Piron let him play and told him to go to Old Man Tio (not Lorenzo Jr, his uncle Luis Tio). So he's taking lessons from the old man and Sidney gets to feeling good and starts hitting high notes and making them slurs on the clarinet. When the old man hears this he shouts in his strong Mexican accent, "No, no, no, no, that is not the way. You don't make the cat meow and the dog bark on the clarinet." He'd learned the different keys and was getting smart. He just thought the old man would like to know the progress he was making. He'd cut loose in those lessons.

After I'd lost trace of him for about two years, one day Bob Lyons or Frankie Duson had a funeral job. Sometimes Big Eye or Tio used to play with them, but for some reason they didn't have a clarinet player that day. Sidney was around then and somebody suggested him. He didn't have a clarinet with him. Jake Fink, who ran the pawn shop, had an old yellow wooden clarinet with one key missing. Jake had had it for about five years in a showcase. Jake let Sidney borrow it. Sidney wet the mouthpiece, stopped up the hole of that missing key with a piece of cord and played the funeral, played the parade back and cut up a breeze.

Buddy Bartley had a joint at Franklin and Gravier. He bought Sidney a clarinet and bought him a brand new set of clothes. He hired Sidney and a piano player to play in his joint. But Sidney was a wino. He started getting all that wine and someone stole that clarinet from him. He got another one and then started pawning it. Bartley had to get it out for him so he could play his joint. When he started playing with Frankie Duson in the Eagle Band, Duson got him another clarinet from the pawn shop. I heard him play with Duson's band. He was really kicking then, sensational. Then he left for Chicago and then New York.

I played with Tio out at Tranchina's about 1916. The Piron records didn't show

how the band sounded. The engineers didn't have the technique of balancing the band for recordings. Tio and George Baquet were the best clarinetists. Baquet was more brilliant. He played louder, but Tio was more on the legit side.

I feel that we had more vitality then. We didn't get to bed as much then. If a man has got a job tomorrow he'll go and get his rest – he has to. Sometimes I'd get so tired playing music I slept 12 hours! Didn't move, just like a dead man – 12 hours straight. These days all I need is 6 hours.

I played alto horn with the Tulane Brass Band and a few jobs with Old Man Henry Allen. David Jones taught me to play alto horn. He was self-taught. He learned to play saxophone right on the boat. I believe he got a few lessons from Norman Mason. He went right on from there and became one of our best saxophone players.

If you were working for the Streckfus steam line they would let you buy any instrument you wanted. They would get it at a cash discount and you paid them back by the week. When Louis Armstrong came to join the boat, Ory had stood guarantee for his horn, but Louis wasn't through paying for it. Ory said, "If you go on the boat I'm gonna take your horn back." So Louis met me at the boat on the rehearsal morning and said that he couldn't make the job. I told him we'd talk to the Captain after the rehearsal. We went to the purser's office with Fate. Captain Roy said, "Can he play?" Fate said, "Yeah, he can play." The captain said, "Don't worry, we'll buy you any horn you want. Just be here next Tuesday noon and catch the train. (In 1918 and 1919 we travelled up to St. Louis by train to join the "St. Paul".) When we got to St. Louis, Fate, Baby Dodds, Louis and myself went to the office and there was a telegram from Captain Roy authorising Louis to go out and buy a horn. Louis tried to blow the bell off the horn.

*"S.S. Capitol" band. Left to right: Henry Kimball, Boyd Atkins, Fate Marable, Johnny St. Cyr, David Jones, Norman Mason, Louis Armstrong, George Brahear, and Baby Dodds.*

Once we were playing and Louis came to an abrupt stop. Fate said, "What's the matter, Louis?" Louis said, "Man, I had to stop and let some of the notes get out of this horn." He was making so many!

On the "St. Paul" were Joe Streckfus Jr., piano, Captain Roy, violin, Johnny, trumpet, Verne, the youngest, violin. When the old man was in the excursion boat business, Verne was just a kid, but his older brothers were accomplished musicians. So when they got the first boat they had only three instruments – violin, trumpet and piano. Old man Streckfus was pilot, captain and everything else. They took over old boats and gutted them to make a big dance floor. The first boat was the "Sidney", the smallest; the "G.S." was larger; the "St. Paul" was 300 feet long and 50 feet in the beam, extra wide. 2,000 people it took when you got that boat loaded. The vibration from the two side wheels shook the boat bad, so they cut 25 feet off it. They did it all themselves. All of them were ships' carpenters, boat draughtsmen, electricians, engineers, pilots, and navigators. They really knew the business.

Captain Joe was a big strong man. Four deck hands were trying to lift a piece of timber 12" x 12" x 20 feet, and they were trying to turn it over to get their hands underneath. They weren't doing it fast enough, so he said, "Get away, get away," and he picked it up and walked off the boat with it. That was the beam for the "Capitol". He bought that hull and after he checked it he thought the beam wouldn't hold out, so he bought a new beam. Boats wintered up in Davenport, Iowa.

We took the train up to St. Louis; half of us did not belong to a union. Baby Dodds, Louis Armstrong, Sam Dutrey, Joe Howard, Bebé Ridgley and me, had to join the local. We didn't live on the boat – we had rooms nearby. I was the cause of Sidney Desvigne coming on the boat. When they asked for a trumpet player after Louis, I suggested Peter Bocage. Pete didn't want to leave town, so I suggested Desvigne.

After I finished on the boats, I went to Chicago. I was staying in the house where Lil Delk Christian roomed. It was a good-time house that sold bootleg liquor. Guys would come in and get Lil to sing. I was playing guitar so wouldn't expect anything for my services, but they would often get Lil out of bed and expect her to sing. All Lil would get out of it was a belly full of liquor. Guys wouldn't even tip her. She didn't mind but I thought I'd try to get her to sing on a record. I said, "If nothing comes of it then you have nothing to lose." I spoke to Fern at Okeh – "Are you in the market for new talent?" "Sure," he said "you rehearse two numbers with her and call me up. We'll cut a record and send it to New York (Okeh's headquarters), and if they don't accept it, you've lost nothing but time. If they like it you'll be paid for it." I rehearsed her on two numbers: *Sweet Man* and *Sweet Georgia Brown*, and then I called them up and we went down to cut the record. They liked her, and said she had clear diction.

We ran it through and I timed it. So they said, "Let's cut a master." We cut two masters and two weeks later Fern called up. "Come out and get your checks." Well, I had been recording with Louis and I thought they were for that. I went to the office and they said, "Where's Lil?" "She's at home, I guess." "Why didn't you bring her down with you?" "Why?" "You cut two numbers, didn't you?" So they rang Lil and drew up a contract for her at $50 per side as a staff artist. "Come down in half an hour, there's a check for you and Johnny." (I got $15 a side as a musician). She looked at the contract and said, "Well, as I got the job through Johnny, whatever Johnny says is all right with me." So the next time we cut four numbers and she got a check for $200. Mine was $60. When we got the checks I took them to the bank to cash hers, and went back to the house and gave her the money. She said, "You're the cause of this, take what you want out of it." So I just took $25.

I was working with Jimmie Noone at that time, so I had asked him if he'd like to cut a record with us, just him me and Lil. We cut *Lonesome and Sorry* and *Baby O'Mine*. After that recording I said, "You're on your own." But she was very grateful for what I had done for her and wanted me on her next two sessions. Then they asked Lil if she would record with just a piano. She was very loyal, she said she'd have to ask Johnny. But I said, "Go ahead, if they want to use a piano player, fine." She made the session with Richard M. Jones and the next one after that with just me and Jimmie again.

Her husband, Charlie Christian, was a gambler. He used to go out to the automobile industries in Michigan on pay days. He told me how these fellows came in and got Lil up at all hours of the night and none of them would offer her a dollar. He said, "You are the only one who helped her. I want you to know that anytime we got a place, you've got a home with us." That was very nice of him to say that.

Eddie Heywood was visiting Chicago from New York, and the people from the Okeh Company in New York gave him a letter of introduction to record in Chicago. A woman from Detroit was singing in a sanctified church and they booked Eddie Heywood to play piano accompaniment for her. So when she got to the studio she said, "Where's the guitar player?" They said, "We're going to use a piano player, we're not going to use a guitar player." She said, "I don't want to sing with a piano, I want a guitar player." I had recorded a session with Louis that morning. I was playing at the Dreamland from 8 until 12. Then I went over on the southside to the Apex Club and played there from 1 o'clock until 6 in the morning. I had to record with Louis at 10 o'clock. I wouldn't go to bed as everybody who lived by me was working and I was afraid I might oversleep. I decided I would stay up and go to bed after the recording. While we were in the studio, Erskine Tate came to record and he had no banjo player. He was recording right after Louis and he asked me if I would stay over and work with his band for the recording session. So I told him, "Yes, I would." We finished with Louis about 11.15. Then I ran over the numbers with Tate and recorded with him. We finished around 1 o'clock. By the time I went downtown and made lunch it was about 2.30. I'd just got into bed and they called me up and told me about this woman wanting a guitar player. He said, "Johnny, can you come down?" I said, "I've been up all night, I've done two recording sessions." He said, "We paid this woman's expenses from Detroit and we got to pay her expenses back and we've got to record her, we can't waste the money. You would do us a favour if you would come down here and work with her." "O.K." I got down there about 3.30. They introduced me and I ran over the number with her. We made one test record, played the test over, and then cut a master. She was just wild about the way I played guitar. I got back home around 5 o'clock. I had to get to be with Cook's band at Dreamland at 8 o'clock, so I told my landlady to wake me up around 7 o'clock. She said, "Johnny, you gonna kill yourself." I said, "I didn't want to do it, it was a favour." I was never interested in records. A record date was just another day's work for me, just another job. I never dreamed that record collecting would be what it is today.

Regarding the New Orleans style: musicians from New Orleans have a certain rhythm for certain numbers. I noticed when I went to Chicago that there was very little variation in the tempo. All fast music. I believe that was why Joe Oliver was such a sensation – he had such a variety of tempos, and the rhythm was always perfect, right there with the beat. That was one of the things that made Joe very popular. They had some good bands in Chicago but their tempo didn't vary. Some of the bands those days played so fast, you couldn't tell what the melody was. Joe's fastest number was slower than most of those Chicago bands. You couldn't have danced or marched to those fast tempos they play now. Then they played to a dance public, and the people wanted to dance. Nowadays they play so fast it's like an exhibition of their skill – but you can't dance to that. You'd be burned out before you'd dance three or four dances. We'd play all what you'd call "easy tempos". We'd play all night and wouldn't tire the people out who wanted to dance all night. Easy tempo. We'd play one-steps, two-steps, and the blues would be draggy. Lots of waltzes and lots of schottisches. The Scottische was a very beautiful dance. The tempos of *Sophisticated Lady* or *Stars Fell on Alabama* were perfect for the schottische. We had the Round Scottische and later the Promenade Scottische. On the old Scottische, the couple were holding each other all the time, where in the Promenade Scottische they let go and moved from side to side, 1-2-3-4, formed a ring, and it was beautiful to look at. It would make a wonderful movie, starting with the Penny Parties for the kids, with two instruments, then the fish fries and on up to the balls. We played all the latest numbers as soon as they came out, as fast as we could get them. We would work them out to suit our fancy. If it was written in a fast tempo we would play it as written and if it didn't sound so good to us we'd say, "Let's take it at a slower tempo. Sounds better that way." I think the New Orleans bands were the only ones who could pick the right tempos. That's what appealed to the public – they had their own ideas about tempo, regardless of how the number was written. They also had their own ideas about improvisation. If a guy had something that was good, let him give out with it. If it's good, it stays; if it was no good, then let's try something else with it. By the time they had got them working on the number, they had it right where they wanted it. We enjoyed playing more for dances than for people just sitting around a table. The melody was always predominant and there was one instrument in the band that kept that melody. We'd play the number straight, then we'd start kicking it around. We had a solid tempo. You take bass players and drummers: now they got that four-beat on the bass drum and the bass player got four beats throughout the number. We didn't use that. We got a solid 1st and 3rd on bass; guitar used 4 and when they began using piano, it used 4. The snare drum used 4, bass drum 1st and 3rd, bass violin 1st and 3rd. Then in the last chorus, everybody got in – "Hot chorus." There was what we'd call "Boston Rhythm": one of the Jelly Roll numbers had the whole band hitting on the afterbeat; no 1st and 3rd, just a 2nd and 4th beat.

Musicians then were a very agreeable group. They were all happy, they were all friends and they loved the music. It made them play better. There wasn't as much petty jealousy in bands as there is now. In those days bands stayed together for years. They had a big field to pick from and they all spoke the same language. Some theory and some hot style, but they were all good. They all fitted together. You can always feel it right away if something is not right in the band, and especially in the rhythm section. The trumpet or the trombone player might be lazy – you'd notice it, but you'll notice it even more if you get a bad drummer. Some drummers are pulling for a faster tempo all the time. They may never reach it, but you can feel it if they are just a fraction ahead of the banjo or guitar. Sometimes piano players will do the same thing. It's got today when sometimes the drummers, if they get happy, they get fast. We also used to riff a lot. Not like the swing bands when they are doing that all night, but just a novelty in the last chorus. We'd call it "doing the Joe Petit." Guys would put in anything they felt like, sometimes it would be terrific stuff. The pretty part of it was when the band came down to piano level. You could appreciate the balance in the band. Nobody tried to blow each other out, it was always balanced. Everybody tried for a good tempo and harmonizing. The violin would play the lead and then they'd play obligatos. They played the straight lead: the verse and then the chorus and then go back into the verse again and then the final chorus. On certain numbers they worked out an introduction. Some bands used to work out some little novelty introduction. They would often modulate (change key) from the first strain into the second strain. There were times when the whole band would modulate and times when only certain instruments would make a modulation. Often the winds would take down while the modulations were going on – to rest their lips. If the whole band made the modulation, then they would come down very soft, clarinet in low register, violin, guitar, bass, drums. They didn't have wire brushes then, they used sand blocks and rubbed them together. They'd play about two soft choruses like that and the winds would have a rest. Then they'd pick up and play two more choruses; the last one they'd just kick around. It was good music. There were always at least three men in the band that could read.

Old man Cottrell had a beat called the "Steady Roll." And it was a steady roll. He had the accent on the second and fourth beats and he could hold that roll all night. You couldn't detect a flutter. Those babies would get soft: the cornet playing in the derby, the clarinet in the lower register, the trombone muted and that lets the strings stand out. When they all came in for the last chorus, the violin would go up high. But they never got so loud as to drown the violin.

I owe a lot to Jules Baptiste who got me started, and I grabbed a few tips from Bud Scott. I learned to read around 1918 and would advise anybody wanting to take up music as a career to learn to read.

If someone wanted to take up guitar or banjo today, I'd advise banjo; it's what the public wants. Personally I prefer the guitar. It's the first rhythm in a dixieland band. Banjo has been popular since around 1917. It was already popular out east, before that the guitar was always the foundation. I play a four-string tenor banjo. I still use the same banjo that I bought in St. Louis in the 1920s. I also play a Martin guitar, which I used on the recordings with Jelly. I prefer the round clef hole, as it throws the sound more. The shallow depth gives a better tone. I make my own pick out of old toothbrush handles. Jules Baptiste made his out of bone. They were thick like a finger and solid.

Nowadays bands just jump off from one key to another. Then we used to modulate, about 4 or 8 measures from one key to the next. With a succession of chords we could slide from C to A-flat. Ed Garland could be playing and if someone came up and talked with him, he wouldn't miss a beat and his fingers would automatically find the right chords. The New Orleans style is based on originality. We played our own way and didn't try to copy bands from outside.

# GEORGE GUESNON

George Guesnon
banjo/guitar

Born: New Orleans, Louisiana, May 25, 1907
Died: New Orleans, Louisiana, May 5, 1968

*"Creole" George Guesnon was one of the best known New Orleans banjoists. His first job was with Kid Clayton in 1927. He later played with many famous New Orleans musicians including Buddy Petit, Chris Kelly, Kid Rena, Oscar "Papa" Celestin, Sam Morgan and George Lewis. He composed and recorded many blues. George Guesnon was interested in writing, and several of his articles, short stories and poems have been published.*

My father was part negro and French, my mother was Spanish and negro, so that makes me Creole. Just like jambalaya, all mixed up. They say a creole is a direct descendant of a Frenchman and a Spaniard, and I speak both languages fluently, as did my grandfather and grandmother. I was born in New Orleans at 2114 St. Ann Street, May 25th 1907. My early childhood was just like the rest of the kids of that day, selling papers and shining shoes and helping to unload the boats that used to come into old Basin Street. We would spend time running around behind the different bands and you know, a funny thing, as a small boy, I remember hopping on the truck that Sam Morgan's band was playing on to advertize something. My father didn't play an instrument but I had an uncle that played guitar with Slow Drag years ago. His name was Emile Guesnon and they had a little spasm band. My father was actually a plasterer. Sometimes I went to work with him and Johnny St. Cyr's stepfather, old man Sam Augustine.

One night I was sitting at home and who comes along but a guy from off a show, a very good friend of mine, Gilbert Young. He asked me if I wanted to go out with him to the Humming Bird Cabaret on Bienville and Marais. I went out there. It was St. Joseph's night 1927, and what I saw out there I ain't never seen before. They had Baby Dolls out there and all the whores with their asses sticking out, stockings full of one hundred dollar bills and all them bitches was ballin' back there. I was raised up from a strict family that went to church and different things. I didn't know nothing about that. Once I got a taste of that life I never did go back home. Sure enough, I went in that place and from then on I practically lived there. Professor Sherman Cook was the master of ceremonies with his wife, Evelyn. He and I got to be good friends and he gave me a chance to do little odd jobs around the place. I made more money doing those odd jobs, and with what those whores would give me, than when I was working out in the hot sun with my daddy, so I made up my mind I wasn't going back to that day work.

While I got to sitting around the Humming Bird between tasks, I got to the point I would sit up and listen to the band. Especially the banjo player, Earl Stockmeyer. The band in there was called Kid Clayton's Happy Pals. Clayton played trumpet, Peter Badie played alto, Tink Baptiste played piano, Earl Stockmeyer on banjo and George Williams on drums. Now I played a little ukulele but I didn't think it would fit into any musical group. Earl Stockmeyer and Clayton and I became friends. I got to talking with Earl and he told he that I could tune a banjo up like a ukulele and sit in with them. Hell, they

# CREOLE GEORGE GUESNON
## SOUTH'S GREATEST TENOR GUITARIST
### AND THE COMPOSER OF SUCH
### OUTSTANDING RECORDINGS
### AS

DECCA RECORD ARTIST

HUB RECORD ARTIST

IBERVILLE AND FRANKLIN
EMPTY BED BLUES
LAST GO ROUND BLUES
BROKEN PLAYHOUSE BLUES
BLACK WOMAN BLUES
GROG HEAD WOMAN
BIG HOUSE BLUES
BASIN STREET SWING
DR. JEKYL AND MR. HYDE
LOVER MAN BLUES
KING ZULU ON PARADE
IN OLE WYOMING
THAT ONE LITTLE KISS
AT THE INSECT BALL
EARLY MORNING BLUES
ROUND THE WORLD BLUES
LONESOME HEARTED BLUES
IF YOU CAME FROM NEW ORLEANS
MY LYDIA GIRL OF MY DREAMS
UP AND AT EM

WORRIED MIND BLUES
GOODBYE, GOOD LUCK TO YO
WEST SANTA FE BLUES
MISSISSIPPI TOWN
BLUE AND EVIL BLUES
SUN FLOWER COUNTY BLUES
LOST LOVER BLUES
CHICO MIA
LOUISIANA LULLABY
SONG OF THE SEA
CARMENCITA
LEARN TO MIX YOUR BITTER
(WITH YOUR SWEETS)
ALLEY CAT BLUES
BLUES ON MY MIND
SOBBING HEARTED BLUES
HOUSING PROJECT BLUES
NOW THAT THE THRILL IS O
THATS WHY I'M BLUE OVER

*To Mr Bill Russell
Best wishes Since*
*George Guesnon*

## CREOLE GEORGE GUESNON
COMPOSER-MUSICIAN
UNIVERSAL ATTRACTIONS N.Y.

DECCA AND HUB
BLUES
RECORDING ARTIST
OF
NEW ORLEANS, LA.

weren't playing in but two keys all night. It got so I was on the stand more than Earl was. I began to like being a musician. So what happened is I said, "While I'm here I'm going to try to better myself," because I knew what I was doing was wrong, playing a banjo tuned like a ukulele. I couldn't read a note and didn't know one chord from another. I had to try to rectify this some kind of way.

One night my cousin Margaret wanted me to take her to the Fairgrounds, to a dance. The band turned out to be Celestin's Tuxedo Orchestra with John Marrero playing the banjo. What a banjo player! Man, this guy had everything. Tone, execution and those beautiful chords that he had. I sat in this cat's lap all night. I didn't dance with nobody, just sat there all night listening to him. At the end I went to him, spoke to him. I said, "Mr Marrero, I would like to take some lessons from you." He told me the price would be 50 cents a lesson and he would give me lessons three times a week. He was living on Dumaine near Claiborne. It was a scuffle getting that money together but as long as I had the job at the Humming Bird it would be O.K. Sometimes I went to him every day but as long as I paid him the 50 cents he didn't care.

Well, I studied hard because I loved music. Loved my instrument. I really got my money's worth from him. There wasn't anything he showed me that I couldn't go back there next time and play for him.

See, years ago the guys – I mean, C minor and G minor had been on that guitar ever since it was made but none of them ever seemed to know it. The average guitar or banjo player was making rolling chords from C to G7, C to C7, F back to C, back to G and that was it. No minors, no augmented, diminished. They just wasn't making them kind of things. But what happened, things began to change. They began playing stocks and stuff. The bands on the boats, why, all of them had a piece of music before them. The handwriting was on the wall. Either you learned to read and play or you wasn't going to play no music at all.

I went to John Marrero for about seven months. Seven hard and full months. The majority of things he gave me to learn, I just ate up. One night he had a misunderstanding in the Tuxedo and he quit. You know they called me to take his place. Then I knew I had it made and was on my way. I stayed with that band about a year and a half. Me and Guy Kelly went in the band at the same time. Jeanette Kimball was the pianist, Sidney Carriere played tenor. I just don't remember all of them. John Porter was on bass, Chinee Foster was the drummer and Herman Franklin was playing third trumpet with Celestin and Guy Kelly on the other two horns.

After about 18 months I left Celestin to go with Sam Morgan. See, Sam was going to travel and I liked that part. When he said, "Pass Christian" it looked like that was over the seas. Maybe up in Wyoming or somewhere. I had never been no further than here. Never been out of New Orleans in my life. But, hey, we was going to Pass Christian, Mobile, Biloxi and we even went on an excursion to Chicago. I joined Sam right after they had recorded. After Sam had to leave the band we tried to stick it out with his brother, Isaiah, but Isaiah didn't have Sam's popularity. Sam was well liked no matter where he went. People just flocked out to see him. That was after Sam got paralysed. Now all the time I stood with them. It was the finest aggregation I ever played with, but they never

Sam Morgan

Isaiah Morgan

got a break. As they were all poor together, they were happy together. You see, they had uniformity, they had brotherly love. They had so much feeling for one another. See, when Sam had the band there wasn't nobody in the band like no Mozart or no hell of a great reader, but everybody in there was a great musician as far as playing from his heart went. When they got stock numbers, why, everybody struggled together. Sam would let Earl Fouche take Andrew in the corner. He would say, "George, take the rhythm section in a corner and work out. Me, Isaiah and Jim Crow, we'll work out our part together." They all struggled and stumbled until they got it together, and once they got it in their ear, they added their own feeling to it. He told me, "You are one of the best banjo players I ever heard but you are like a deer. As fast as I hit, you are gone. Your timing isn't good. But, when you leave my band you are going to be able to sit in with anybody's band." He kept a slap stick on us in the rhythm section, to be sure we held our time correct. See, our drummer Roy Evans, he was real powerful and he had a cymbal, looked this big. When he would hit that thing it looked like the whole house would shake. Good God, him and me, we was just flying through these things. When I left could sit in any band and they would say, "George, you are a nice timekeeper." Well, charge it to Sam. That's the cat who showed me everything. Everybody was willing to listen to everybody. I was with the Morgan band for about seven years.

Now as far as New Orleans style banjo players, the ones that stood out to me were John Marrero and Caffrey Darensbourg. That's one man you don't hear too much about, but you never heard a sweeter banjo in your life. He used to work with Manuel Perez on the Roof Garden. He was 20 years ahead of his time in taking solos and all that fast execution. Another fine banjo man was Percy Sevilla. I used to feature a solo on *Doll Dance* and this Percy, he says, "Well George, that's the prettiest thing I ever heard." Anyway, Johnny St. Cyr had just recorded that solo of his with Louis' Hot Five on *Heebie Jeebies*. The cats around here all said that it was made on a six string banjo and nobody could make that with four strings. Percy said, "I'm going to make it on four strings. Just give me time." Sure enough he got it down and that was real hard to do. I heard him playing it and I told him, "Man. That just knocks me out. I would like to learn that." He told me that if I showed him how to finger my solo on *Doll Dance* he would show me his solo on *Heebie Jeebies*. Percy Sevilla was a real fine one.

After Sam's band broke up I went with Little Brother Montgomery and His Southland Troubadors. Brother was the finest blues player I ever heard in my life. He has one number that is outstanding and will go down in history as being a classic. That's the *Vicksburg Blues*. Well, before he put this band together he had not worked with a group where you had to make all those chords together. But see, I showed him how to make all his chords like all the 7ths and 6ths. Kept him in a room until he had it down. See, a friend of mine, saxophone player named Lucien Johnson had gotten a letter from Brother Montgomery from Jackson, Mississippi, wanting him to come up there and make a band up. Naturally he wanted to take me too so he told Brother and that's how it all got set. We had a trumpet player out of Conway, South Carolina named Doc Palmerdy. Howard Roach, Ross Emerson out of Meridian and Jesse Steele out of Kansas City. Oh, we had a wonderful band. That lasted about 14 months and then Little Brother decided to go up to Chicago. We was all set to break up when a funny thing happened. Nat Towles, the bass player, come through Jackson with a bus and no band. We had a band and no bus, so from then on we continued under the banner of Nat Towles. We stayed out on the road hustling and struggling for about 18 months.

Another funny thing in my career. I got with Celestin after they had made their recordings, same thing with Sam Morgan. They had made their two sessions. Looked like I was going to be shut out all around. I was never going to make a record. I had wrote many, many blues songs but I didn't want to sing 'em. I never wanted to sing blues, I never wanted to give up my status as a jazz musician to be a blues singer. But you never know what's around the bend. Little Brother came back to New Orleans in 1936 and he had a recording contract to do a few sides up at the St. Charles Hotel. He and I were good friends from the years with his band and he asked me to come there with him to the recording date. He had these sides to make for Bluebird and he said when he got paid he would give me a few bucks. Well, we went up there and I got a real break. When they had like an intermission, I told Brother that I had this little blues song that I wrote called *Goodbye, Good Luck To You.* Little Brother was trying it out and who should hear it but

"I know that Brother Coleman was with one of those big-name bands, but don't you think he ought to change his style if he's going to do the Lord's work?"

2-TO1-SAYS THIS CAT IS FROM NEW ORLEANS, AND THATS THE ONLY WAY HE KNOWS (BOOT IT UP)

*Cartoon sent to Bill Russell from George Guesnon with comments*

*"Strictly N.O. Dixie-land here" – 1949*

*Right to left: Albert Francis (dms), Jim Robinson (tbn), Kid Howard (tpt), Albert Burbank (clt), Alcide "Slow Drag" Pavageau (sbs) & George Guesnon (amp. gtr)*

Eli Oberstein, the guy who was cutting Brother for the record session. He says, "What's the name of that number?" I told him, and he says, "Well, I like it. You want to sell it for ten dollars?" "Man. You've got yourself a deal," I said. "You go ahead and sing it on that record and I'll give you the ten bucks." That was the first record I ever made in my life. I sang it and Brother played the piano. When I got through he gave me the ten dollars and Brother gave me seven. That meant I had 17 dollars and he had a song. He gave me a contract that long but I never got another quarter out of it. Those were the days you had to learn, man. Little by little you learn this game. It's a rough game but I wouldn't change it for nothin' in the world. It wasn't just the money. That was a secondary thing. See, some felt that way and some just did it for the money. One guy felt that way, and wherever jazz is mentioned you're gonna hear his name. That's Manuel Perez. When those guys came around here to write those books, Manuel wouldn't talk to nobody. He resented all that. They come asking him was "so-and-so a drunk?" See, he wouldn't even talk about it. Now if they had come to him as an artist, he would have given them the full detail. He was a very proud and a fine musician. His brother had a second-hand shop on Orleans, between Villere and Robertson. I used to see Manuel there all the time. 'Course he was older than me but a fine old man. He was very sincere about his music. When a cat get with him, you had to play what was there, like it was there. If you could bring out the beauty within his construction, he loved you. Just don't mess up his music. Don't come to him with no bullshit.

I'm like that too. Music is my life, always has been, and as long as I'm able to play it, always will be. I've lived by this code . . . If you don't do nothing and have nothing, that's alright, but if you do something and have nothing, that don't make sense. I'm ready to pitch a bitch when that happens. So they said I was temperamental. Maybe I was, but in my book that's better than going down in history as a damn fool.

# LAWRENCE MARRERO

Lawrence Henry Marrero
banjo/guitar

Born: New Orleans, Louisiana, October 24, 1900
Died: New Orleans, Louisiana, June 6, 1959

*Lawrence Marrero was born in the 7th Ward of New Orleans around Mandeville and Prieur Streets. His father was William "Billy" Marrero, a well-known local musician, who died around 1917, at the age of 47. Lawrence's father's main instrument was bass violin, but he also played guitar. He did not read music. In the family were five boys and two girls. Simon was the oldest and played bass, John was next and played banjo, then came Lawrence and finally Eddie, who played bass. Little is known about the fifth brother. The Marrero family, father and mother and the brothers, would get together in their house and play musical instruments together. His mother was a good singer and guitarist. Her maiden name was Jeannette Frazier and her brother was the father of Josiah and Simon Frazier.. Paul and Emile Barnes were Lawrence's first cousins, as their mother and Lawrence's mother were sisters.*

*John Marrero, who was about three years older than Lawrence, became one of New Orleans' most famous banjo players. He was largely self-taught, but got some pointers from his father. He went on to play in the city's most celebrated bands including Piron's and Celestin's orchestras.*

*Lawrence started on sousaphone and guitar, before becoming a fairly proficient bass player. He finally took up banjo and played his first professional job on it in 1917.*

My brother, John Marrero, was the leading banjo player here, but he didn't start me on banjo. I just picked it up. My first instrument was a guitar and my first number was *Under The Double Eagle*, but I can't play it now. See, that march is hard because it changes so many different keys. Then I left guitar and went to playing bass violin, then I went to banjo. Tenor banjo and then bass drum. I've been fighting all them things all that time. I mean, I did come up with music. I read music somewhat, but I'm not a very good reader. I learned by ear at first then learned to read later, when I formed my own band with Bush Hall, trumpet, Paul Barnes, clarinet, my brother, Eddie, bass violin, and Josiah Frazier on drums. My brother Simon, he played bass violin, and bass drum in brass bands. I start playing bass drum in street bands because of his influence.

I began playing music jobs of my own and filling in for my brother John. I was a regular member of Chris Kelly's band with Eddie Marrero and Emile Barnes. I was with Buddy Petit's band in Pensacola, Florida and I filled in for Johnny Dave, of the Sam Morgan band, when he couldn't make some of the trips.

When I was a child, around 1910, all the bands I knew about were using guitar, not banjo. The use of the banjo became popular around 1915. Now, I prefer banjo and I think John preferred banjo as he was more popular when he began playing that. He had a lot of scholars, white and colored, and girls too, after the switch to banjo. Other than my brother John, the guitar players I liked were: Willie Santiago, Louis Keppard and Richard Payne. I remember Tom Benton too. You see, the old-time musicians took more

pains with their playing. The young musicians today begin playing jobs when they can play two numbers. In the old days, if a musician wasn't good enough on the job, he might be sent home. Sometimes two bands would be called for a job and the better one was kept, the other was sent away from the job.

In the old times, the '20s and thereabout, Kid Rena was the jazziest. Fast fingering and lots of notes. Sam Morgan played the sweetest, and Chris Kelly was the king of "ratty" low-down music. When they would meet on corners, having music battles, the bands would stay there playing. Rena would signal his good friend Kelly to leave, as Kelly couldn't take care of the others, but Rena could.

You see, when I played guitar, we didn't make such things as those 9ths and 10ths, 11ths and 13th chords. Because we didn't have all that. Mostly it was the minors and majors and flats. But now, the guitar player got a hard time. I mean, the easy way is always the best way. Now, if you can't get it the easy way, you get the hard way. I don't know much about music, but I've always felt that you get the basic ingredients first, you know, the foundations. Then you can really get technique. I'll tell you, I don't have much wrist work, but it all depends on wrist. But you see, my banjo playing is chordin' and heavy accompaniment. Then when the trumpet get soft, I'll get soft. That's the way I do it now. That's the way the people taken a liking to my playing, because I play different from everybody. I don't try to get up there and try to play banjo solos all night, see. Because I can't do that. I mean I could do that, some things, but I don't play banjo solos. Try to be doing that, the people think you're crazy. You got to keep it up and exercise your wrists.

You know, if they is low, you can get low and if they're heavy, well, you can get heavy too. See, this mute . . . it gives you a nice tone. Get somebody like George Lewis, be playing low register, well I put that on there and move it closer to the bridge. I have a short neck banjo and you've got to reach further in fingering some of these things. And whenever you finger your banjo, always finger your strings. You see, I've got a different tone from plenty of guys because I always do finger my strings behind the fret. Don't finger them on top of it. Finger right behind it like that. That's got to give a tone. You see, that's what the fret's for. Be sure that's right behind the fret and your tone will be alright. Now what you've got to do is learn how to get that tone. If you get the tone right, and if you get the tone of your banjo right, that give you a better hearing.

This Epiphone, I've had it over twenty years. They are hard to get. One fellow come down, then two colored boys come by here last week. Wanted to get a banjo. Wanted to buy a banjo from me. I say, "I'm sorry. All gone." And if you get a good resonator, it'll be alright. It would sound much better to you. It improves the tone. Get a good book too. Morris' book revised by Nick Lucas is good. I have some of MacNeil's back there, but they're really too hard. Too hard for me, to tell the truth about it. The things that I know of, I don't know everything, but the things that I know of, I'd be glad to help anyone out on.

As for teachin' . . . well, now, Manetta, he is one of the best we've got in town. For teachin' everything. He is really a professor and I played with Manuel Manetta at the Black and Tan on Iberville and Burgundy. I played with him and Metoyer on trumpet, Udell Wilson, piano and Alex Bigard, drums. It was open all night. That's years and years ago. I was a really young man then. Now I teach a few of them myself. The boys are young when they come here. Say, Billy Huntington. Man, he plays like hell. He didn't know how to hold a banjo, but now! And there's another little white kid, they call him John Chaffe. That boy could play some banjo. Bill was more of a jazz banjo player but Chaffe's got more music. Now he teaches banjo himself. He wants to come around and talk with me but he keeps me up too long. I say, "Look here John, I can't make it." He keeps on coming back because he loves banjo. Him and his music. Nothing but banjo.

I'll tell you. I'm going to tell you about it. I used to be a mattress maker at one time. The mattress come in and my finger got caught in the machine. Got cut in a gin. A big cotton gin. That's why I don't use this finger much. When you're stroking a banjo I really don't think it make much difference. You see, I play my own way. I don't try to copy-cat behind nobody. I play so I give everybody a heavy accompaniment. I'm not too much of a soloist, very little. I'm more of a solid beat. We had one of the best rhythm sections there was: Alton Purnell, Joe Watkins and Slow Drag. One of the best rhythm sections I think they had around here, with George and them. We had Tony Parenti too for a while, when George got sick. That's a good clarinet player too. Tony can play, but I don't know . . . there's something about George Lewis. That fellow can play some clarinet. I swear, I can't find nobody to match him. I've got my cousin Paul Barnes, he is just as good a clarinet player as they've got, but he can't touch George Lewis. I oughtn't to say that, but he can't do it. Man, George is . . . there's things he don't know . . . but George is the prettiest. I put George with any of them since I've been playin'. What I like about him, he's a man don't knock nobody else, don't make fun of nobody. And when he works, he works. Oh, he works a band, man, he works you. He work himself though. If he's sick, he works. You've got to give him that. He's a good clarinetist. One of the best.

Like George Guesnon. You see George Guesnon, that's a son-of-a-gun man. I wish I had the wrist George has. And you know, my brother taught George Guesnon, but George could teach me. I'm telling you the truth, I wish I'd know half as much as George know. He's really a good banjo player and guitar player too.

Now I've got old, and I'm starting to get sick. My mind don't be on music so much no more. I just had my mind to pick me a good band, but then, the travelling. Nothing but travelling all the time. I don't want to go far away from home no more, and I'm afraid I might get sick or something on the road.

# LOUIS KEPPARD

Louis Keppard
guitar/tuba

Born: New Orleans, Louisiana, February 2, 1888
Died: New Orleans, Louisiana, February 18, 1986

*Brother of Freddie Keppard. Around 1906, Louis joined the Magnolia Band and then he formed the Cherry Blossom Band. Later he re-formed the Magnolia Band, which included at various times Joe Oliver, Honoré Dutrey, Frank Goudie, and Arnold and Dave Depass. In 1917, he organized a band which appeared at the Grand Theater in Chicago and toured the Pantages circuit for a year. In the 1920s he worked with Papa Celestin, Manuel Perez and "Wooden" Joe Nicholas, and played alto horn with the Young Tuxedo Brass Band. In the 1930s, he joined the W.P.A. Band, and in the 1950s and '60s he played tuba with the Gibson Brass Band.*

I was born February 2, 1888 in the city of New Orleans. My father was a chef at a place on Dauphine and Canal. His name was Fred Bertrand Keppard. No one in my family played anything, outside of my brother. He was one year younger than me, born June 15th 1889. My first instrument was guitar when I was about 14 years old. Freddie, my brother, played mandolin first, then violin. He took lessons with Adolphe Alexander Snr, then later he played with Mr Alexander's band on violin. Freddie had a job at Michael's jewellery store on Royal and Bienville, then later he started in music and went with Joe Petit. My daddy had bought him a little brass cornet so he could work with Joe. Adolphe Alexander showed him how to play it, so I took his job at the jewellery store. He really played cornet from then on, but he played on the accordian too.

As for me, well, Manuel Perez and Hyppolite Charles gave me my music lessons. Not on any instrument, though, just lessons of music. Bud Scott was my guitar teacher. He played great guitar and also the violin. When I started playing professionally it was with the Magnolia Band. Maurice Durand played trumpet, Sidney Vigne clarinet, and I remember Arnold Depass was the drummer. After a while we formed a group called "The Cherry Blossom Band." I went up on 3rd and Magnolia, where Joe Oliver was working as a butler and doing garden work. I talked to him about playing music with us. We got Honoré Dutrey to play with us and Eddie Dawson on bass, then "Red Happy" Bolton on drums. They put me as manager. We decided to get some uniforms from Sears and Roebuck so we gave the money to Joe, who was sort of the treasurer. He used to hang out every day playing pool, so it come we find out Joe had spent all of our money. We called him on it, made him put all the money back and finally we got our uniforms. We played all over. Out at the lake, at Lucien Pavilion and at Hunts'. Sharkey was playing out there at the lake at the same time as us. He was a good man, and if I'm not mistaken, he studied with Manuel Perez. He gotten so good that my brother used to say, "Between Sharkey and Bunk, I don't know which one I'm more scared of."

Like I said, my brother was taught music by Adolphe Alexander Snr, but he had a great ear. One of the best ears. He would hear a piece once and could come on down with it. When Fred left here first he went with the Creole Band. Bill Johnson, the bass

*Freddie Keppard sending greetings to his brother*

player, sent for Fred and he left here to go to Chicago. There was four of 'em left here, half of his own band, Jimmy Palao, violin, George Baquet, clarinet and Eddie Vincent, trombone. He got in the union in Chicago and went to playing cornet there. He was going with Jimmie Noone's sister. That was his girl friend. He never married her. When Fred left here we lived at 1813 St. Ann Street and seems like my mother grieved herself half to death when he left, he was so young. Later, the band sent word to me in New Orleans to see if I could do anything about his drinking. He was a good fellow, a great mixer, but he used to drink too much. When I went to Chicago in 1917 he had left and gone to New York.

But to get back to me in New Orleans. There was a man, Mr Locaze, I think from across the river. Well, he come over to see me. He wanted to get a band. In other words, to go to Chicago. We would be booked from New Orleans to Chicago and then use that as a base of operations and travel all over. It was a long contract and we had two lawyers from here to draw it up. I tried to get Joe Oliver to go, but he wasn't for it. I had Lawrence Duhé and Roy Palmer, then I talked to Johnny Smith, "Sugar Johnny" we called him.

Johnny was more than willing. He had a furniture store and he had bought furniture from a man and sold it before he paid for it, so you know he was willing to go. I got Herbert Lindsey and then I had a cable from Mr Locaze saying that the bookers wanted a drummer to make up the full pieces. I got Red Happy to go. We had a whole year contract. We had a deposit. It was $15, the same for all the men. When I turned around, here come a second cable saying they had decided to cancel the drummer and use one from Chicago to cut down on expenses. Happy kept the deposit money but didn't go. When we got up there they had a drummer waiting for us but, for some reason, he didn't play the first night. After a while we didn't keep the drummer. We

*Mamie E. Lane and her New Orleans Jazz Band, Grand Theater, Chicago. Left to right: Roy Palmer, "Sugar" Johnny Smith, Lawrence Duhé, Mamie E. Lane, Herbert Lindsey, Louis Keppard, and Edward Garland.*

played for colored first, then white. Mamie E. Lane was a white girl that blacked up to imitate a colored girl. Her husband was the manager of the show. She could dance, though. When the contract was up for that show I was sorry. We got $25 per third night each. Three nights a week and one matinée. We had all our transportation paid, of course. We left Chicago to go to St. Louis, Missouri. Then we went all over, far as Cedar Rapids, Iowa. We only stayed in one town two or three nights. I stayed with that show for a year. When it ended the men could get a ticket to New Orleans or the money instead. I took the ticket and went home. I had enough of travelling for a while. Next year they sent me a telegram about going with that show to New York, but I didn't go.

I stayed here and played music all through. I played with Wooden Joe Nicholas and all the guys round here. Now I got a way of hitting that guitar. It's like a double rap. Shuffle beat, you know. Plenty of those drummers couldn't play with that beat. Now, Happy Goldston and I, we were a team. Happy could follow that double rap beat. But music round here has changed. We used to play lancers, polkas, quadrilles, schottisches and waltzes. Of course I don't hear the boys play that no more. That was the music in them times.

Everything in New Orleans was competitive. People would always be betting on who was the best and greatest in everything. That's where the battles of music came in. Lots of the bands couldn't read too much music. So they used a fiddle to play the lead – a fiddle player could read – and that was to give them some protection. The banjo then was strictly a rhythm instrument, Buddy Bolden would say, "Simmer down, let me hear the sound of them feet." The New Orleans bands, you see. didn't play with a flat sound. They'd shade the music. After the band had played with the two or three horns blowing, they'd let the rhythm have it. That's what Buddy Bolden meant when he said that. The rhythm then often would play that mixture of African and Spanish syncopation – with a beat – and with just the rhythm going. They'd let the people use their imagination for the other sounds.

**Danny Barker**

I joined John Robichaux in 1904. There were seven men in the band (no piano): guitar, violin, Jim Williams on trumpet (he used to use a mute), cornet, Baptiste Delisle on trombone, Dee Dee Chandler on drums, and the greatest bass player I ever heard in my life – Henry Kimball. They played for the élite and had the town sewed up. In about 1908, Robichaux had a contest with Bolden in Lincoln Park and Robichaux won. For the contest, Robichaux added Manuel Perez. Bolden got hot-headed that night, as Robichaux really had his gang out. On other occasions, when Robichaux was playing in Lincoln Park and Bolden in Johnson Park, about a block away, Bolden would strip Lincoln Park of all the people by slipping his horn through the knot hole in the fence and calling his children home.

Each Sunday, Bolden went to church and that's where he got his idea of jazz music. They would keep perfect rhythm there by clapping their hands. I think I am the first one who started four-beat for guitar, and that's where I heard it (all down-strokes – four straight down). Bolden was a great man for what we call "dirt music." Let me tell you, he was pretty powerful. Even with all that power, the trumpet players of that day would have their notes covered, and they would not hurt the ear the way rebop does now. You could hear every instrument in these bands – every instrument. The drummer had his drums tuned – he would tune those drums like they were a piano.

**Bud Scott**

A jazz musician has to be a working class of a man, out in the open all the time, healthy and strong. That"s what's wrong today; these guys haven't got the force. They don't like to play all night; they don't think they can play unless they're loaded. But a working man have the power to play hot, whisky or no whisky. You see the average working man is very musical. Playing music for him is just relaxing. He gets as much kick out of playing as other folks get out of dancing. The more enthusiastic his audience is, why, the more spirit the working man's got to play. And with your natural feelings that way, you never make the same thing twice. Every time you play a tune, new ideas come to mind and you slip that on in.

**Johnny St Cyr**

New Orleans Style:
STRING
BASS

# EDWARD GARLAND

Edward Bertram Garland
String Bass

Born: New Orleans, Louisiana, January 9, 1885
Died: Los Angeles, California, January 22, 1980

*"Montudi" Garland played bass drum and tuba with many different marching bands in parades until about 1908. After switching to string bass he worked with Frankie Duson's Eagle Band and later the Excelsior Band. Around 1911 he joined the Imperial Band, then the Superior Orchestra and The Security Band. He left New Orleans in 1914 and worked in Chicago at the Deluxe Cafe, and subsequently with Emanuel Perez, Lawrence Duhé, Freddie Keppard and King Oliver.*

*In 1921 he travelled to California with the Oliver band and joined Kid Ory's band when Oliver returned to Chicago. When Ory left for Chicago in 1925, "Montudi" worked in "taxi dance" halls with Mutt Carey, and then led his own band at the One Eleven dance hall from 1929-1933. In 1944 he rejoined Kid Ory when Ory was making his comeback, and remained with the band until 1955. After spells with Andrew Blakeney and Joe Darensbourg, he toured with the Legends of Jazz in the 1970s.*

I was born January 9, 1885 in New Orleans, right where Parish Prison is on Saratoga, between Tulane and Gravier. I don't remember about my mother because I was only four years old when she passed. I had an older brother named John. He played violin mostly but also trombone, mandolin and guitar. I heard music in the church when I was real young. I went to the St. James Church on Roman, between Iberville and Bienville. When I was a young boy I used to hear the old Excelsior Band and that band across the river, the Pacific Brass Band. The band I was always crazy about was the Imperial Band. You know, well, I was a good size then because I used to "pinch-hit" for Jimmy Brown, the bass player with them. But I'm getting ahead of things. My brother used to keep all these instruments lying around. He could play a few little numbers on them, the mandolin, the guitar, but it was always for me to be a bass player. I started fooling with the guitar when I was around nine years old. My brother had a bass. It had three strings. Henry Kimball was the man who taught me to play a four-string bass. He was the bass player with Robichaux's Orchestra. Believe it or not, I was the only one that could go and sit in with Robichaux's band. He didn't allow no sitting in. Not with those guys, but Henry was good to me and he showed me the bass. In those days we was all bowing. Wasn't doing any picking. Just bowing. If the bow broke down I'd buy a spool of No. 8 thread and thread it on my own bow. I'll tell you, I really don't know who was the first one to pick a bass. It was just one of those things. It just come to all of us. Many times we would break our bow and just go ahead and pick. Just automatically come to us. Just like that slapping. We would do it 'cause we seen someone do it. In those times we had some pretty good bass players. Sam Nickerson was a pretty good bass player, and Oke Gaspard, but in my book, Henry Kimball was tops. He was actually a good musician, read and everything. Jimmy Brown was also a good bass player. Jimmy Johnson was all right too. He used to play with Jack Carey and also with the Crescent Band. Now before he played with the

Crescent Band he used to play with Buddy Bolden. I played in Bolden's band too, for Jimmy. He used to work in some furniture factory, and lots of times he would be late and couldn't make it, and I'd "pinch-hit" for him. They played a lot at Kenny's Hall, the one they used to call "Funky Butt" on Perdido and Liberty. They played the Saturday night dance there. Would go all night till Sunday morning and twenty minutes afterward, it would be a church. They finally turned it into a church. Old man Kenny owned the place.

Buddy Bolden used to play in there. Now, I can't tell you everyone in the band, but there was Frank Lewis played clarinet, Willie Cornish played trombone, Jimmy Johnson played bass and a fellow named James Phillips played drums. He used to have a toothpick always in his mouth, a toothpick or a match, and he wouldn't be there ten minutes before he would get sleepy. Dee Dee Chandler finally took his place on drums.

Now I remember the first job I ever played. It was with Cornelius Jackson. He was playing guitar, my brother John played violin and I played bass. Just the three of us. A little party on a Saturday night. Some kid had hired us and the people was all dancing. Well, I had to be home at nine o'clock. That was supposed to be my bedtime. Nine o'clock come around and I began to get sleepy and really did fall asleep. The people came around to see this little fellow asleep at the bass. Someone hollered, "Put some ice up to his eyes." But they finally said, "Let the little fellow sleep." So they continued on with just guitar and violin. I never knew how much money we got.

I always used to run with older fellows. I'd slip in the dances like at the Oddfellows Hall. I used to play a few numbers for Dandy Lewis, who played the bass.

Finally they give me a job. I used to make like a dollar or maybe six bits. So then I started to play with Manuel Perez and his band. Manuel was kind of sick then. I think he had stomach ulcers. I played quite regular with Manuel, right after Jimmy Brown left them. Georgie Baquet played clarinet and George Filhe trombone, and this boy Henry Nickerson, that's Professor Nickerson's son, played violin.

When I was playing with the Imperial Band and Manuel Perez and all, George Filhe said, "Say Ed, they got a young fellow here just come out from La Place named Ory. You'd be just the guy for them. They got a good band and them guys need a good bass player. Go on down there and help 'em out." At that time Ory's brother Johnny had a saloon on Conti and Claiborne. That was the same brother that Ory had the chicken farm with in later years. Anyway, I went over there to see Ory and he asked me to come to a rehearsal. So I went to their rehearsal, but I didn't know any of the tunes they were playing. They was nothing but some make-up tunes from out in the country. Like *1919 March*, you know. I played with them and they said, "Oh man. Can't you stay with us?" I told 'em I'd think about it. That's how it all happened. I joined them but they would get all messed up. Sometimes they wouldn't get any money. Nothin' at all. Me and Johnny Dodds would fight every night. Sometimes about music or something. One time I wapped Johnny in the mouth. We didn't mean harm to each other but kidded around fighting and all. See, Lawrence Duhé was the clarinet player with Ory and them. Then they took Johnny in to replace him. During that time, and when Ory really began to get noticed, we played all around. Lots of the time we played out in the country. St. John, Donaldsonville, Lake Charles. For years we worked at a place called "Cole's Lawn" at

Willow and Jackson. We worked there Saturdays and Sundays and all holidays. It was a lady who ran this place. She was crazy about Ory's band. She always said that if she died she wanted Ory's band to play for her funeral. I don't know which band played for her, but when she died she was the only woman that had a band play for her. These parties at Cole's Lawn, they charged 50 cents to get in there. It was a big pavilion and they served beer and food.

In 1917 we took a band from here to Chicago. It was "Sugar Johnny" Smith, trumpet; Lawrence Duhé, clarinet; Roy Palmer, trombone; Herbert Lindsey, violin; Louis Keppard, guitar, and myself. We were supposed to have Red Happy play drums with us but just as we were going to get on the train, the agent, who was taking care of the business at this end, comes up with a telegram that said they had to cut the drums. Poor Happy was in tears, but we went on the train and up to Illinois Central. When we got to Chicago the booking agent was called Lee Kraus, I'll never forget him. He had us rehearse and we had a white girl named Mamie E. Lane. She'd make up a black face and would dance in there with those wooden shoes. There was a big bale of cotton in the center of the stage and she sat in this bale and when we start to playin' she'd come out. The bale of cotton just opened up and she could go. We had a beautiful cover with a steamboat in the background. The band was called Mamie E. Lane and her New Orleans Jazz Band. We went up there and played and everybody was just crazy about the New Orleans Jazz Band. See, we had a regular routine. Numbers we used to play for her to dance by, you know, like *On The Robert E. Lee* but then we played some of the New Orleans standards and pretty good it was too. Then I went with Joe Oliver and started really travelling, all out to the coast and then I went back with Ory out there. We made those records out there in 1921.

On the bass, I had a lot of lessons. I started out faking around New Orleans, but the little reading I done was started at Old Man Jackson's, in Chicago, at 31st Street. Henry Kimball showed me the fingering back in New Orleans. Henry showed me how to use the E string, which I had taken off the bass, too many strings, that was my way, but he showed me the finger board and lots of different bass players with more experience than I give me a lot of ideas. When I started playing we played most always two beats to the measure but later on we started to double up and make four. As for that slapping against the fingerboard, it's O.K. But for a true tone from your instrument don't touch the fingerboard at all with the strings. When I was young I practised scales, scales and scales. Now I practise solos. I play a three-quarter-size wooden bass. Now once I tried an aluminum bass but they ain't no good. This bass I got now, I've had since 1921. As for strings; I use a gut G and D, a steel A and E. I tried one of those electric basses, like a guitar, in a store, but they're no good for my line of playing. I just couldn't get all I need out of one of those basses. Not for dixieland. I mean it's a different tone altogether. In fact, in my line of playing you have to have the soundpost adjusted right to get the tone and the bridge too. You have to keep your bass adjusted from the floor too. It ain't too good to have no bass too close to the floor 'cause the tone goes down and it kills it. It's like trying to play on carpet. That kills your tone and muffles it. You set a little board underneath it and set your bass right on it. Well, a lot of people plays too hard. Works

Ed Garland's 1929 firearms license. The age given on the certificate makes him six years younger than the age he always gave.

themselves to death playing the bass. You don't have to, you know. Now you take the fellow that plays with George Lewis' band. What's that old man's name? Er, Slow Drag. He works it hard and Joe (Darensbourg) would tell him, "Look at Tudi. See how easy Tudi's playing." I sit there and play just as calm and I'll be hitting notes too and getting a tone out of it. That's one thing I praise myself for. Ory was crazy about that. I played a solid bass. Bud Scott said the same thing.

When I play, I'm not thinking about the chords, like, this is a B-flat, next comes an A-flat. No, no. You know what you are doing. I can be playing and talking about something else at the same time. If you know it, you know it, but if you're playing something you don't know the melody to, then you got to keep your ears open. All I want to hear is that melody and I can put the right basses in there. If he's a right piano player and playing the correct basses, I'll play with him, see. I'll play with that piano player. I like to be next to the piano player's left hand in a band. I always take my bow on a job. I always got my bow. I like to use the bow behind someone singing, especially on those sweet numbers.

Now I enjoyed working with Bud Scott. He played chords and rhythm too, and he loved to sing. He made some awfully nice arrangements for Ory, did Bud. We used to talk things out that we were going to make. Bud could play his solos too. In Ory's band, Mutt used to be the leader. He used to knock off the numbers. After Mutt left, Ory used to knock off the numbers, that was after we left The Green Room. But, you know, Ory knocked off on the wrong foot. Knock off with the left foot. Boom, boom. We used to think that was a cannonball, so loud. I tap my heel when I play but not loud. But to get back to Bud. His wife's name was Alice. Ram Hall stayed right around the corner from them. Bud lived on the south side of the street and they had a nice back yard. They had a big tree right out front of the place and they had it cut down and they fixed their home up. Well, Bud was writing a book that tells all about Robichaux and them. He was always walking around with that book under his arm. Some lady was writing it for him. See, I played with Bud back in New Orleans, but Ram never played with him till he got out here. When I first played with Bud, he was with Robichaux. I played in Henry Kimball's place a few times, and Bud was in there with them then. Another thing, Bud played a little bass, you know, and trombone too. Lots of folks don't know that. Bud was way older than me. He was older than Mutt too. I first met Mutt when I was playing with Ory. We had a trumpet player called "Chif", and Mutt came to town. He was working at the Cotton Exchange down on Common between Baronne and St. Charles. Mutt was working for one of those offices, cotton samplers. George McCullum used to work there too. Well, so they got Mutt in Ory's band. I don't think Mutt used to get along much with his brother, Jack Carey. We used to give Jack's band the devil. We used to play over in Gretna at the "Come Clean" hall. They used to come way over there to play sometimes.

It would be two bands. We'd be on the stage and this man Oscar, I guess he was something to do with the place, Oscar De Pris or something, he'd be at the door and when he saw Jack and his boys coming he'd come to the stage and tell Ory, "Play a march. The Crescent Band is comin' in." Ory told the guy, "If they march in, let 'em march by their own music. We'll never march 'em in here." See, the people was already dancin' and Ory didn't want to stop that. So they had to slink in. Lawrence Duhé was playing clarinet with us at that time. In the old days we all had some kind of uniform to wear. They had bands called, "The Boys In Blue" or such names. Frankie Duson had his band which was called the "Eagle Band" but everyone called them "The Boys In Brown". But with Ory we had blue uniforms. Our cap said, "Ory's Band." When I first joined Ory he used to play a bit for lawn parties, private affairs, you know. Lots of times we played out to West End or out to Milneberg at the camps. In fact, every Sunday we stayed out there from nine o'clock in the morning till six o'clock, then come right back to play at Economy Hall till four in the morning.

Now you take now. I mean lately. A lot of those bands just play the chorus of certain numbers. Back then, they would play the whole thing. Verse and chorus too. As years went on we changed it to maybe just the choruses, but we played it all in our own style. We "shaded" the music in New Orleans. Let's say, the introduction or the first chorus loud, then the next part softer. That's one thing about Ory's band, even in the early days, they would call us "the sweet and soft band." We used to play so soft, then maybe come up on a chorus medium. He'd say, "Let's hear just the beat," and that's one thing Ory was always good for, shading. Another thing, the tempos. Today I notice they play things so fast, like *The Saints Go Marchin' In*. In New Orleans we never did play anything so fast you couldn't dance to it. They didn't bother with so many solos like they play now either. I know I never did play too many. We didn't do much of that. All we did was give the beat. The horns, well, if a clarinet was playing the other two would give background.

My advice to bass players now coming up is to start out right. Start from the bottom and get a foundation and come on up. You can't put a house on naked ground, you got to have a foundation. After you get that foundation, you can come up as high as you want to, but you've got to have the foundation to build it up. Start out right and keep your head buried in that book. In a band you can maybe fake it but you can't have everybody faking it at the same time. I can play *Home Sweet Home* and it'll come out dixieland style. Whatever you play if you're into that style it will come out as dixieland.

# George "Pops" Foster

George Murphy Foster
string bass

Born: McCall, Louisiana, May 18, 1892
Died: San Francisco, October 30, 1969

*George Foster moved to New Orleans from the McCall Plantation in 1902. He began playing around 1908, and a little later joined the Magnolia Band with King Oliver. He worked on the Mississippi River Excursion boats with Louis Armstrong and Baby Dodds, beginning in 1918, stayed in St Louis awhile and went to California in the early 1920s.*

*In 1928 Foster went to New York with King Oliver and soon joined Luis Russell's band. He helped revolutionize New York jazz by inspiring all the tuba players to change to string bass. In the late 1930s he began playing again with Armstrong, this time on a touring basis.*

*"Pops" Foster became the best known of all New Orleans bass players. He was also a great talker and wrote an interesting autobiography.*

I was born May 19, 1892 in Assumption Parish, McCall, which is 68 miles north of New Orleans and three miles from Donaldsonville. My brother, Willie Foster, will be 69 this Christmas. He's up in Baton Rouge. My mother made 106, the 3rd of February this year [interviewed in 1958].

Before we came down to New Orleans, we had a three-piece family band – me, my brother and my sister. My sister played mandolin, my brother played guitar and I played the cello. I started learning music when I was seven. I'd stand on a box and play the cello like a bass with a bow. Then my brother got me a nice string bass. The people who my mother worked for were the McCalls. They were the cause of my playing music. The mother played piano and she would see that we rehearsed on certain days. They used to give a dance – they called 'em "balls" – they'd get one big room and ask 25 cents at the door or 15 cents if they'd buy a ticket beforehand. They'd sell wine and gumbo. They had a table of chewing gum. You'd take a pack and split it. They also had bananas and other things. Now you had to play a march whenever you catch that floor crowded, then you stop playing and grab a girl and she hold on your arm and march you right to that table. They gotta thing in 6/8 movement for this march. Now whatever she pick up you gotta pay for it, a piece of gum at some of the dances was 25 cents or one slice most likely was a nickel or a dime. Orange 25 cents or 15 cents. The guys used to watch the dance as the floor get more crowded right after you play the march. If he figure you're goin' to play another march – he's goin' to go right in as she ain't goin' turn you loose. She's goin' to hold on your arm and watch until they play, another march. We had to play slow polkas, mazurkas and quadrilles. But if you ask somebody about polkas right now, they don't know what you're talking about. Different tempos. Then they come up with one they called the "Chicago Glide." Now whatever dance the people wanted, why you had the music to play that dance – and they'd dance and we had to play them waltzes – the *Merry Widow Waltz* and all them waltzes. And you'd better play those waltzes in the right tempo 'cause them dancers will tell you if you don't. When I come out to Los Angeles, they used to have guys to introduce the dances – tell you what dance. In New Orleans they didn't

introduce no dance, you just played the introduction to the dances.

Outside those dances, the brass bands made more money in them days than your orchestras made in these days. They played funerals and parades all through the week, 'cause back in them days they didn't bury people on a Sunday. The bands, like Louis', in the late days, came up with playing *The Saints* and all that stuff, but in the old days, *The Saints Go Marching In* – they played that when they're going to the funeral with the body. They played that in a very slow 4/4 tempo, it was gorgeous. In the later years, they come out and played it in ragtime style. See, 'cause we played places in the South right in Texas, and Lord, they wouldn't let you play *The Saints*. 'Cause if you play it the place is raided. Preachers wouldn't let you play it. Like *Just A Closer Walk With Thee*, we didn't play them kind of things – we didn't play nothing like that in no dance hall. We played strictly dance songs – and those hymns belonged to the church. When my mother came down to New Orleans she worked for some people called W.G. Wilman. She stayed on the premises. She and my sister stayed there with my daddy. This was round 1902, for the Mardi Gras and we never did go back. Then we moved to Octavia Street between Liberty and Howard. Right back there was just like country – nothing but fields. It wasn't built up at all.

I went to school at New Orleans University, uptown. Bunk went there too when he was a kid. I didn't learn nothin' in school 'cause I was playing music all the time. When we came to New Orleans, we formed a three-piece band called Rozelle's Band. Roy Palmer was our first guitar player, then later we converted Roy to cornet player when we had Joe Johnson on guitar. My brother had a E-flat cornet 'cause all the cornets was E-flat around there in the brass bands. Joe couldn't fool with his E-flat cornet so he learned how to play guitar. Then we had a trombone player called Ovette Jackson. We didn't make it until Ovette switched to trombone and Joe went to B-flat cornet. And they both turned out being very good. After Joe quit, Roy was our cornet player for a long time. Roy first started on trombone.

Then I got acquainted with Louis Keppard and Eddie Garland's brother, Johnny Garland. He played violin and a little "hurry up" trombone. We called it "hurry up" trombone, as when he couldn't play, he looked like he was in a hurry to make his notes. Johnny had a job. Ed Garland had to go on with the Ory band that night, so Ed Garland sent me. Louis Keppard was playing and they had a little band downtown, the Magnolia Band. So they asked me to play with 'em. This was a Saturday night and then they asked me to play with them on Sunday. I went down and played that Sunday and then they started raving about my playing. We got this little band and we called rehearsals once or twice a week. Our rehearsals were like a party. The band rehearsed in this room and a bunch of girls wanted to dance. They didn't interfere with our rehearsing. Every once in a while they come with lemonade, cake and red beans and rice, man, just like a party. When you played a dance in those days you had to get a 50 cents permit. But at one of these rehearsals, we was making so much noise, with the barbecue, wine, beer and everything, that the cops come along to see if we'd got our permit. So we had to get a permit for our rehearsals.

I always lived uptown and I did all kinds of work when I wasn't playing music.

Louis (Armstrong) worked for the Tennessee Coal Company and I was working for the Pittsburgh Coal Company. We both drove coal wagons. When he was going uptown to deliver coal and I was heading downtown, we would meet and buy whiskey. Some morning it would be my turn to buy and the next morning it would be his turn. We'd get a big bottle of 10 cent Southern whiskey. Then I worked at longshore for a while. I was also playing music most nights. I worked pretty hard in my younger days.

We used to play what we called ragtime music. St. Louis should have had a lot more credit than it did. We bought most of our music from St. Louis, but they didn't have no bands to play that music like we could. We beat 'em to the punch.

In a band of six or seven guys, everyone would join a club for a $1 a month and buy the music. If two had the same number, we would trade with other bands if they had a number we wanted. If you hadn't anything to trade, you could borrow the number or the book. Bands got along, downtown bands I'm talking about.

Downtown there's a different class of musicians. Buddy Petit wasn't in a class with them. Downtown you had bands like the Superior Band, the Olympia Band and the Magnolia Band that I was in. We had the Silver Leaf Orchestra. That was led by Albert T. Baptiste, a violin player. His uncle was one of the best trombone players we had in New Orleans. Baptiste DeLisle – he used to play with John Robichaux's Orchestra. He and my cousin, George Williams, from Donaldsonville, were the first guys to switch from valve to slide trombone. George's brother was Claiborne Williams, he's my uncle. When I was in New York I used to go and see Clarence Williams. I told him: "Man, I should have stayed around my uncle's a little longer." He say: "What d'you mean your uncle? I'm from Plaquemine." Plaquemine is near Donaldsonville and it turns out we were cousins. After Clarence quit the music business he was the only negro in the country to have a pawn shop.

We had drummers downtown that could fit in with my band. In the French Quarter, 'Old Man' Cottrell, John MacMurray, and Jean Vigne. The stuff that drummers are doing right now, Jean Vigne was doing that years ago – the shuffle beat. You see each of the guys had their own style. Nobody copied behind each other – everybody had their own style of playing. Bunk had his style. Bunk had a style out of this world when he was a young man. "Wild Ned" had another style, he played high pitched, way up there. He played with Bolden, and his brother was a tuba player. He was with the P.G. Lorell show. That was a circus band. If you couldn't read, there was no use going in that band. Yeah, see, George Baquet was the greatest clarinet in the world and George was a nice man. I don't care where you was playing, if he knowed you was in a band from New Orleans, he'd come and see you. George got up out of his sickbed after he first got that stroke and come down to when I was playing in Philadelphia. Saw him a couple of times. George and Jim Williams and Baptiste DeLisle were three real top notch men in Robichaux's band. That was a band. John Robichaux passed out the music. They'd get all the new numbers – waltzes, rags, blues, anything, play anything. When John first come to New Orleans, they tell me they had another drummer before Cottrell. He lived uptown, he was a boozehead, Dee Dee Chandler. He played with Buddy Bolden when Frankie Duson got in the band. I remember they played at Johnson Park, when John Robichaux was next door at Lincoln Park. I'd slip into Lincoln Park in short pants and hide from the cops 'cause they'd chase you out. On Sundays, Robichaux had his orchestra on a big outdoor stage playing from 4 to 7 p.m. Then they knocked off to eat, and then they went into a big hall and played from 8 till 4 a.m. Margaret, Kimball's wife, played piano with them in the afternoon. But at night, they didn't use no piano. They got inside and played till 4 o'clock.

Easter Sunday used to be a big day for musicians, also New Year's Eve and Christmas. People all went to church and then they'd go to a dance. Mardi Gras day was another one. Everybody worked on Mardi Gras Day.

Most of those musicians in New Orleans, back in those days. were either carpenters, or plasterers or cigar makers. They had something they would do through Lent 'cause you didn't play from Mardi Gras to St. Joseph's night (March 19), then we played a dance on St. Joseph's Night. George McCullum was a sampler in the cotton business. He'd take cotton and trade it. He taught Sidney Desvigne. He was another nice player too. There's a lot of misunderstandin' in them books. Now you take Ory's band. That band didn't have no regular job in them days. The only bands that had regular jobs was the downtown bands, Magnolia Band, Superior Band, Imperial Band and the Olympia Band. A lot of them bands had night jobs in the District. Manuel Perez was at Rice's, Freddie Keppard and them was at Billy Phillips'. We was at Nagel's and Groshell's place. Eddie Groshell and Hans Nagel were partners and ran a saloon and dance hall at Custom House and Liberty. When Manuel Perez had his band down there, we used to work with the Superior Band. When the Superior Band used to go off on gigs, we'd work in there. We'd always have three or four nights in the District. The Superior Band and the Magnolia Band also worked

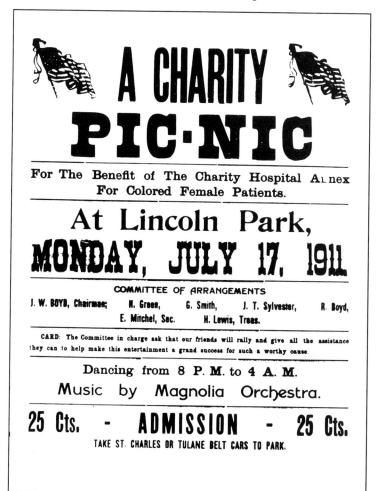

*Handbill advertising a dance featuring the Magnolia Orchestra at Lincoln Park – July 17, 1911*

for Hans Nagel. Big Eye Louis played with us first in the Magnolia Band, then we had Dave Depass. We'd have kept Dave, but we wanted to get rid of his brother, Arnold, who was our drummer. We couldn't get rid of Arnold unless we got rid of Dave too. They used to put letters under your door when you got fired and when you wake up the next morning you find your letter and you ain't got no job! Dave Depass played clarinet and he was very good but we wanted another drummer, so we got "Quank" – Ernest Trepagnier.

When we worked in the district I'd go over to Billy Phillips', Billy Marrero or John Lindsey might be there and I'd play there awhile, then they would come over and play in my place. Sometimes we'd get off at 12 and I'd run like the dickens to get to dance the quadrille. I used to get a kick out of that quadrille, just looking at them guys dance. Now if you walked in the place and Manuel Manetta was playing violin or piano, everybody was dancing. The first part of the night at the Masonic Hall was supposed to be "dicty" dancing, they played nothing but waltzes, but after midnight then they would do the blues and quadrilles, slow drag and more. That was all honky tonk. You would see all them sportin' women come in after they'd finished their work. They were really rough women. That's about the time I would be in there. The quadrille people were the rough gang, most of those guys were uptown. They had two different class of people that came to dance. In the early part of the night they'd dance waltzes, then they'd leave when the rough ones would come in at midnight. The sportin' women wouldn't come in till after midnight. because they never played no blues before then. Back in those days, if the band couldn't play no blues, they couldn't play the rough halls like the Funky Butt Hall.

I used to play in those bands in places like Come Clean Hall, the Number Twelve Hall

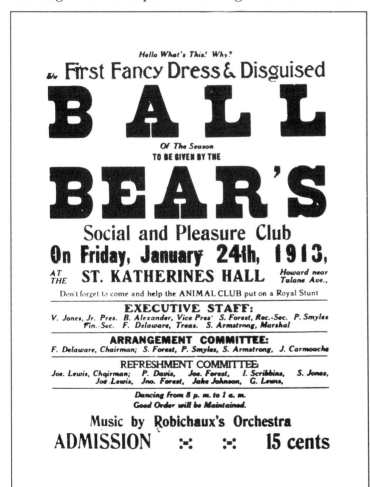

*Handbill advertising a dance featuring John Robichaux's Orchestra at St. Katherines Hall – January 24, 1913*

and the Big Easy over in Gretna. They used to have dances every Saturday night and they made plenty of money. A glass of beer or wine for a nickel and everybody was happy. Uptown, Edward Clem had a band. Bab Frank had a band with his brother, Alcide, who played violin.

In the first band I worked with, we had a cornet player called Harrison Gugee. He could play anything that was put in front of him, but he couldn't play head music. Bunk had a nice sound when he got with them creole boys in the Superior Band. When he got with them uptown boys like Frankie Duson, he started drinking – stayed up all night. For months and months he didn't go home – slept on pool tables. The only trouble that Bunk got into was himself. Bunk just didn't stop drinking; he was drunk for a long time. After he left New Orleans, I didn't see him again until 1937 and I didn't recognize him. I was with Louis Armstrong and we had this dance in New Iberia and he came and sat in with the band.

Johnny Dodds was working in the rice mill when I first heard him. He wasn't playing with anybody. I picked him up and took him over to Globe Hall where 'Old Man' Toca was playing. Duhé was leaving for Chicago and I got Johnny that job.

The best reading clarinetists uptown were Charles McCurdy and Sam Dutrey. In the Eagle Band, Phillip Nickerson was the only one who could read – that was a ratty band. They played the number that Ory said he wrote, *Muskrat Ramble*. They were playing that around 1910.

Buddy Bolden could read a little, but Cornish and Duson and the rest of those guys couldn't. Duson and Lorenzo Staulz were real ratty guys. They wore their braces down with their pants half falling down. Three men in that band went crazy – Bolden, Frank Lewis and Dandy Lewis. Jimmy Johnson was the best musician in that band. We didn't class the Bolden Band or the Eagle Band as anything special.

In them days everybody had their own style. Manual Perez had his style, Arnold Metoyer had his style, Freddie had his style, Buddy Petit, Sam Morgan. No one copied anyone, they stayed in their own style. You could be outside a place, or maybe a couple of blocks away, but you could always tell who was playing. Today everybody tries to copy each other. In later years, Louis ruined many a good trumpet player. Gus Aiken was a good musician until he got to fool around with them mouthpieces trying to get those high notes Louis could make. Louis had a trumpet player called June Clark. He used to stick his head out of the window to get a cold so he could talk like Louis. He still talks like Louis today and he can't help it. June was a nice trumpet player till he started doing all that stuff. Today everybody is trying to follow behind the next man.

In those days in New Orleans, everyone was real friendly, not like today. John Robichaux and some of 'em organized a union around 1900, but everybody I knew weren't in no union – we didn't need no union. Things were stricter then. We didn't work no scale, but if you didn't want to hire me you go to another man and he's going to tell you the same thing. We all worked for about the same money. Ridgeley had a job at the Perseverance Hall and I was late coming on the job. He got Oke Gaspard to come in. When I got there, Oke said: "Foster plays, or you ain't got no bass." Me and Oke were like family. Another time when I was working with Ridgeley at the St. Charles Hotel, they had two bands:

Ridgeley and Manuel Perez each had a band. Oke was supposed to play with Manuel that night, but he never made it. So I played with both bands that night. Manuel tried to give me the money, but I told him to give it to Oke. Those guys from uptown were used to working like we worked. We all got along real good. We all had fun playing music.

I played with a lot of those downtown bands too. Those bands had plenty of work. The District was only a sideline, because they had enough other work. They would play in the District during Lent. You made your money from all those people coming off the boat and we used to play from 8 till 4 a.m. Bands didn't stay in the District too long – just a couple of months – just enough time to make their money and leave.

We used to play them "banquets." The last banquet I played was with George Baquet and Freddie Keppard at the Perseverance Hall on Villere Street, when Freddie and them was fixing to leave to go to California. They used to have a long table the full length of the hall with gumbo, ham, salad, barrels of wine and beer. Nobody told you when to have an intermission, you just got off the stand and get a cup of beer. At 12 o'clock, they would feed the band. Whatever was on that table you could have, didn't pay for nothing.

The Economy Hall was high class compared to other halls like Hopes Hall. When you made the Economy Hall it was like working at Carnegie Hall.

We used to have some fun playing those all day picnics out at Milneburg. Freddie used to play these on Saturday and Sundays. He played right off the boardwalk where the train stopped. There might be 20 or 30 bands up there at weekends. When you get off playing, you would go and listen to the next band. They had a lot of camps out there and people would sell beer and food, and the people would come around and if they liked you they would hire the band for their picnic. I remember when John Robichaux broke up his band, he went up there to play with Freddie at them picnics.

When I first got on the boats, Frankie Duson and a drummer called James Alexander was working there. Then Manuel Perez and Charlie McCurdy, Tio and Andrew Kimball got that job. Then Zue Robertson came on the boat with Johnny Lindsey. They played trombone together and when I couldn't make it Johnny would play bass. Sometimes people would think it was me behind that bass as Johnny and I look similar.

They tried to get Peter Bocage for the boat, but Peter didn't want to leave town, so they got Joe Howard. Our drummer was James Alexander, but he wanted to go off with a show, that's when I went and got Baby Dodds. Then they wanted another cornet player. Louis was playing with Ory on Claiborne Street and Johnny Streckfus heard him there and wanted Louis. Louis learnt a lot from Joe Howard about music. Joe was from St. John's, Louisiana – a lot of good musicians come from 'round there: John Robichaux, Papa Celestin, Eddie Atkins. They're all what we call Frenchmen – "creoles."

I joined Charlie Creath in St. Louis in 1922, then I went back on the boat with Dewey Jackson's band in 1923, to take the boat back to New Orleans. The next year I went out with Sidney Desvigne on the boat and they sent for Manuel Perez to meet us in Memphis to work with us back to New Orleans. We had some fun on that boat, but we got sick of that food and we would go and buy our own. We worked on the "Island Queen" up to Cincinnati a lot of the time. When the water was too low you couldn't move the boat and when it was too high, they had to fold back the smoke stacks to get them under the bridges. I worked with Sidney Desvigne, until Mutt Carey sent for me to come to California in 1927.

When I was in Los Angeles, nobody was playing string bass except "Montudi" Garland and me. Everybody was playing tuba. When I went to New York, I was ashamed to carry the bass 'cause I couldn't go more than a block without people laughing. Every bass player in New York was playing tuba.

When I left New Orleans I wasn't playing tuba, so when I came back the guys were surprised when I had my tuba. I didn't stay long enough on the tuba to do anything but fake it. The last job I played on the tuba was in Los Angeles in 1928. When Luis Russell sent for me in '29, I was back with Dewey Jackson, but he didn't want me to leave and he wouldn't give me Luis Russell's telegram for two months 'till his wife got salty.

The string bass is best for swinging a band. On the tuba, when you hit a note it's gone. The string bass has got a mellower vibration – it sustains a note longer. A tuba never did fit in no orchestra, but they tried to make 'em. A tuba is made for brass bands. I only learnt the tuba so I could sit down with the rest of the guys!

Out in Los Angeles I had a tuba and was working in this little dance hall. One Friday night I brought my string bass down and played the job. After that the leader told me to keep on the bass.

When I got to New York I sent my tuba back to the music store. Guys who take solos on tubas sound nothing to me. It's a bass instrument and should be played as one. If I take a solo on the string bass, it can sound like I'm playing the melody, but I'm not, I'm playing straight chords. If you know the numbers you can sing to the changes that I'm making. These guys who try to play the melody, there's no foundation behind what they're doing. I don't like playing solos. I'd rather play behind the other guy and let him blow. If you got a good rhythm going, you can have as much fun as the guy playing the melody.

When we went to the Roseland Ballroom, we didn't always have much of a band, but we sure had some good rhythm. Me and Paul Barbarin, Will Johnson, the guitar player from Ohio, and Luis Russell. People dance by rhythm. On Easter Sunday night we went into the studio to cut a number. I thought it wasn't anything, but *Mahogany Hall*, that's the number that made the string bass famous. Louis just holds that note and I'm just walking behind it. Then everybody started buying string basses. Everybody was trying to play it. All the tuba players would come around to my house and I give 'em lessons. In the next three years you didn't see nothing but string basses. All them four and five hundred dollar tubas were left around the hallways. People didn't want 'em no more.

The string bass wasn't nothing new in New Orleans – we'd always used 'em. Jimmy Johnson in the Bolden Band used to pick the string bass as well as bow. And before him they had a man out at Donaldsonville, Louisiana, who played string bass and violin – Henri Baltimore. He picked but didn't slap the bass like I do now. Albert Glenny told me the first one he heard pick a string bass was Johnny Predonce. Henry Kimball was the best of those old time string bass players. When I was coming up, we always bowed the slow numbers and picked some of the fast numbers. On some jobs you would bow all night. We always used that bow and gave a note its full value or whatever was written. When I was teaching in New York, they would tell me that Braud told them not to use a bow, but I told 'em that any good bass player should learn how to bow. When they come to me, I first tell 'em how to tune their bass and I won't teach them anything else till they know how to do that. When they got that I tell them to run the scales very slow. They've got to learn the right foundations if they're going to play.

One guy came to me and said his fingers got sore. I say don't put nothing on 'em – don't put no tape on your fingers, nothing, just freeze 'em with ice. Put some iodine on 'em and stick 'em in ice. I don't care how bad they hurt, in time they'll get hard.

I pick the bass with two fingers together, first and second together. With both together you get more volume and grip. You gotta grip those strings to get intonation.

*Emile Barnes (left) with Albert Glenny in the 1920s*

The first bass I had was a three string bass. Most of them old basses were three string. Then I learned to play with four strings where I had to pedal C. Today some guys are using the five string bass and come up with that high C, real high, but it don't sound like no bass to me. They used them five string basses in theaters long ago.

My ideas come to me right on the stand. If you feel the music you get your ideas to put with it. I remember one night we were playing with Louis' 17-piece orchestra up in Massachusetts. We had some new fancy arrangements but nobody was dancing. I told Mr. Glaser that we're playing the wrong music. He say "What should we play?" I said, "Play *Sweet Georgia Brown* in jig tempo and stay right there." Everybody started dancing. He said "Best music I've heard all night." "No" I said, "we just play what those people understand." Some of those fancy arrangements

107

were over the people's heads. So Louis said "Close the books and play." I played out of my head for the rest of the night and the people enjoyed it much better than the big arrangements.

When I worked with Luis Russell, I used an aluminum bass. It was good for running around the country, 'cause you didn't have to worry about it getting banged up, but I didn't like it too much as it had a very metallic sound on some of the notes like B-flat. The old style basses had a flat back, but now-a-days I use a round back.

In a band, I always prefer to stand close to the piano. The bass belongs on that side of the band. Sometimes they put the drums between me and the piano, that doesn't sound right. In the old days they used to line up with the drums at one end and the bass at the other. That balances a band.

In the old days they mostly played a good solid two beats, except for a few numbers that needed four beats. A solid two is better than four. I play one and three, what piano players long ago used to call "oom-pah" rhythm. What they call "antique" right now.

Manuel Manetta was the one that got me started playing solos. He played *The World is Waiting for the Sunrise* with one finger on the piano to give me the notes.

I never did copy anybody. Guys come up to me and say they want to play like me on those records. I say "Why don't you get some of your own ideas. Don't try to play like me, use your ideas."

Bass players now try to play too many notes, that don't swing a band. Clarinet players today play too many notes and they make notes that don't fit. They're playing like they'd got piccolos, right up there. Clarinets are beautiful instruments. Charlie McCurdy, George Baquet and Lorenzo Tio played in the middle of the clarinet. Some of the clarinet players now are just screamers, they don't get that clarinet tone.

There are hardly any drummers left today, only cymbal beaters. Some of them make a mistake buying drums, all they need is two sticks and a cymbal. Our average New Orleans drummer was better than the best we have now. Sid Catlett was the one that came close to the old New Orleans drummers. Paul Barbarin was very good, but when I played with his brother, Louis, I thought he was better. The average drummer now doesn't know how to work with a string bass. They also don't know how to tune their drums. They don't understand, drums have to be tuned just like a bass or piano.

I would rather work with a piano player now as they don't have no good guitar rhythm men now. None of them can play the full chords. I prefer the guitar in a band than the banjo. Years ago they had them plectrum banjos on the streets, but they weren't in no bands. Around the twenties they started bringing the tenor banjos into the bands, about the same time as they got the saxophones in to kill the clarinet.

I don't regard myself as anything special, just another bass player trying to make a living. Louis and me used to call each other "Pops" all the time and after a while the name just stuck with me.

I try to keep up the good work for all the old guys who didn't get away from New Orleans. I try to remember them in books and things. They didn't get a chance. I'm lucky enough to get a chance to say things on their behalf these days.

# WELLMAN BRAUD

Wellman Braud
(originally Breaux)
string bass

Born: La Place, Louisiana, January 25, 1891
Died: Los Angeles, California, October 29, 1966

*Wellman Braud began playing violin when he was seven. After moving to New Orleans in 1911, he worked with a string trio at Tom Anderson's Cabaret, playing violin and later bass. He also marched with various brass bands playing trombone. He moved to Chicago in 1917 and worked with Freddie Keppard at the Pekin Café, and then at the Dreamland and DeLuxe Café. In 1922 he joined Charlie Elgar's Orchestra and, in 1923, visited Europe with The Plantation Orchestra.*

*Wellman Braud is best known for his spell with Duke Ellington (1926-35), where his driving string bass style became a hallmark of the band's early recordings.*

*After leaving Duke, he worked with Jimmie Noone and the Spirits of Rhythm, before forming his own trio. He left full-time music in 1945, but continued to play weekend gigs around New York, including dates with Bunk Johnson in 1947. In 1956, he moved to California and joined Kid Ory's band. In 1960 he worked with Joe Darensbourg, and although he suffered a heart attack the following year, he continued to work until he suffered a fatal heart attack at his home in Los Angeles.*

*This interview was recorded whilst he was visiting his childhood friend, also from St. James Parish, La Place, Lawrence Duhé – see photograph on page 216.*

I'll start from the beginning. I was born St James Parish, La Place, January 25th 1891. My father owned a rice farm. I played in a little brass band called the D.I., around Jamestown. My first instrument was mandolin, but I played guitar and drum too. I started to learn drum under Professor Claiborne Williams, out of Donaldsonville.

In 1911 I moved to New Orleans. My surname was really Breaux, but my father changed it to Braud. There was so many of us in that family that the mail would always get mixed up. So he changed our family name to Braud. I never played in the District. I was too young. You had to be 21 to go in there. I played out at Bucktown with Willie Humphrey's daddy's band. John Joseph was their bass player and it was him that started me on mandolin, but I played guitar with Humphrey's band. Joseph was a fine bass player and still is today. He and his brother, they had a barber shop. I began to watch the bass players from then on and my favorites were Billy Marrero and Henry Kimball. I also liked to watch the trombone players. Really that was my favorite instrument. Ory and Zue Robertson were the best trombone men. Zue took lessons from Baptiste Delisle. He was a real good trombone player, and a lot of people don't know this, but he was a fine piano player too. Baptiste Delisle was one of the finest trombone players from here. Bolden used Delisle after they kicked him out of his own band. See, Bolden was tops in New Orleans and he had the pick of the musicians. Frankie Duson kicked Bolden out and took over the band, calling it the Eagle Band. They used Frank Keeling on trumpet for a couple of weeks out at the Lincoln Park, then

Duson got Bunk Johnson to play with them. Duson had Lorenzo Tio, Brock Mumford and Jean Vigne in the band. I remember all that too.

In the old bands like Duson's, they never had any bass solos. Just two beats to the measure all the time. In fact, most of them old bass players played three-string basses. They tuned the strings to A, B and G. Duson's band was real good at that time, with Bunk. See, Bunk in his older days was no comparison with when he was young. I know because I heard him so much with Duson and I made his last record date in New York. In his younger days he was on the order of Bobby Hackett with that tone and swing. I mean, next to Bunk in his young days, Bobby is now. In fact Bobby told me that a lot of the old timers say he sounds like Bunk.

They had a family living over in Algiers, the Lindseys. They all was musicians. The father, John Snr, played guitar, and the sons, well, Herbert Lindsey played violin and the little one, Johnny, played bass. He was so small they had to stand him on a box so he could even hold the bass. Jimmy Palao, he come up with them and he said they sounded real good. Johnny later went on to play trombone.

I played around New Orleans until 1917 when I went to Chicago with the Original Creole Band. It was called the Olympia Band here. Keppard, Baquet, Roy Palmer and Tubby Hall was in there with us. I played bass but my favorite instrument was the trombone. I used to play like Ory. In fact, the people used to call me "Little Ory" for a while. See, in the country, we all faked. I was a faker till I went to Chicago. I studied there under Professor Jackson. He had a place on 31st and State Street. Clarence Williams had a publishing place right on the next corner. Professor Jackson taught a lot of them boys. Milton Hinton, Eddie South and Darnell Howard were all pupils of his. See, I was working then so I could afford proper lessons. At the end of six months, well, I didn't have to fake no more.

I gave up trombone in 1919 when my lips went bad and concentrated solely on the bass. A bass is a very fine instrument when it is played right. Milton Hinton played it right and so did Jimmy Blanton.

Now I can play my part on bass reading or I can play it faking. That has been my success in the music business. I played the first note in every bar then I'd run my changes. A man got to know his instrument.

I have a great friend, Sidney Bechet. He doesn't read at all, but he can play everything from Grand Opera down. We call it "soul." One time Jim Europe asked Sidney to sit in with his orchestra and they played *Poet and Peasant Overture.* Sidney ran that clarinet cadenza on down and Jim Europe's twelve clarinet players couldn't do it that good. See, Sidney is a sensitive artist and he has a certain feeling. He's like me, if he hears something wrong in a section, it drags him.

Some places in music, I take a eighth note and make a thirty-second out of it. I think I'm the first person to start the walking bass. The old guys in New Orleans played two beats to the measure and a whole lot of bow. The young guys today hardly use a bow. They don't know what it's for. Steve Brown of the Goldkette Band was one of the finest bass players from here. He couldn't read anything but he sat in Paul Whiteman's Band and played on some of their greatest records.

There's nothing in Dixieland music that can compare with a guy from New Orleans. Like I say, it's what you call soul. Everything they have today, like Buddy Rich and Gene Krupa with their drum solos, they had all that here. There's nothing new about it. Why, they had a boy here, "Happy" Bolton that played at the Lyric Theater. He was doing all that drum solo stuff way back. The best clarinet player for me was always Barney Bigard. For banjo I would take Buddy Christian. As for trumpet, Freddie Keppard played the best second trumpet I ever heard. He was really the best. Buddy Petit could play good second too, but Freddie would play so low in there. He'd play F on trumpet that I'd play in the fourth-position on the trombone. He could also play very high and never miss a note. When I played with him in Chicago, he was just playing alone but I heard him play second trumpet in Carroll Dickerson's Orchestra behind Bobby Williams. That's George Mitchell's teacher. He was strictly a first but he was better than Mitchell. That was at the Sunset where I heard Freddie and Bobby Williams together. Freddie would play straight second mostly but sometimes obligatos behind him. Freddie took all the solos too, with that band. He was the best trumpet player I ever worked with.

The best rhythm section I ever played with was in the Creole Band. Lil Hardin, me and Tubby Hall. The second best was Duke Ellington's rhythm section. I don't care how good the soloist is, if that rhythm section ain't right, it's no good.

I joined Duke in 1926 and stayed till 1935. We made records for Okeh, Brunswick, Victor and all, plus many, many more. I'm kind of cranky about tone on a bass. A lot of fellows play it and it sounds like someone knocking. To make a good tone you must run the chromatics for hours. Practise whole notes. You must not overplay. The way I play is very pleasing to the ear. On some of Duke's old records I did overplay with all that slapping. On my first record date we played *Saturday Night Function* and I was overplaying because there was no drum, but on a record like *There'll Be Some Changes Made* that I made with Ory, you can see how smooth I play. Smooth, just like drinking a glass of water. I always played for tone, just like when I'm playing sousaphone on *The Mooche*. I was always curious about things in music. Always asking questions. Anyhow, one day I went over to the Rochester Theater and got talking to the sousaphone player. He was hitting four tones at once on the horn. He said that he had been first brass bass with John Phillip Sousa for twenty five years. I knew he had to know what he was doing and in fact, he made that horn sound like a string bass. You have to take the dumb side if you want to learn with a professional, so I asked him how he got that tone. He told me it came from the stroke of the tongue and so I went home and practised on that for a long while. That's how I got the effect on *The Mooche* with Duke's band. While I was in the band I wrote *Double Check Stomp*. I got the title from Amos 'n' Andy. I guess that was around 1931, when we made that movie with them. The movie was called, "Check and Double Check", but my first record date with Duke was when we made *Birmingham Breakdown* and *Black and Tan Fantasy*.

On the bass, the beat is the main thing, especially when it's with phrasing and tone. In a dixieland band I never patted my foot to keep time. Maybe in a concert group for the count but never in a dixieland band.

In later years when I was with Ory we had a good New Orleans rhythm section. I was in there about a year. We had Minor Hall and Lionel Reason. Lionel used to play the intermission sets with George Lewis' band at the El Morrocco Club. He is on Oliver's record of *Mule Face Blues*. So being from New Orleans, or at least around there, he knew just what to do. He had that New Orleans way down pat. If you listen to the record of *There'll Be Some Changes Made* with Ory's band, on that record I was using the beat Steve Brown used. He was one of my favorites. Of course I took it and improved it some. You can hear me going down to the 7th position on that record.

I think that bass solos are very good in a band, but I only like to play eight bars or so for a solo, otherwise it gets monotonous. Some guys are playing cello parts for a bass solo and it gets over-done. Lots of bass players pick with one finger only. I'm pretty powerful 'cause I use two fingers to pick with. I use the second and third finger to pick mostly. See, I have flexible wrists. My whole body is not jumping up and down like you see some bass players do. I play with ease. If a musician relaxes, he can give. When you put your fist around the strings, you muffle the tone. My left hand is free holding the bass. I don't need my thumb back of the board. It all comes from your schooling.

I don't much go beyond seventh position on a bass. I like to play a lot of bow.

For me, I get better results out of thin strings. Heavy bass players use heavy strings. They don't have any control. I use a bass made in Italy. It's a full size three-quarter bass. Like I said, I don't go much beyond seventh position. I like to play low. I use tape sometimes but it is better if you can go without it. I use alum water to soak my hands. It makes my fingers harden up. I never had callouses. When I bow I use the French system, not the German system. The French system causes you to play with the hand like a violin.

I played with all kinds of bands and recorded with all kinds too, but you know, the best small band records I made was with Sidney, Muggsy and Carmen Mastren. Those 12" platters were tops for that kind of thing.

My advice to the young kids coming up, say I was starting someone, I'd teach him to play using the bow and work on one string. I'd show him his chromatics, but most important, I'd teach him how to use his wrist. How to utilize it. Buy a method book because if you go by the method you won't overplay 'cause the man who wrote it, wrote it right. All in all, it's just like the tune Duke wrote, *It Don't Mean a Thing if It Ain't Got That Swing.*

654 ST NICHOLAS AVE
NEW YORK CITY
JULY 19-1957

dear mr russell, just to let you know
i recive the photos and i was very glad
to get them and all so very happy to hear

from you i told the boys in george lewis
band whot a very nice time we had i route
to new i bery to see the old man lawrence

mr russell i was over to the central plazer
to hear george lewis band he sound very good
and he pull a very big house and they like him

well he started the old time jazz around new york
with bunk johnson so he is a very good felow
and every one a round like george very mutch i

think he is tops and slow drag is a show a
lone just a live old man and he hav his little
dance and a few jokes that he tell and it is a

lots of fun well things is very slow in new york
i heard from alvin alcorn he is at the beveley
caven with edward garland band he said things is

very slow out thair well this is all ever well
i will see you this fall because i will not
be in new york for the winter i will stay in

kenner all winter and from thair to los angeles
well this is about all for new and remember me
to the boys my very best wishes to you by new

you ers very truley
wellman braud

p.s. tanks a lots for the photos and
leads of luck to you and may god bless
you dear sir you are just a very fine man

*Letter from Wellman Braud to Bill Russell*

*Note the rhythmic spacing.*

# ALCIDE "SLOW DRAG" PAVAGEAU

Alcide Louis Pavageau
string bass

Born: New Orleans, Louisiana, March 7, 1888
Died: New Orleans, Louisiana, January 19, 1969

*Although Alcide Pavageau began as a guitarist, he became better known as a dancer in the 1920s, and most musicians knew him only as "Slow Drag." He began to play bass in 1928, on an instrument he made himself, and worked with Buddy Petit and Herb Morand. He began working regularly with George Lewis from about 1943, and remained with the band into the 1960s. During the last few years of his life he acted as Grand Marshall for several brass bands.*

I was born on March 7th, 1888. I learned to play guitar in 1916, and played it up to 1927. From 1928 I played bass. That's over 30 years ago. No one showed me guitar or bass, I learned myself on it. Now I know what to make on the bass. I picked up a barrel on Orleans, between Robertson and Villere, by Maude's grocery, and I made me a bass, a little bitty bass. I'm more than glad that I'm kind of feeling good and that I'm willing to do the best I can with my playing. It's not the bass, it's the man behind the bass. You know I kept the little three string bass for years and then Nick Gagliano asked me for it and I gave it to him. 'Course I played a regular bass too when I was young. They was all three-string basses then. I played on my cousin's bass. His name was Auguste and he kept his bass upstairs, always had it tuned up.

I had many family people, but can't remember their names. I know Marie LeVeau is my father's first cousin. She died on St Ann, between Burgundy and Rampart. The house is still there, but nobody been livin' in it. She was buried right next to my father and my mother, and my sister. See, my father's name was Joseph Pavageau and my name is Alcide Louis Pavageau.

As for the name "Slow Drag", well, I won many contests dancing the Slow Drag. They had around ten different dances in New Orleans those times. Had Mazurka, Polka, Waltz, Schottische, Quadrille. In the contests, they had no prize for the man, only for the woman, and she would get an umbrella. The bands that played for the contests were, The Golden Rule Band, they had a trombone player named Bouboul [Valentin] and a trumpet player called Adolphe [Alexander] , who was a shoemaker. They is all dead now. Manuel Perez, he was the leader of The Imperial Band. First it was called "The Boys In Blue." Manuel, he would play all the dances that was called for, Cakewalks, Slow Drags, any dance you wanted. He had a band that could fill all that out.

Now my cousin Auguste, we called it "Augooste", he was playing at the "28." They used to have a "kick the ham" contest there. The "28" was on Franklin Avenue. Well, his guitar player got sick, so he turned around and he took me, put a pair of long pants on me and I played there with them three nights. I surprised all of them on guitar. See, I had up till then been playing in a sandpaper band. We had a boy called Armantan Picou and this boy Buddy, he was playing washboard and Joseph Davis played sandpaper. See, we mostly played for good-time people. I used to do all other work than music. I

used do paper hanging, plaster work, bricklaying and slating work. Then we had a little band with Albert Glenny playing bass. He's the oldest bass player I ever heard. Alphonse Picou played clarinet and his baby brother, Ulysses, was singing. Billy Marrero was the best bass player I ever heard, then comes Billy's son, Simon. Oke Gaspard was great too. He used to use the bow and all. Billy Marrero he used a four-string bass but they had a guy called Jimmy Brown, he used a three-string. He played with The Golden Rule Band. See, that band was older than Perez and "The Boys In Blue." But Jimmy Brown, he was the only one who slapped the bass strings. But, like I say, Billy Marrero was about the best bass player I ever heard. He would pick the bass and he used the bow a-plenty too. He had a touch on the bass, it went to you, 'cause he played with feeling, you understand. That's where I used to copy, watching him.

See, I mostly stay with trades in work, up to when I met up with George Lewis. He turned around and asked me. He say, "Man you're getting too old now." He say, "You want to play with us?" 'Course I said yes. He told me, "Well I can use you anytime you want." I started to work with him in a trio with Lawrence around 1942.

I was still playing my home-made bass then but the one I got later, with George, was from a bass player called Joe Morris. He had three basses, then his mother died and he went into the church. Lawrence told me about the bass he was selling and I went there and gave him $90 for it. He wouldn't give me the bow or the carrying strap with it. So we had some records to make at George's home on St. Philip and I used it on them.

Years ago when they had the three-string basses, they had the A string, that's where you tuned it from, then the D string and last the G string. Now the bass I got has four strings with the E. Now I use my finger to snap the strings. My left thumb behind the neck. I use sometimes one, sometimes two fingers to pull the strings. Then I take my right thumb away from the finger board when I get active like that. This is a three-quarter size bass.

When I get going I shake my left leg. That's my timekeeper. I leave my toe down and pat my heel on the floor. Also I can slap this bass here while I'm holding the bow. There's many "right" ways to hold the bow but the Dixieland way is to grab it any way you can. I always use tape, too. Around the first and second fingers, otherwise this finger would be split wide open. I use all gut strings and keep them about an inch from the fingerboard. In fact, I need a new fingerboard right now.

When I first met Bolden, he came to my house. He asked me if I was playing regular. I told him no. He asked me to be a member of his band. So I played with Bolden for four or five years.

Bolden was a strong trumpet player. You couldn't help from playing good with Bolden. He was crazy for wine and women and visa versa. Sometimes he would have to run away from the women. I used to take his horn away from him sometimes and bring him to my house. When he went mad, he would walk up and down the street talking to the wrong people – foolish – about this gal and that gal.

**Albert Glenny**


I was born in Jamestown, Louisiana. That's about eleven miles outside Donaldsonville. When I was eleven years old, my uncle, Philogene Joseph, had a little band. I played three-string bass, and one of my brothers, Nelson Joseph played guitar. [Wellman] Braud played mandoline, and my uncles, Eusand and Philogene Joseph both played the violin.

Then I played with Claiborne Williams in Donalsonville. If he had two jobs I would play in his second band. He usually had violin, clarinet, cornet, valve trombone, bass and guitar. They didn't have no drums, just used bass and guitar, and no piano. They always had a violin in the band in them days, that was the lead instrument, that was before they were using cornet for lead.

Buddy Bolden was the first one to play the blues. That's what made him so popular with the colored people. Jimmy Johnson, played bass with Bolden; he was a bow man. He wasn't much of a picker. All that came up later – that pickin', you know. Once in a while you had a passage for pick; you hold your bow in your hand and pick. And when this pickin' started, my cousin, Eddie LeBoeuf and Jesse Clem were the best. Of the old time bass players, Henry Balimore, from Donaldsonville, was about the best. A good reader. He was one of the best readin' bass players I heard at that time. He could sing and he could play. People ain't looking for that now; they're looking for that fancy stuff – "fly". Just like Duke [Ellington] told [Wellman] Braud, he told him, "Forget about the music; just use your own judgement. That's all it takes for bass, if you got this." [Touching his ear]. That's right. He used his ears; if you've got good ears that's all that's needed.

**John Joseph**

NEW ORLEANS STYLE:
PIANO

# MANUEL MANETTA

Manuel Manetta
multi-instrumentalist and teacher

Born: Algiers, Louisiana, October 3, 1889
Died: Algiers, Louisiana, October 10, 1969

*Manuel Manetta was an outstanding pianist in the "Red Light" District before World War 1. Albert Nicholas, one of his pupils, called him "one of the greatest musicians of all time." "Fess" or "Hoss", as he was called, started as a violinist but played almost all instruments professionally. He played with Buddy Bolden, Frankie Duson, Jack Carey, Celestin, the S.S. Capitol band (doubling on calliope), the Kid Ory-King Oliver band, and many others.*

*After 1922, most of his time was spent teaching in his Algiers studio. He was interviewed in depth (more than 100 times) to obtain his full life history in music.*

I was born in Algiers, Louisiana, third day of October 1889. I had two uncles, Jules Manetta and Duce Manetta. They were the "professionals" of the town. Jules was a cornet player and Duce played trombone. My first job around here was with 'Old Man' Tom Albert. That should have been around 1909. I played violin, that was my first instrument. The job was on the pleasure boat that ran from Esplanade down to Chalmette. It was a four-piece band. Tom Albert played trumpet, me on violin and a guitar and bass. After a while I had taken up piano. My sister was a pianist but she gave up on it so I took it up. My teacher was a lady named Laura Albert. She would go around visiting houses, teaching on Tuesdays and Fridays. At first I played the violin and she accompanied me on piano. I remember the first time we played in public. We played *Waves Of The Danube*, which was a waltz that Al Jolson later took and made it *The Anniversary Waltz*.

After a while I gotten so I could join Jack Carey's orchestra. It was called The Crescent Orchestra. Jack Carey was the manager and trombonist, Oscar Celestin was our cornetist, 'Old Man' Willie Humphrey played the clarinet and Bebé Matthews, that's Bill's brother, was the drummer; Jimmy Johnson played bass and Charlie Moore played guitar. We played for dances, picnics out to the Lake on Sundays and house dances during the week. One place we played regular every Sunday was Eastman Farm. They gave a lot of picnics there, it was back of Carrollton. Sunday nights, when they finished with the picnic, we would play at the Come Clean Hall for a dance, over in Gretna. See, Jack Carey, he was well liked on this side of the river and he drawed a crowd. They charged 50 cents to get into dances then. That was the lowest price. On Mondays the Wolfs' Club would give a dance. They had their own hall, they called it "Wolfs' Forest." They would advertize a dance by having us play on a wagon. They'd rent a wagon, a furniture wagon, and hitch about three mules to it. There would be the driver and they would have a fella up in front with the driver. He'd be hollerin' out to the people. Then we'd have three or four boys carrying "dodges", notices, like handbills. We sat down on little round-seat chairs. The wagon had three short sides and a tailgate. The drummer would sit right behind the driver facing towards the back of the wagon. Opposite him would be the bass then the brass. I'd be up there with my violin and one side of me

would be the clarinet and the guitar would be on my other side. So, these boys would follow us and when we'd stop at a business corner, like, maybe a saloon, they go pass out all those advertizements.

You see those "bucking contests", they really happened. We had it uptown. The people all liked Jack's band. But when you got to come downtown . . . most everybody was for the Olympia. We was all scared of Freddie Keppard.

Anyways, one Sunday on the corner of 8th and Howard, a gentleman called me out of the wagon, on our break. He lived on 8th Street. His name was Ike Jackson and he had played for Tom Anderson for years. He had played with my uncles and had visited the house when I was a small boy. So, he asked me how would I like a job in the District.

He worked at a place called MacIshes, on the corner of Marais and Iberville. It was a saloon and Mr. MacIshes was the proprietor of it. So Ike Jackson had the band in there. Used three pieces. He had a mandolin player with him and guitar and he played bass. He liked my violin playing and asked me would I accept a job playing every night. See, he knew my people so I told him it sound good to me. I went to work with them. We had to wear little white coats, like waiters' coats.

Well, one time the Shriners was in town. The popular piece for the Shriners was, *It's A Long Way To Tipperary*. People was buying that music like hot cakes. They had a day bartender in MacIshes and a night bartender. The night bartender's name was Johnny Rice. He and his lady friend had been out shopping that day and here they come with this music of *Tipperary*. "Say Ike, we was out and here's the popular song of the Shriners. Play this and we'll have the barroom filled with 'em." Well, the mandolin player we had, he was an ear musician that played his own way, what he heard and stuff. Ike says, "Say, listen. Our violin player will play it for you." So they opens up the player piano and took off the rolls and I played it. The Shriners started piling in there plus all the shipmens. I didn't have to touch the violin at all, just played that all night for the people. The rest of the band was kind of embarrassed all night. There was a drummer in the audience who turned out to be Lulu White's old man. So he says, "Listen. How would you like to play a job in a parlor? You wouldn't have to wear no white coat, you could stay dressed." When I knocked off I went home and told my family about the offer. They didn't like the idea at first but I guess they warmed to it, and finally I went to work at Lulu White's.

They had about three storeys to that place. I played upstairs. At first, when you came in, they had a real plush entry hall. Lulu herself, she'd sit like in a box right where you came in. It was to the left of the entry where you went in. It looked like a ticket office for a theater but bigger. She would sit there all the time. They had about 12 or 15 girls there at the time. You'd see different faces a lot. I played in the parlor on the second floor. They had an upright piano and I played for them when they would come up there. They had sofas and stuff and then the customers would want to dance with the girls. There was three or four waiters on hand and the girls all wore beautiful costumes and such. Long evening gowns. Then they would pair off and go up on the third floor for their pleasure.

Lulu herself looked very grand, when she was all dressed up. She was very large, you know. Had a real large face. She wasn't from New Orleans. In fact she told me that she was from White Castle, Louisiana. That's a little town up the road from Baton Rouge. When a customer came in, he'd have to stop in at the box and chat with her first. She liked all the big-timers, nothing but big-timers visited there. I started at nine o'clock and played till three. Sometimes I wouldn't get out of there till nine the next morning, though. I would make plenty in tips. The girls would tell the customers, "Be seated and give the Professor something for his next selection." Some of the customers had their regular lady friends in house while others had just to get acquainted right there. See, Lulu liked me because I could play all different songs. There was never anything but piano players in the house but most of them were entertainers and sang their own songs. I never was a singer but I made up for it by playing all their requests. Some of the girls were graduate songstresses, too. They would bring music for me to play while they sang. When I played alone, I would play a lot of Joplin's material, *Maple Leaf Rag* and *Grace and Beauty;* then I played a whole lot of popular rags like *Black and White Rag.* When I played blues like *Memphis Blues* or *St. Louis Blues* I would make a whole lot of tips. The customers liked that stuff better because they could dance. Another thing, see, the customers would all be white. No exceptions to that rule. They would come in there always in their evening clothes. I stayed at Lulu White's for over a year and eight months.

Soon after I left Lulu's, I went to work, well, in fact Mr. Tom Anderson, he sent for me. His lady friend, Gertrude Dix, ran a house called, "The Brass Rail." It was right next to Mr. Anderson's Annex saloon and I went to work there for Miss Dix. I played there for eight or nine months. Then Tom Anderson's son-in-law, Tom Dulcy, opened a cabaret on Rampart, between Canal and Iberville. Mr. Anderson, he says, "Now I'm gonna change. I want you to go over and play for my son-in-law." Anyway, so I hired the band myself, Peter Bocage on violin, me on piano and my drummer was Chris Minor. I hired three entertainers too. Willie Jackson, I knew him from my days with Jack Carey, because he lived in Gretna then and he always told me, "Times come that you get a job for me to sing I'd like to have it." So I kept him in view and hired him when we opened up. The other two entertainers were "Nooky" Johnson and Alfred Wynn. They sang and danced right on the bandstand. I stayed on that job for over two years till I got sick. Then I hired Paul Dominguez to play violin and Freddie Washington to play piano and Paul, he hires Louis Cottrell. They played there till the job ran out.

Meanwhile, I played with Arnold Metoyer at the Cadillac, on Conti and Rampart, once I got well again. Albert Nicholas played clarinet, Arnold Depass, was our drummer and we had a banjo player they called Joe Robertson.

During these times there were many great piano players around New Orleans, but the greatest piano players were Tony Jackson, Albert Wilson and Albert Cahill. The last mentioned was from Miss Lulu's hometown, White Castle, Louisiana. He played piano with John Robichaux's band as well as solo. I heard that band when I was young, still in short pants, but I put on my brother's long pants and went to a place where John Robichaux's Orchestra played regularly. His was the most famous band in the town and they played up in Carrollton at a place called Lincoln Park. He was mostly the only band that played up there. Dances would start at 4 o'clock in the afternoon and they had a fella Buddy Bartley, that would go up in a balloon. That was a large place, the Lincoln Park, and you know what, there was no trees, just the ground. This Mr. Buddy Bartley would go up in his hot air balloon and come down by parachute. This was around 4.30 in the afternoon. Man, that guy was like a monkey but it was a great advertizement. Anyways, getting back to Robichaux's band. He had a full band. Hisself, violin, Jim Williams, trumpet, Baptiste Delisle, trombone, George Baquet, clarinet, Bud Scott played guitar and sometimes sang, Henry Kimball, bass and Louis Cottrell, drums. They played music like Scott Joplin's. They didn't do nothin' but read. In fact the only one number they played by ear was, *Home Sweet Home* and that was at the end of the program.

I struck up a friendship with Ed Ory and later got to lead their band, Ory and Joe Oliver's band I mean. When I say lead it, I meant from the violin. The band consisted of Ory, myself, Oliver, Johnny Dodds, Lorenzo Staulz, banjo, Bob Lyons, bass and Happy Bolton was the drummer. I never knew his name at first, we all called him "Red Happy." He had just gotten out of the Jones' home, him and Louis Armstrong. We had a lot of work with that band. It was the preference band of the people. The people really liked that dixieland that we played. We played all over in picnics, house parties, halls such as Economy Hall, Cold Pup Rings Hall and The Wintergarden.

In fact we cut the band down, or rather, Joe cut it down after the records come out by the Original Dixieland Band. I heard those numbers like *Livery Stable Blues* and *Fidgety Feet* from the Dixieland Band. They are supposed to have originated those songs. I'd never heard those pieces before. So, I'll tell you, that's what made Joe mostly want to use a five-piece band. Joe borrowed his style from the Dixieland Band by cutting the bass player, Bob Lyons out, then Lorenzo Staulz he cut out, you know. But he always tried to keep me with him because I could work with him with this too. He put me on piano. I told him, "Now that's hard to do, that kind of thing." Joe said, "We've got to follow suit. Follow suit." Ory went for that too, him and Joe.

After a while Joe and Ory began to fall out with each other. See, Ory liked Joe Lindsey for his drum playing and Joe liked "Red Happy". You know how those things go.

Sometime around the early twenties I bought a saxophone. Bob Lyons used to have a bootblack stand at Rampart and Perdido and one day he told me that Big Eye Louis had come back to town with a saxophone and had pawned it. It was a C Melody. Anyways, Bob Lyons says, "Go see about that saxophone." So I went over to the pawn shop on Gravier and Rampart and they wanted $60 for it. I bought it and became the third musician in New Orleans to buy a saxophone. Louis Warneke was the first, then Sam Dutrey second, then I was the third.

Now I always worked around here because the fellows all liked the way I played. That's how Joe Oliver and all them fellows got their touches from the style I used to play my piano in. I always knew the music and could show them all how it went. It always pays to learn right. Learn right from the start. See, I started with Professor Nickerson, but he didn't teach me right, I changed to Miss Laura Albert. She taught me all the right things. You must know the right things in music and use them.

# "Sweet" Emma Barrett

Emma Barrett
piano

Born: New Orleans, Louisiana, March 25, 1898.
Died: New Orleans, Louisiana, January 28, 1983

*Although Emma Barrett never learned to read music, she was a regular member of the city's premier reading bands. In 1923, she joined Papa Celestin and went on to work with John Robichaux, Armand Piron and Sidney Desvigne. Following the death of Papa Celestin in 1954, "Sweet Emma the Bell Gal" became one of the best known bandleaders on Bourbon Street. In the 1960s she appeared regularly at Dixieland Hall and Preservation Hall, and survived a near-fatal stroke in 1967. Despite being paralysed on her left side and confined to a wheelchair, she continued to perform regularly until a few weeks before her death.*

When I was little, when my mother was living, we stayed at 516 Dorgenois, around Tulane and Broad. Did you ever hear of a trombone player named Ulysses Jackson? Well, he lived right across the street. He was a tall, heavy-set blackskin fella. If you heard of Honoré Dutrey, we used to call him "Noré." Well, his wife, a big, stout, cross-eyed woman, was Ulysses Jackson's sister, Olga. All these musicians used to come to Jackson's house to practise. He and Dutrey were friends, and all those people, Johnny Dodds, Baby Dodds and them, they would come over there. Dutrey was the ace on the trombone, for those times. I mean they had such as Frankie Duson, but he never was no hell of a trombone player.

When they first brought a piano in the house, it wasn't for me. It was for my sister. She never did learn it. Took lessons and everything, but it just wasn't in her. I used to play with one hand. Music was in me. I must have been around seven, and played in a band when I was around twelve. Anyway, my Daddy, he wasn't no musician, noticed I used to play along with my brother singing. He had a beautiful voice. My Daddy sent me to Professor Nickerson for lessons. He lived on Galvez and I used to go right to his home.

I guess I made good in music, being a girl, on account I was never timid, just went along with the program. I got to be called "Sweet Emma," because I always went along with the program, never got contrary. Whatever the band went through, I went through. When I played with Ernest Trepagnier and them, we missed the train back to New Orleans, They all got up there and slept on the tables in the depot. Well, I got up there and slept right along with 'em.

I been around Percy and Willie Humphrey since they were in short pants. Their grandaddy played nice trumpet. Yes, Jim Humphrey played nice, sweet trumpet. Straight, but each note come out perfect. Not all this fancy stuff. He didn't use mutes like Percy, no slurring of notes. Percy is about the best around here now. Not that the others aren't playing good, but Percy, that dixieland is all he plays. That's the way he was taught, and that's the way he come up. Now I played with Charlie Love too. He was a nice trumpet player but he was a scary man. Scared to blow that horn. Another nice

trumpet player was old man Joe Howard, but like Charlie Love, he always doubted himself. He played tuba later. Now, Louis Dumaine, he never played fancy. Never from the head. He just had his music. I played with him and "Fats" Houston's band. I played with Lee Collins too, many times. He was pigeon-toed. Always walked that way. They tell me that Louis was very good to him when he got sick. Paid all his doctor's bills and everything. A nice trumpet player. Worked right down here with him. Spot jobs and all.

Now, Kid Rena's wife used to be my neighbor, up in Carrollton. She played good piano too. He was a good powerful trumpet player, but he got that liquor and his eyes all popped up. He played all those high notes. Hot man. Loud and powerful. A great "get-off" man. Turn him loose and he would go. Get right off that lead and go. See, I always did love to play. It wasn't just the money. Music is something you got to put your whole heart and soul in. If you go there with no pep, or feeling, that don't go. That don't take over. Lots of people think you can't play, 'less you got liquor in you. That's not so.

Peter Bocage, I played with him years ago, in the Lyric Theatre. He had his own band. Used to stand in front of them with that violin. He played wonderful violin. See, all that was back when Lorenzo Tio was living. Tio met Peter's sister and married her the next day. He could play, really play that clarinet. Looked like a Mexican. Tall, but he let that liquor get the best of him. Played all out of the side of his mouth. He was tops around here on the clarinet. Barney Bigard was another great clarinet player. Nice looking, bright fella. 'Course he was a younger man, but Tio was tops.

Any qualified musician here, I played with 'em. By being so young, I played with, oh, so many of them. I never did dissipate after a job. Never did go in for "bumming". I always came home after a job, to get my rest. That is what's kept me going till now. Take good care of yourself. I seen so many musicians, they hung out drinking and such, then they went out like a candle. You got to take good care. Now, with this one hand gone, it's hard, but I do it. You don't know what this doctor thinks of me. Playing in this wheelchair and all.

Now Ricard, Ricard Alexis, that's my son Barqi's daddy. He played the real dixieland. Not like they're playing today. He got beat up and had to have his jaw all wired up. He couldn't play no more trumpet. I met Ricard out at the Lake, at a picnic. I was playing out there with Anthony St. Ledger, the trumpet player, and Ricard was out there. Later years, he had a monkey. This monkey, he'd go in the people's back yards and take all the clothes off the line and drop 'em. Go in the kitchen and pour coffee grinds all over the people's food. He had to get rid of that monkey. Paid $50 for him, too. He was just too devilish. Anyway, he couldn't play his trumpet no more so he switched to bass violin. Sylvester Handy has his bass now. I'm not superstitious, but I don't want no dead people's instrument. Like Willie Humphrey, he's got Louis Warneke's clarinet.

As far as piano players go, Fate Marable was a wonderful piano player. He used to work on the steamer "Sidney". You know what he used to do? It was really kicks. He always had his own piano. He wouldn't let me play on that piano, and when he'd get off, why, he'd lock it up. See, I worked with him when they had two bands on the boat. Fate played so good. Played the calliope and the bells and all that. I used to hear that calliope from where my mother used to live. That's where Baby Dodds and them used to come to practise. See, drummers like Ernest Trepagnier and Baby Dodds, they had a different beat than today. But they kept perfect time. Cié Frazier is one of the best dixieland drum players they have here today. Got a good beat and keeps perfect time. In those days, Cié, Ernest and Baby Dodds were tops. Ernest sang nice and we teamed together with vocal duets. I'd always sing lead. We had numbers we'd worked up, you know, like *Telephone Me*, and another pretty waltz we used to sing. *Let The Rest Of The World Go By*. I first heard Baby play, on a job, at Jack Shehan's Suburban Gardens. Later I played with him out there. Salary wasn't good, but the tips were good.

Lots of bands didn't stick together, they just played around. But see, Celestin, and also Piron, had regular bands. Unless musicians had a regular job to go to they all moved around. When I started with Celestin, Manuel Manetta had been with them. When I went into the band, Bebé Ridgeley was the manager and Celestin was the leader. Ridgeley wasn't no top trombone player. They used to call him, "Gloomy Gus." The band was The Original Tuxedo Band. The band was named after the Tuxedo Dance Hall, not because they wore tuxedos. They didn't wear tuxedos on every job, just like later at places like, out at Tranchina's. Most respectable jobs. They wore them in order to go to those places. I started out with them at Jack Shehan's place. Jack was a guy that never smiled. You never saw him laugh, but he was kicks, though. Celestin had heard so much talk about me, by me being so young and having a head for music. He was very nice. Of course, he got his knocks, but he was always the perfect gentleman, and I loved his trumpet playing. When he played, *Maryland, My Maryland* he would go off, way off, to play the bugle part.

He used to carry a big grip of music around on the job. I didn't play from any music with them. Neither did Willie Bontemps, the banjo player. With Celestin, all of 'em wasn't tops, now. They had some of them in there that could play real good. The band overall sounded good, and Celestin was great with the public. They were crazy about him. He played in a lot of brass bands too. Now a lot of people play good in a brass band, but in an orchestra they just don't fit in. Take, like, Albert Warner, he's no red hot trombone player but he's fine in a brass band. Celestin was good, either way.

When Shots came in the band, he wasn't even getting a salary. He just came in and played second trumpet under Celestin. He wasn't no great musician but he got all that sweet second stuff out of his head. Cié played with Celestin way back too. They didn't have all those drum solos in the bands then. Just had general assembly. They didn't fool with all that bass solos and stuff. None of that commotion. Just lately they came with that. Anyway, Celestin used to carry this big grip of music around and one night, he just set that grip down and quit. Ridgeley and Celestin separated and I stayed with Ridgeley. That girl, Kimball's first wife, another fine piano player, took over with Celestin. Ridgeley had a sign hung over the drum. It said, "William Ridgeley's Tuxedo Band." Later Ridgeley got on the drums. He wasn't too much though. See drums, bass, piano and banjo, works together. That's time, see. I didn't do all that with my right hand then, mostly, it was four-beat rhythm.

Piano is the foundation of a band. I've played jobs with just two pieces. When you're playing, you got to think of things. Like when you come back from a break, you've got to open with something peppy, and you can't play "Racehorse" stuff that the people can't dance by.

I always had a heavy bass. Heavy complement. I've always been strong from a youngster coming up. Stronger than some men. Any music, it's got to be in you and you've got to take interest in it. If you love music, you'll learn that horn. Learn it right. You'll do better if you pay attention. Now take Willie Humphrey, he really masters that horn. Plays in any key. George Lewis don't play in any key. I'll tell you his keys, and I

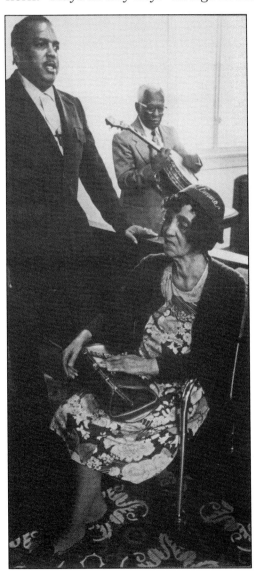

*"Sweet" Emma with her son attending Billie Pierce's funeral. Narvin Kimball is in the background. (Photo: Josephine Sacato)*

don't work with him much. His keys is F and B-flat. If you had a piano that was too low, I used to "cross-chord." That put you in a lot of sharps and naturals, but the band is in tune. This piano player later played with Celestin, Mercedes Garner, she would just sit there. Couldn't cross-chord. I was a wizard at that, made all the horns be in tune.

I didn't care for a lot of loud beating. You just don't play loud behind, like a singer. I'm not no great strong person hittin' the piano, but I got strong arms and hands. Little hands, but strong hands. I never tried to copy anyone either. When you're playing to back someone else in the band, well you just comp, but when you go for yourself, like getting ready to take a hot solo, well, that's different. You use your right hand a lot, make something like the lead in your right. When you're just comping, not no lead, never no lead, see. That electric stuff is lazy, you hardly have to touch the instrument. Like the strings on a bass. See this boy here, Chester, he loves to play his bass and loves his instrument. I think a bass violin swings a band more than a tuba. There's more pep when you're pulling them strings. Years ago they all played with the bow. It's harder with this picking they do now, but it makes a band swing. When a man takes a hot solo, you've got to be under him. I mean the whole band.

The main thing about a banjo, it's the chords. See, a bass, banjo and piano, they got to stick together, stick to those chords. We work directly together and if the drums is going ahead of us, it's pulling on the other instruments. A lot of people don't pay attention to that. It's got to be right. A good guitar, if you hit it right, is good in a band. Four beats rhythm. One, two, three, four.

Another thing is the tuning. You got to tune up, in order to harmonize. Say, if the clarinet is too low, it works the others to death. A piano should be at four-forty. That's international. Tune to that and it will come out good.

I never did practise much. If you want to hear me play something, pay me. I never did play much piano at my house. Not with my piano.

---

We always had some kinds of musical instruments in the house, including guitar, drums, piano, trombone, and so forth and so on. We had lots of them and everybody always played for their pleasure, whatever one desired to play. We always had ample time that was given to us in periods to rehearse our lessons, anyone that was desirous of accepting lessons. At the age of six, I gave up the jaw's harp and took my first lessons on the guitar with a Spanish gentleman in the neighborhood.

**Jelly Roll Morton**

Clarence [Williams] really wasn't much of pianist though, he'll tell you that himself. When he was back home in New Orleans he played piano in one of those honky-tonks and could only play by ear – maybe knowing a half-dozen songs. Then some inebriate might come in and ask for a song he didn't know, and Clarence would say, "Come back tomorrow night." The next day he'd go down to the five-and-ten-cent store, to the sheet music counter, and pull out the song for the piano player to demonstrate. He would hear it once and know it. If that customer came back, Clarence would play the song and maybe pick up a dime tip. It was like some of our hillbilly artists say about songs, "I can write them down, but I can't note them."

**Frank Walker**

New Orleans was the stomping grounds for all the greatest pianists in the country. We had Spanish, we had colored, we had white, we had Frenchmens, we had Americans, we had them from all parts of the world, because there were more jobs for pianists than any other ten places in the world. The sporting houses needed professors, and we had so many different styles that whenever you came to New Orleans, it wouldn't make any difference that you came from Paris or any part of England, Europe, or anyplace – whatever your tunes were over there, we played them in New Orleans.

**Jelly Roll Morton**

New Orleans Style:
## Trumpet

# WILLIE "BUNK" JOHNSON

Willie Geary Johnson
trumpet

Born: New Orleans, Louisiana, December 27, 1879
Died: New Iberia, Louisiana, July 7, 1949

*For many years, since his death in 1949, it has become very fashionable for jazz critics to berate Bunk Johnson and say he was a "real phony" and a "notorious liar." Almost without exception, those "critics" never met Bunk or heard him play.*

*The highly esteemed pianist Don Ewell, who played with many of the greatest musicians from New Orleans and other centers, once remarked that the only genius he ever worked with was Bunk Johnson. Several years of association with Bunk, hearing his music and fascinating conversations, and checking the facts, convinced me that his memory was the most remarkable I have ever encountered in my life.*

*Bunk was never interested in becoming a "jazz expert" or writer, but there is enough evidence, which was also confirmed by musicians I spoke to, that Bunk was telling the truth about his early life in New Orleans.*

I was born in uptown New Orleans, December 27th 1879. I was one of 14 children, seven boys and seven girls. I am the only one living. Every day at 11.45 we had 15 minutes at the chapel with Professor Wallace Cutchey. He was a Mexican who played the chapel organ and gave us our music lessons. I learned the rudiments of music first and then singing. I sang four years before I touched an instrument.

We had two days a week devoted to studying an instrument. Mr. Cutchey taught me how to play cornet. I played in the school band which played all street marches, overtures and waltzes. The school band used to play at all the ball games. Now if I was to teach anyone to play an instrument, I would have to learn him the rudiments of music first and how to sing. Then I would teach him the delivery of wind through an instrument, how to produce tone; then to execute on that instrument and start on the first scale in C and go on from there. That's the way I learned.

I finished school in 1894 and I joined Adam Olivier's band at $2.50 a night. It was a good band that read music. The band had Adam as first violinist, Tommy Olivier, his son, second violinist, Kattos, drums and his brother, Fabbion Kattos, guitar, Charles Bazile, bass, John Pembleton, trombone, George Caldwell, clarinet, Ned Knute and myself, cornets. Tony Jackson was not in yet. Olivier had the best reading band. John Robichaux had a good band. The Golden Rule Band was a good band but Bolden was best because they played by ear, by head, and made up their own pieces. King Bolden's style was what I liked at this time and I wanted to play with his band. Bolden knew my parents well. We were then living on Tchoupitoulas between Aline and Fourcher streets, facing the old docks where grain was loaded and unloaded. Bolden had his headquarters at Mustache's saloon at Perdido and Franklin. I joined Bolden's band in 1895, which had Cornelius Tillman, drummer, Willie Cornish, trombone, Frank Lewis, clarinet, Brock Mumford, guitar, Jimmy Johnson, bass, Alcide Frank, violin and Bolden and myself, cornets. I was the youngest of them all. We played such tunes as *St Louis Tickle, Didn't*

*He Ramble, Sammy Samson, Lazy Moon* and *Brewery Buck* in addition to quadrilles and all kinds of blues.

Bolden could play his horn in any key, but he didn't know the compass of that horn. Any key was his key. He would play in four, five, six sharps, E and B and F sharp, all hard keys. He could execute anything. When he played in some hard key, Mumford and some of the men would ask, "King, what key are you playin' in, Buddy?" Bolden would reply, "He who fall down, stay down." But I played with him, 'cause I read. I was "suckin' blood" all the way, 'cause I could go like 500. Bolden played the first part of *Tiger Rag* to get the partners ready. There was no Original Dixieland Jass Band. Later these "smart fellows" took T*iger Rag* – the first eight bars – and turned it into the number what we dancin' today, what we call *Tiger Rag*. What made Bolden's band the first that played jazz was that he had a band that couldn't read. King Bolden had everybody in the city of New Orleans real crazy and standing on their heads. In later years Robichaux set up the union to freeze out Bolden, as he couldn't read. Buddy found out that the union, which was a "one man" union was killing him, so Bolden broke up the union.

*Alphonse Picou – c1905*

I joined the Superior Orchestra about 1902. Here are the names of the men in the Superior band: James Phillips, drummer, Buddy Johnson, trombone, Peaco Forrester [Alphonse Picou] clarinet, Jimmy Scriggs [Jimmy Palao], violin, Richard Payne, guitar, Billy Marrero, bass and manager. Later Scriggs left the band and they got Peter Bocage, violinist, for leader. The old Imperial Band never did like the Superior Band much, because wherever they played, we would close them down on the street. We would run them. That's the way the Superior Band treated the Imperial Band. That's what caused the hatred. They were good sight readers, but I had them some. I could play a sweeter cornet than they could play, and finger out of the good book. That good old diminished fingering. Now, to make the grade playing cornet or trumpet, you must use that diminished fingering.

I played with the Superior Band a great number of years and it broke up in the neighborhood of 1911, I think. I know for sure the band did not stay together not more than a year after the Jack Johnson fight. The fight was July 4th 1910.

The second week after the Superior Band broke up, Frank Duson came to my home, where I was living on Burgundy Street near Spain Street, to get me to join the Eagle Band. I accepted. Here are the members of the Eagle Band when I joined it: Henry Zeno, drummer, Frank Duson, trombone player and manager, Lorenzo Tio, clarinet, Bab Frank, piccolo and leader, Brock Mumford, guitar player, Dandy Lewis, bass player. Now in the year of 1911, Bab Frank left the band, and also Tio, so there was no leader and clarinet player. Finally, Duson went to see Armand Piron and was lucky to get him and we had a leader but no clarinet player. Sidney Bechet started to play clarinet in the Eagle Band regular, and in a short while Sidney became real good. Then Frank had a good band for a long time.

My friend Clarence Williams came to me and told me of a job he had in Alexandria for a four-piece band. That we could make good money playing in a dance hall across the river in Pineville. Well, I went with Clarence, also my friend, Alvin "Zue" Robertson, so that made Clarence in need of a drummer to complete the four-piece band. He tried to get a drummer and couldn't get any, so we got together and went to Alexandria, to our own little job. Clarence got a drummer in Alexandria. We broke into Harry Walker's band and took his crack drummer, "Baby" Lovett, then we had the best band in Alexandria. We were all good readers and we were handling Scott Joplin's red back book and all of Clarence's arrangements. Joplin's book contained *Maple Leaf Rag, African Pas, Sunflower Slow Drag, Cascade Rag, Easy Winners* and other high class standard rags. After a few months that little band broke up and I came back to New Orleans and went back to the Eagle Band. I played with them a short while again, then in the beginning of 1914 I started teaching a little in Mandeville, Louisiana. In about a year and a half I left and went to Bogalousa. About a year later I went to Lake Charles and played with the Royal Band.

My friend Walter Brundy got me to join "Toots" Johnson's Band and I played with them about a year. I have been up and down the road ever since. I was a member of the Banner Band here in New Iberia for some years.

I had an outstanding style of playing from every man in town. Played my own style, just my thoughts, used my ideas about it. Of course I would listen to other cornet players play; I'd take their ideas and put it with mine. Made me have greater ideas. And I found out I was about topping all of them. Everybody liked my style of playing.

# Louis Armstrong

Louis Armstrong
trumpet

Born: New Orleans, Louisiana, August 4, 1901
Died: Corona, New York, July 6, 1971

*There seems little need to introduce Louis Armstrong, as he was the most famous of all New Orleans musicians. At the time of his death, the media claimed that Armstrong was better known throughout the entire world than any other American.*

There was so much music when I was growing up in New Orleans, that you couldn't help but hear it. I lived with my mother in Jane Alley, in the heart of what they called "The Battlefield," between Gravier and Perdido. There was all sorts of honky-tonks on every corner of Liberty, Perdido, Franklin and Poydras. Mostly, they just had a piano player working there, but sometimes they had other instruments as well. There was Spano's, Red Onion, Kid Brown's, Henry Ponce's and Matranga's. Just around the corner on Perdido Street was the Funky Butt Hall. On Saturday night the band would play for about half an hour outside to advertize themselves, so the people would know about it. Then they would go in for the dance. It was a beat up old place with big cracks in the wall and we would go down and look through the cracks and see all them chicks dancin' and shakin' everything.

Buddy Bolden had the biggest reputation, but he just played loud. Don't think he really knew how to blow his horn right. Bunk Johnson was very different. He had a beautiful tone, the best imagination and the softest sense of phrasing. But my favorite was Joe Oliver. I thought his tone was every bit as good as Bunk's and he had wonderful ideas and such a range. Joe was so good to me, even when I was just a kid. When he was marching with the Onward Brass Band, they'd stop for a rest, he would let me hold his horn. He knew this meant a lot to me, so he shows me how to put my mouth to it and get a note. Joe was always real nice.

In the evenings, people would give parties on the lawns in front of their houses. They'd have beer, lemonade, sandwiches, fried chicken and gumbo. The band would sit out in front on the porch and all the people would dance and have a good time. Mrs. Cole was famous all over New Orleans for her lawn parties. She ran them two or three times a week, and it was almost impossible to get in if Kid Ory's band was playing.

Music was everywhere. The pie man and the waffle man used to have their little hustle. The pie man had a bugle and the waffle man had a big triangle to attract people. The junk man – called him Lonzo – had a long tin horn, and man, he could play some blues on that horn. I used to love to go with him into those rich neighborhoods to buy old clothes. He'd get out this horn and blow, and I'd be hollerin', "Old rags and bones, old rags and bones."

The best brass band I ever heard was the Onward Brass Band with Joe Oliver and Emanuel Perez on cornets. Big tall Eddie Jackson booted the bass tuba. A bad tuba in a brass band can make work hard for the musicians, but Eddie knew just how to play that tuba. On funerals, Black Benny would beat the bass drum with such a soft touch,

and Bebé Matthews would put a handkerchief under his snare to deaden the tone. They would play *Nearer My God To Thee*. It didn't matter who was being buried, when they heard that music played so beautifully, everyone couldn't help but cry. On the way back, they would strike up with something like *Didn't He Ramble*, and all the people would leave their worries behind. Particularly when Joe Oliver blew high register in the last choruses.

It was a big thrill for me when I got old enough to play in those brass bands, and with old-timers like Joe Oliver, Oscar Celestin, Roy Palmer, Kid Ory, Oke Gaspard, Sam Dutrey and his brother, Honoré, and Jack Carey and his brother, Papa Mutt.

I learnt cornet while I was attending the Waif's Home, and after I got out I got a job playing at Henry Matranga's honky-tonk on Franklin and Perdido. At first I used to rent a horn. Then I found a little nickel-plate cornet for $10 in Uncle Jake's pawn shop. It was all beat up, full of holes in the bell. But I cleaned it up and, at least, I was able to make a living with it. Later when Papa Joe would get off after his job at Pete Lala's, he would come around. One night he brought me an old York cornet he had, and then I started going up to his house and taking lessons from him. I owe Joe everything, if it hadn't have been for Joe, you wouldn't have heard of me! I'll never forget what happened to him in the end. The doctors said he died of a heart attack, but I think it was a broken heart.

Then Joe Lindsey and I formed a little orchestra. We had six pieces: cornet, clarinet, trombone, drums, bass violin and guitar. Joe was a good drummer and we had a good little orchestra. In the end his woman made him quit playing, and after that the band broke up. That was a real shame, 'cause if you're real serious about music, that has always got to come first.

When I was a kid in New Orleans, I used to do a whole lot of figurations. Man, I was crazy on that. Joe Oliver would tell me, "Play the lead, boy, play the lead so people can know what your doing."

These cats today couldn't play a straight lead to save their lives. When I was coming up all you had to do was to play what you see on them cards and you was a hell of a musician; you were swinging. Nowadays cats try to make the music as hard as possible so you think they're really playing. They ain't. How many musicians today could play a rag, a funeral march or a blues like they did when I was a kid? Had to be beautiful, 'cause they were thinking as they watch those notes and phrasing that music. Like when I play, maybe *Back o' Town Blues*, I'm thinking about one of the old, low-down moments – when maybe your woman didn't treat you right. That's a hell of a moment when your woman tells you, "I got another mule in my stall." You got to draw on your experiences.

It's too bad that a lot of them old cats in New Orleans didn't take care of themselves. Whisky, wine and beer was cheap, and many of them couldn't handle it. You get a picnic job out at the Lake – Spanish Fort or the West End – and they would have a pint of whisky before they unpacked their instrument. Whisky in them days was 100 proof and raw. That's no good, you can't play like that. Your mind's better without all that, and it affects the stomach and the lips. Then you got nothing.

You got to stay healthy. When I was a kid, Mama used to give me all sorts of medicines, boiled cockroaches and herbs and all sorts of things. I later found out that some of those medicines didn't always do too much. But it got me in the way of thinking how to keep away colds and illness. Nowadays, I take my Swiss Kriss to keep me cleaned out, and lip salve to keep my lip in shape. You got to eat right and live right, and always try to please the people. Like an old timer told me when I left New Orleans, "Stay before the people. Please the public." Well, I'm with him.

---

That was the Crescent City in them days, full of bars, honky-tonks, and barrel-houses. A barrel-house was just a piano in a hall. There was a piano player working. When I was a kid, I'd go into a barrel-house and play 'long with them piano players 'til early in the mornin'. We used to play nuthin' but the blues.

**Bunk Johnson**

As many bands as you heard, that's how many bands you heard playing right. I thought I was in heaven playing second trumpet in the Tuxedo Brass band – and they had some funeral marches that would touch your heart, they were so beautiful. **Louis Armstrong**

*Punch on Louis, 1919:* No, that's the style of New Orleans. Everybody play that style, everybody. Maybe somebody who's a plunger, say a man didn't play in that order 'cause he learned a way of doing it . . . Chris Kelly and Kid Rena – they was high note men. They could hit higher notes than could even old Louis. Oh yeah, way above Louis. Chris Kelly's a high note man. **Punch Miller**

Lee Blair said several times that all the Louis Decca's were out of tune. Louis always tuned up sharp. They'd ask Louis, "Aren't you a little sharp?" and he would say, "No, that's the way I want it." **Francis Squibb**

Louis Armstrong told me, "Don't try to imitate me or nobody else. Do your best to develop a style of your own. Play to satisfy yourself and the people you playing for." He said, "Don't worry about what anybody else thinks. Only the people you workin' for, and the people you playing to, and you happy with it." **Percy Humphrey**

Who was the greatest trumpet player in jazz? Louis Armstrong – there's no question there! Louis played from his heart and soul, and he did that for every thing. You see, he tried to make a picture out of every number he was playing to show you just what it meant. He had ideas, enough technique to bring out what he wanted to say, and he had a terrific lip. **Mutt Carey**

Everytime Louis puts that horn to his lips you're hearing jazz, real New Orleans jazz. **Preston Jackson**

# Natty Dominique

Anati Dominique
trumpet

Born: New Orleans, Louisiana, August 2, 1894
Died: Chicago, Illnois, August 30, 1982

*Natty was a cornet pupil of Manuel Perez in New Orleans. He went to Chicago as early as 1913 and in the 1920s played with many New Orleans musicians, including Jimmie Noone, Johnny and Baby Dodds, Louis Armstrong, Honoré Dutrey, Zue Robertson and Jelly Roll Morton. From 1928, until Johnny Dodds' death in 1940, Natty was a regular member of Dodds' band. He left music in the early 1940s and became a Redcap at Chicago airport. After appearing at a jazz concert in Chicago in 1949, he returned to part-time playing and led his own band during the 1950s.*

I was born in the year 1894 at 1721 Urquhart Street, New Orleans, Louisiana. When I was a child, the first time I heard music, was my father and mother singing in harmony. My mother and father both had beautiful voices. My brother, Ferdinand, had a beautiful voice. He's won many contests but as he grew older his voice left him. I got interested in music, first, by my sister taking piano lessons; second, my brother Mervyn, taking violin lessons under Piron – Armand J. Piron. I used to go to the French Opera House, and I was crazy about a lady harp player there, playing beautiful harp. It's a wonder I'm not a harp player instead of a trumpet player! Opera music was in our blood. My father didn't like jazz. He never did. Even 'Old Man' Tio – old Papa Tio – when he heard jazz, he put his hands up to his ears and say, "It's a disgrace to music in anybody's house." In those days, bands used to advertize dances during the week, and they'd tie wagons together, just buck each other. Their music would sound good to me. I'm a youngster. One day, I took a liking to Louis Cottrell on the wagon, playing with Manuel Perez. I liked his drumming, real smooth, beautiful press rolls, like he was tearing a piece of paper. I told Mr. Perez, "I like that drummer." So I took a few lessons under Mr. Cottrell. Many years later, in Chicago, Baby Dodds was sick and couldn't play. I said to Johnny Dodds, "I can play the drums," and I played the rest of the night. Johnny said, "Where did you learn that?" I said, "I took a few lessons."

The first job I played was with Manuel Perez's Orchestra, when Cottrell couldn't make it. My feet were too short for the pedals so they had to sit me on a low box. I was pretty good. One night I had a jam with Buddy Petit, way up around Louisiana Avenue. I had to walk, as I could hardly ride on the street car with drums. So when I got to a pawn shop I put the drums in pawn. When I got home, my father whipped me. He gave me a terrific whipping. I'll never forget that as long as I live.

At school I'd play all kinds of games. One day I was in a marble game, and Manuel Perez came by, it was about 4.30 or 5 o'clock. He looked at me and said, "Come here, Sonny, pick up all those marbles. I'm going to make a cornet player out of you." I told him I didn't want to lean how to play cornet. He said, "Yes, you've got to learn. Now, if I go tell your father . . ." I said, "Please don't." So I went into the house with Mr. Perez and sat there, just as stubborn as a mule. I didn't want to take any lessons, I

didn't want to learn cornet, I didn't care for it. I sat there, and my first lesson went till 12 o'clock at night. I had a book called the Solfage book, and he made me sing the scale. I didn't do it right. Every time I did it wrong he made me do it right, and that's the reason why I stayed there till 12 o'clock. When I went home he went with me, and said "Mr. Dominique, I want to teach that boy cornet." Now the lessons would cost $12 a week, but he didn't want to take any money. He said, "Seeing as how your boy's head is hard I've had him in my house since four o'clock in the afternoon till 12 o'clock at night." My father said, "All right son, get ready for bed." Then my father gave me a thrashing I'll remember all my life. Then every day when I came home from school my father would be there, and he'd say, "Son, study your lesson." So I didn't have to make a decision. Eventually, I got learning and got interested. I even got to like singing – that whole Solfage. I studied for about seven months, and then Mr. Perez said, "I'm gonna tell your father to get you a cornet." The old man went around to the pawn shop and got me a cornet, all patched up with lead. "Pop," I said, "that's not like Mr. Perez's cornet. It's not pretty." I think he paid $8 for that horn. I said, "Well, I don't know how I'm gonna blow it." He said, "Son, you're gonna blow it all right." When I went on over to Manuel and he looked at the horn he said, "Good enough for you to learn on." But I was so disgusted –

*Manuel Perez*

I wanted a cornet like Manuel's cornet. I said "I can't blow it." He said, "I'll show you how to blow it." The first thing he taught me was how to handle my tongue. You tongue the instrument and let a long breath behind it, which is right. So I practised for about three hours, and he had me going on a note they call G. Eventually he said, "That's enough, and you come back in a couple of days. You practise A, B and C." Well, I practised and practised and I got up to C. Then I went for my lesson and I went up to C. Mr. Perez then taught me to sustain the notes, whole notes, and give them all the full value. He said, "That'll help you someday." So I sustained the notes – I went on and every day I sustained different notes. He'd say, "Come on, I want you to sustain G, I want you to sustain A, B, now that's an awkward note to sustain, and also sustain D." Mr. Perez made me sustain every note. He said, "The reason I'm doing this, getting you to sustain the notes, is so that you get tone. If you don't have tone you have ta - ta - ta, but when you have taaaah . . . that's your tone. When you have tone it makes it more brilliant, more clear." When I had got to sustain all the natural notes he had me sustaining sharps. That was after I got beyond that first stage in my Solfage book – he had me sustaining sharps. Then he had me sustaining flats. That's very awkward. Any musician will tell you, a flat is hard to sustain.

As I proceeded learning music and sustaining notes like Mr. Perez told me, I developed a marvellous tone, and I would advise any pupil that's taking lessons – please learn sustaining notes, because nowadays they will not hire you, regardless if you're a good musician, if you haven't got tone. They don't want you in no brass band, still less in an orchestra.

One day I went along and I didn't know my lesson. I went from the left hand corner – <u>almost</u> to the bottom. That's one thing I liked about Mr. Perez, he was a teacher. I missed one measure. He closed the book. He said, "Son, come back again." I said, "Why, Mr. Perez? I'm able to play the lesson, I just missed that one measure." He said, "You're not supposed to miss anything. You study your lesson at home. When you come here, you should know your lesson thoroughly, without a mistake. I will not stand for it." And I admired Mr. Perez. As a teacher he was a marvellous man. He wanted you to do right, because he said, "If I let you get away with that, you may come across the same measure in music, you may make a mistake. When I was learning music I was treated the same way and I'm going to treat you likewise, because I made a good musician myself." Another thing about Mr. Perez, I never heard him miss a note ever. In no form, regardless – brass band, opera, even *Thais* and *Faust* in dance form, I heard him playing with my own ears, and look at him – a great musician. And please, young men, if you get a hold of a good teacher that's very strict on you, I advise you to stick with him, because these teachers nowadays trying to give you lessons in one room or another, you're not going to learn anything. I once had a boy under my supervision who had learned under a man in Chicago – I daren't mention his name because he's a good musician, but the way he gave that boy a lesson, he had him keeping time with his left foot, and not his right foot. Now if you keep time with your left foot, you'll vary. The proper way is with your right foot. I took that boy, trying to keep time, and I said, "Snooky, now that's not right." He said, "Well, that's how they've been teaching me." So I took the boy myself, and tied that left foot up against a chair leg. OK, he was taking lessons quite a while with me, he was well advanced, but it was just his time. So when I got to the 6/4 lesson, he could not play it unless I give it to him over and over. Every time he come he couldn't play it. When I played it with Snooky he played it with me, but I didn't want that – I wanted him to play it alone. I kept on giving him that lesson for three months, the same lesson. I was determined he would play it. So he got tired, the poor feller, he quit. He said, "Mr. Dominique, I just can't play it without you." I said, "I'm sorry, son, but I'm not changing. But if you come across again that same tempo, 6/4 time, tell them that is why you quit. That don't make me a bad teacher. Tell 'em you quit of your own good will, 'cause you got tired of the same lesson." Supposing I'd got tired when Mr. Perez gave me the same lesson – I wouldn't be the musician I am today. I can read music, I can compose music, and I can write music. I write all my own compositions. And as far as I know, every lead-sheet I sent to Washington D.C. to copyright, I always get my copyright. I never get my lead sheet back saying there's a mistake.

I'm very proud today that Mr. Perez is the cause of my being a trumpet player. But coming back to my subject, that's the advice I'm giving to you young boys trying to take lessons – please listen to your teacher. And don't try to play . . . Bop music! Bop music is no good. It's what you call – a noise, that's all. One man have a conception of bop, the other man has his, but viewed together it's nothing. I know what I'm talking about, and if any bop player read this article in this book, I am sorry, but it's nothing. Learn music, play your melody. You'll have your tone when you practise intonation, sustaining notes, you'll sound beautiful.

Coming back to when I was taking lessons from Mr. Perez: there's a trumpet player that died – Mr. Freddie Keppard. He was sitting on the step talking to Mr. Perez when I was coming for my lesson. He said, "You taking cornet lessons? Manny, can you teach him that? 'Fella here, he'll never be a cornet player." I looked down, I was a young boy and of course I couldn't tell a grown man anything or my father would chastise me. Manny said, "Go in the house." I went in the house. Manny saw I was downhearted and said, "Listen, Natty, don't listen to that guy. I'm gonna teach you to play music better than him and read music better than him. You're gonna find out one day that you're gonna be a better musician than Freddie Keppard." So I continued with the inspiration that Mr. Perez gave me. I studied, I studied hard and every time I picked up that horn I'd think about what he'd said that I'd never be a cornet player. I studied and I passed the Solfage good. Then Mr. Perez sent to Paris, France, for a book. It took three months to get that book. The book had 150 pages, and I regret today that my nephew Don Hubbard lost that book – it was a terrific book. So I kept on and practised, and now and then he'd say, "Well son, you learnt the horn – let's sing some music together." He would get his horn out and we'd play together. That book that come from Paris started off very hard on the first page. And he said, "Well, Natty, this is your first lesson. You take it, and I'm going to give you a lesson once a week. I know it's hard." I went home, and I studied and studied, and I practised and practised, and I knew my lesson. And when I went back he took me to the next page, and then next page. I went along, gradually and gradually getting better, and then one day Mr. Perez was playing a picnic at the fairground that night, and he also had a job at Economy Hall. He couldn't find a cornet player to go in his place, so he sent me. That's another night I'll never forget. Big Eye Louis Nelson was playing in Manuel Perez's orchestra at the Economy Hall. I took my horn and I went up to the hall. When I opened the door there was a big crowd in there. As I entered Big Eye Louis looked up from the bandstand and said, "Why, look who Mr. Perez sent." I was hurt and I turned right back and went home. I got his point, I was only a kid. When I got home I told my father about it and he whipped me again, and said, "You shouldn't have done that to Mr. Perez, 'cause Mr. Perez is a good man. He don't want no paying, he's teaching you for nothing and you are taking up all his time. You should have stayed right there." The next day Mr. Perez heard about it and he scolded me about it. But one thing I'll say, I'll give a clarinet player credit – Alphonse Picou. That was another job I went on – the only thing I could do was read music a little because I was still taking lessons. So I went on the job, and Mr. Picou told me, "Come here son, gee I'm glad Mr. Perez sent you." Well, that was encouraging. He said, "I understand you're getting on real nice with that instrument." Buddy Johnson, trombone player, a fellow I'll never forget, he said, "Come on Natty, I know all about you, you can play." "Well, gentlemen," I said, "I'll play what I know and what I can read, but it's quite difficult music you have on this bandstand, because I know what Mr. Perez play, but I'll do my best." He said, "Don't worry." So they played the five or six numbers that I knew. Then Mr. Picou pulled a number out of that book. He said, "Natty, if you see anything in there that's going to hurt you, tell the orchestra and let me know." So I showed him a couple of measures, and he said, "Forget that measure, I'll take that measure." I played down to where that measure was, and he'd take it away from me. And then I played, and he'd take away the next measure – well, that was a lot of encouragement – it was better than Big Eye Louis putting me down. Eventually I found out that Big Eye Louis couldn't read music – he only could spell the music. I said "Well, well, how can a man say in those very words: Look who Manuel's sent!" Later on, Mr. Perez had another job – that was also with Big Eye Louis. He told me Big Eye Louis would be playing. I said, "Oh no, I'm not going, Mr. Perez." He said "Yes, you're going, you're going to go on that job." Buddy Johnson was there, Albert Glenny was there, Jimmy Palao was playing violin and Walter Brundy was playing drums, myself on trumpet and Picou was there with Big Eye – they had two clarinets in the band that night. So I goes in, and Big Eye looked at me like he wanted to say something, so Buddy Johnson looked at him, and Picou looked at him. I said, "All right, I'm all right, Mr. Louis." He said, "I hear you can play, you played with Picou." Picou said, "Yeah, the man can play." 'Cause Picou's playing the lead clarinet, and I found out that Big Eye Louis was faking. I got on the bandstand, and started playing, and people started dancing. I was very glad, and thought that's quite a bit of encouragement for myself, but I was still a bit scared. Then Walter Brundy and Buddy Johnson said, "Listen, Natty, quit trembling, we're with you!" Now Walter Brundy, he was some drummer. If you make a mistake, he's going pick it up right away. So I went along fine. So after that Big Eye Louis says, "Send Natty." Well, it was a novel between Big Eye Louis and Picou – sometimes Big Eye Louis would want me and sometimes Picou. So I told Mr. Perez, I said, "I want to go with Big Eye Louis. I'll tell you why – that man, he don't know music. I want to show him what you're teaching me and I'm going to know more music than him eventually." So I played with Big Eye Louis, and one night they had a clarinet part, strictly a clarinet part, and Big Eye Louis couldn't play it. I looked at him and reminded him, "Mr. Louis, the idea of a man of your ability telling a young boy like me 'Look who Manuel sent.' I'm surprised he'd even have you in his orchestra." Big Eye Louis never liked me from that day on.

So, I went along learning my lessons, and Manuel went to Chicago. I didn't think there was another man in this whole world could give me lessons like Mr. Perez. That's how much confidence I had in him. Because he was exact. He was so perfect, he wanted everything just so. So I stopped taking lessons. Nobody could teach me any more, but Mr. Perez. He stayed in Chicago – so I went to Chicago, taking my little horn, and I got a job with Mr. Perez at the Turner Cigar Factory – Robert Turner at 10 West 35th Street. Mr Perez had been a cigar maker in New Orleans and he and I was making cigars there.

My first music job in the city of Chicago was with Art Steur's Brass Band. He came around to see me at the cigar factory and said, "I need a cornet player." I said, "Well, I play a little cornet." He said, "You read music?" I said, "I read some." So he said, "Do you want to play a job tonight?" I said, "Well, I've had no rehearsal." He said, "I'll give you the trumpet book." So I take the book and practised some numbers that I did not know, and I went on the job. Did you know that the Chicago boys are under the impression that the New Orleans men cannot read music? That's the biggest mistake the Chicago musicians ever made in their life! So, I played this picnic with Art Steur on 36th and Kits. I read through that whole repertoire, right from the front page to the last number. I got so angry, 'cause he kept my head in that music all night, I couldn't even look up at the people dancing. When I got through with the job I said, "Why didn't you go to the Conservatory of Music and pull out all the books and throw them books at me? It would be better than you did tonight! That's the trouble with all you Chicago musicians, you think the New Orleans musicians cannot read music, but I want to let you know – you see that man that's playing at the DeLuxe Cafe, Mr. Manuel Perez – that's an accomplished musician and there's not another teacher like him in the world, for me, because he's a cornetist and a number one genius!" And I regret the day that Mr. Perez died, because I loved him as a daddy. When I look up, his picture comes before me, and I appreciate all he has done for me. Now, I left Robert Turner, and I went to work for George Turner, at 3717 South State Street. Then Jimmie Noone hired me at the Paradise Cafe. I worked there with Jimmie Noone, a great clarinetist, I worked there quite a while. But eventually the place closed, and I went back to making cigars. Mr. Perez was soon back making cigars too when his job with George Filhe closed at the DeLuxe. Then I worked at the Royal Garden with Jimmie Noone. Freddie Keppard had been in New York and he came back to Chicago – that's where I got my revenge on Freddie Keppard.

I'd heard all about the King . . . the King this and the King that. Freddie came down one Saturday night to the Royal Garden. Jimmie Noone had out that Scott Joplin music and we was playing Scott Joplin rags. So Freddie Keppard came to the bandstand and said to me, "Hello there, I see you're with my brother-in-law." "Yeah," I said, "I'm still trying to make it, Freddie." Freddie pulled out his horn and Jimmie Noone pulled out a piece of Joplin music. Freddie looked at him and said, "Play so-and-so." Jimmie said, "No, we got to play that." There's one thing I like about Jimmie Noone, he's a good musician. Freddie was trying to show me up, but he couldn't! So I said, "Well, Freddie Keppard, I'll play that number for you." I played it. Then I said to Jimmie, "Now you can play whatever you want, whatever Mr. Keppard can play. Just let him play a number for the sake of his reputation." So he played about 10 or 12 numbers, and when I was going home, Virgil Williams, the boss of the Royal Garden, called me in his office and said, "Natty, you know Freddie has been working with me before?" I knew what he was about to tell me, so I said, "That's all right, Mr. Virgil, get me my money, I'll take my pay and go."

I went back making cigars again. Then a couple of weeks afterwards Virgil Williams came into the cigar factory and said, "Natty, I want you back." I said, "I don't want to work for you, Virgil. You wanted Freddie Keppard – keep him. He's great, he's the King. I'm only the underdog. He's the King, he stands on top." Then I said, "Mr. Perez, if you want this job working with Jimmy Noone at the Royal Garden, you can have it." He said, "All right Natty, if you don't want it, I'll take it as I'm only working three nights a week." So as soon as he'd accepted the job with Virgil Williams, in comes George Filhe, his trombone player, who also had a job on 22nd and Wabash. So he asked Manny, "Manny, I got a job." Manuel said, "I just accepted a job from Mr. Williams. Take Natty." George said, "All right, I'll take Natty." That was a good band: we had 'Old Man' Willie Humphrey's son playing clarinet, Louis Cottrell playing drums, George Filhe on trombone, a lady by the name of Miss Georgia playing piano and myself. Of course, I didn't know what kind of music it was: I came from a place where they played loud music. So when I went on the bandstand and started playing, the boss came out on the floor and said, "Mr. cornet-player, we're not playing no ballyhoo for advertizing medicine, all that loud music." I said, "Well, I didn't know, I just came from the Royal Garden where I played loud music. If you'd only told me I'll play soft music." So I just walked off the bandstand, but no sooner had I got home than he was there in his big Cadillac. Probably George Filhe had told him, "You should have explained. You got the boy all upset." So I went back and I played soft music and we got along well.

Then I went to Milwaukee. I played with a drummer by the name of Fox. He was supposed to be a great drummer, but there's no drummer in the world like Baby Dodds. I'll tell the world. There's no more Baby Dodds, there's no more Norman Downs. That's the two leading drummers. Now Norman's dead, the poor feller. While I was working in Milwaukee I got a telegram from Carroll Dickerson. He wanted me to go to Chicago. So I came to Chicago, and we opened up at the Entertainers Cafe, that's on 34th between Indiana and Prairie. The Paradise used to be at the corner. I worked there with Carroll Dickerson, I stuck with him, I liked him and we went on the road. We had Willie Hightower, Cecil Irwin, James Hall, Tubby Hall, and Earl Hines – the great pianist. All I could hear on the road from Earl Hines was, "The New Orleans musicians haven't got it!" That vexed me very much. I said, "Some day . . ." He kept saying the New Orleans musicians wasn't as good as the New York musicians, or the Pittsburgh musicians, or the Pennsylvania musicians. I said to myself, "Some day, I'll be able to find out your ability at music." We played all over, and then we came back to Chicago and were booked at the Sunset Café, still under Carroll Dickerson. We played there for a while and increased our repertoire. We had a number called *Tannhäuser*. I'll never forget that number and I'll never forget Earl Hines, he hasn't played that measure yet – that full measure, that is. So we polished that number and everytime it came to the piano part for Earl Hines to take a full measure solo – he couldn't play it! Louis Armstrong was with us. I looked at Louis, and Louis looked at me. I said, "Listen Pops, this guy, Earl Hines been saying we cannot read music. I think <u>he</u> cannot read music!" Louis said, "You don't know that." I said, "I know that." So Carroll Dickerson said to Earl Hines,"Take the part home and rehearse it." So he'd take the part home and rehearsed it, 'cause he's such a great Father Hines.

One night Paul Whiteman's band came in. They came in on Saturday night – the whole band just to hear Louis. I know they came to hear Louis, because Louis is great. Louis can read music. The music that Carroll Dickerson put on us, and Dave Peyton arranged music for the show, it was hard music. And don't let nobody tell you that Louis cannot read music – he's a great musician. I know, because I worked with him for three years. We got off the bandstand at the intermission, and Carroll Dickerson said, "We're gonna play *Tannhäuser* for Paul Whiteman." You should have seen the expression on Earl Hines's face! Right away, we told Cecil to take the piano part, he's supposed to make three-part harmony for the cornet and trombone. He made it. We went back on the bandstand. Carroll Dickerson said, "All right Earl, *Tannhäuser*!" Paul Whiteman had a ringside table right by the bandstand. Earl Hines looked to me like he was crying, with that cigar in his mouth. So we played *Tannhäuser*. When we got to the piano part . . . stop, Earl Hines stopped. The three brass made the part for him. He turned around, and looked and kind of smiled. When we got through playing, Paul Whiteman got up and said, "Fellers, that was very good." But he didn't compliment Earl Hines. He said, "It sounded marvellous, but I wanted to hear the piano make that solo, which is the piano part." We didn't know what to say. Louis and I and Dutrey just looked at each other. Dutrey was a good trombone player. I don't care what you put before Dutrey, he's gonna play it, regardless. He's dead and gone, but I'm going to say it behind his back. So when we got off work I said, "Listen, Earl Hines, you're a great musician. If they'd given me as long to practise the full measures as they gave you, I'd know it by heart. It's a great disappointment in you, but I'm very proud that the New Orleans musicians here are greater musicians than you are. If everybody in Pittsburgh is a musician like you are, that's a pity. When they taught us music in New Orleans, they taught us right. They didn't taught us to skip this, or worry about this later on, because you're gonna come into contact with the same thing in life the same full measures as long as you play piano. I'd advise you to get your own orchestra – that's the only way you can get to suit yourself." He didn't know what to say then. I went on and played with Earl Hines a long time, and that's why today, when I see Earl Hines I call him "Tannhäuser!" and he say, "You never forget anything, do you, Dominique!" "No Earl, because all the time on the road you rubbed it in to me, but the day came and I had to show you New Orleans musicians are good musicians. The best come from there. You take 'Old Man' Papa Tio, a man who never did play jazz in his life. He hated jazz. He was an accomplished musician, a good director. And when you study under those people, like Manny Perez, Vic Gaspard, or for bass, 'Old Man' Gaspard or Piron's brother – they are teachers. They're not half-learned like you are, and you're supposed to be great." They judge people now on musical ability, what they know of music, not what they do on the piano. The reading counts. You've got to face the public, and one day they're going to bring a piece of music. I can remember they brought Sterling Todd – now that's a musician, an accomplished musician, a good teacher. I'll never forget Sterling Todd at the K-Nine club as long as I live. There was an operetta singer come there. With no rehearsal, Sterling played that number at first sight, from top to the bottom, and the woman was very pleased and complimented him. She said, "Young man, you never did see that music before, but that's the best I've ever had my music played."

I stayed at the K-Nine quite a while till it closed up. It was at 9 East Walton Place. We had Johnny Dodds, Baby Dodds, Herb Waters, Ralph Tervalon, and myself. We had a show that needed a Chinese number. That's why I think of Manny Perez today. There was no trumpet part for the music, only a second and third clarinet part. The show was going to open on the Monday and the previous show was closing on Sunday night. They stuck this music on me. I told them, I said, "Mr. Cohen and Mrs. Cohen, I haven't got any trumpet parts." I glanced over at Tervalon's music, he had the piano part, and saw a lead there, so I told them I'd take the part home. Just imagine, an orchestra – a five- or six-piece orchestra, only got second and third clarinet parts, and you gotta find that lead. I found it. I sat half the day transposing from the piano part, to make a cornet part. That night was the opening of the show: Vincent Lopez, Ted Weems, Paul Whiteman . . . they were all there. When they announced that number, they knew it didn't have a trumpet part. I muted my horn and I transposed the second and third clarinets into a three-part harmony of that number. All the musicians came up after and said, "Natty, where did you get that cornet part?" I told them, "From up here." They said, "Who taught you?" I said, "Manuel Perez." They said, "That's that Mexican looking feller who's a great cornet player?" I said, "And a great teacher. A wonderful man." Paul Whiteman said, "That's the best I've ever heard, how did you do it?" I said, "I had to transpose, two notes lower for every note. It took me half the day to get out one cornet part, but I was determined for my orchestra not to fail, and it did not fail." Then he complimented me, and musicians made speeches – Vincent Lopez made a speech, about how Mrs. Cohen and Mr. Cohen were very lucky to have five men like that on the bandstand that play such music.

There was another orchestra at that time that undermined us. They were supposed to be good musicians – Chicago musicians. So, Mr. and Mrs. Cohen gave us our notice. They were very nice about it, of course, they gave us two weeks notice. After three weeks, Mr. Cohen came to the 29 Club on 47th street where we were playing, and begged us to come back! I told him, "Mr. Cohen, under no consideration would I come back. You had something good and you didn't appreciate it, 'cause the other fellers undermined us on the job. Two weeks after that he had to close the place – nobody was going there. When Vincent Lopez' men come into town, and they saw him, they said, "Mr. Cohen, what a mistake you made. Why did you let those boys go? You had everything, and you didn't know it!" "Well," he said, "I had to save a few dollars here and there." They said, "But you had the place packed every night. People was lined up around the corner. Why do you think they came? They didn't come for that show, they come for that orchestra." People living right across the street never complained as we could play soft music, and they could sleep, because we played soft music. He had to close the place, so we stayed at the 29 Club. But there was no music at all for their shows. I had to ask the owner – how do you want it? For dance, medium or slow, or fast? Well, I played the show – it wasn't complicated music like at the K-Nine Club. At the K-Nine Club the performers would hear a record of Paul Whiteman's Orchestra and they would get it and request it. They wouldn't consider my five-piece orchestra. Paul Whiteman had 15 or 20 pieces – violins, cellos, everything. I only had a five-piece. They just get the music and Dominique's got to play it! I patch it, 24-measure rest here, put a lead right there. Coming back to Mr. Earl Hines – I couldn't have had him on the job I had at that K-Nine Club, because he could not read that music. So we got along pretty good at the 29 Club. Then it closed up. We then went to Kelly's Stable's. We had Zutty Renard, Ralph Tervalon, Herb Waters, myself, Johnny Dodds and Baby Dodds – that was our orchestra. We stayed at Kelly's Stables for about seven or eight months. Then he closed the place up, I don't know why, I think the reason was his wife didn't like staying up late at night. We worked there and people were crazy about our music. We had a small combo that knew music, and read music thoroughly. When we left there we went to the Lambs Club, down in the Loop. I had Sterling Todd then. And that was just shows. I had a six-piece band and I had Johnny Lindsey with me in place of Renard. The rest of the group was the same, except for the pianist. I had Sterling Todd and he is a great pianist. So we played some really tough music, some hard music: adagio, Russian music, Simplicity waltzes. It's very seldom you come across that – playing Simplicity waltzes. We worked there – well, I wouldn't like to say what happened. When we left there, we didn't have any work but we were recording then, with Buddy Burton and Jimmie Noone, recording for the Decca Company.

Now, going back to the Sunset: I played with Louis Armstrong there for quite a while. One night May Alix sang a song: *I Wanna Big Butter and Egg Man.* I liked the way Louis played that number. When he taken down for me to play a chorus, I played that number just like him. During the intermission, my pal, my good friend Louis Armstrong, come and sat at the table. He said, "Listen Nique, don't do that. That's a bad idea you have, playing like I play." So I got peeved about it. So the rest of the night I played a solid straight second trumpet behind Louis Armstrong. He looked at me. He was boiling. He didn't tell me anymore. So I got home at 4 o'clock in the morning. I goes to bed. I got up, I turn on my radio, didn't dial a station or anything, I just turned it on. I heard a man say, "Don't be a copycat. Originality will always stand you on top of the ladder, and a copycat will always climb for the rest of his life." So I'm advising you young boys – don't copy after no one, regardless of how good he is. Be yourself. Make up something of your own, that is different, that the public will be able to look up to you as being different from Louis, Cootie Williams, Harry James, and many others, be your own self. That's the reason why, from that night on, I never did try to play like Louis

Armstrong. One night he told me, "I'm going on a vacation for two weeks." So the whole two weeks was on me. I was accustomed to the repertoire and accustomed to the show, I could swing a band perfect. Of course we had a trumpet player, but he didn't know the music, and it was hard for him to catch on. So I got out on the floor and I played the act just like it was supposed to be played, I played that whole night. The other cornetist, I will not mention his name, he was supposed to be a great guy from Chicago. Carroll Dickerson told him to pick out what he wanted in the book. He picked out some numbers and I had to jump from first to second, 'cause he wanted to play first, 'cause he couldn't pick up, seemingly. I thought back what Earl Hines used to tell me, about the musicians of New Orleans, and I felt good. I played the dances, and everybody got up and danced. Carroll Dickerson seemed to be pleased. So I held the band for two weeks, but I worked very hard. You need a lot of strength to play four shows and three sets of dances all night long. Carroll told me, "Dominique, I'm going to call you Iron Lip. I didn't think you were that powerful, that strong. I was looking for you to get down." I said, "Well Cal, the Great has gone on his vacation, and it's my duty to hold the band." I told him, "You know, I was angry at Louis once, he didn't know it. He told me not to copy him. And I'm proud today that I'm not playing like Louis Armstrong." I have my own style, and, so far as I can see, every job I've played, I've pleased the public. They're well pleased and I've had lots of compliments. My dear friend Bill Russell nicknamed me "The Driver," 'cause I play a driving trumpet. I like that name and I hope it will stay with me.

I worked for about a year with Louis. Every time he take down, I played the chorus my own way. Then a bunch of musicians came up from New York. I forget the name of the orchestra – not Paul Whiteman. When Louis took down, I took a couple of choruses, probably three or four, in my own style, not like Louis. One of the musicians in the band walked up to me and said, "What's your name?" I said, "My name's Natty Dominique." He said, "I like your playing very much. I notice you're not playing like Louis." I said, "You don't know. I can play one number like Louis, but never no more. Louis told me not to copy after him." That's why Dominique's got his own style. You get noticed. You won't be noticed by the public as much if you're not being original. The only thing they'll say is, "Well, he's trying to play like Louis, or like Harry James, or so and so." That's no compliments at all. I want to get compliments on my own style. Today I gets it, and I'm proud. And as long as I have breath in my body I will never try to play like no one in the United States of America, or try to be a copycat. I'm going to be Dominique, Natty Dominique – alone!

So we played on, and Louis came back he asked me, "'Nique, how you made out?" I said, "I'm the happiest man in the world to see you. I have to hold the band by myself, swing the band by myself, I have to play the shows by myself, and Carroll Dickerson gave me the name of Iron Lip. But," I said, "you'll always be the greatest as long as you exist in this world. I know they all come here to hear you, but I'm glad I don't copy you any more and I promise you I'll never copy after you as long as I live." He said, "I know you was peeved that night. You was angry." I said, "Louis, I was so angry." But the next night what I done? I come back and apologised to Louis. I shook his hand, and said, "Louis, you're right!" He said, "I'm glad you're sorry, you're a good cornet player. You've got a swing out of this world, you don't know it. Of course I have a different way of playing. But you've got a drive. You carries them with you – they've got to come with you." I said, "I appreciate that, Louis. From now on I will never play like you. I'm going to play like Natty Dominique." So he was happy, and so was I. I said, "Let's get together, on the bandstand to play." So we got together and he played 25 choruses of *Poor Little Rich Girl.* I played twelve second trumpet parts under him, and I tried to play with him, but I got tired. Louis Armstrong will kill you. He's got a powerful lip. That's the reason why he's gonna be great as long as he has breath in his body. So I put my horn in my lap and sit on down and looked at Mr. Armstrong. I was tired, my lip gave down. A man who can play 25 choruses of *Poor Little Rich Girl,* it's got about 74 measures in there, that's playing a lot of trumpet! I say today, Louis Armstrong deserves the golden crown – The king of all trumpet players, with his style of playing. Don't forget, Louis Armstrong is a very good musician. When you sit alongside a man for two years and see all the hard music that Carroll Dickerson put on us, Louis playing first and I'm playing second. Dave Peyton, that's a man arranges music, and he don't arrange no easy music. Hard music, for shows. He put it on us, and Louis Armstrong played everything. Carroll Dickerson would tell you in a minute if you made a mistake, "What are you carrying that union card for if you can't read music? Get rid of it!"

King Oliver was playing across the street in The Plantation. He came in one night with a number named *Snag It.* It had an 8-bar break for first and second trumpet and trombone. We just looked at it, being musicians. We said, "We'll play it for you," and when we got to that break we couldn't finish it, we run out of gas. It was all tonguing. Louis and I looked at Joe Oliver, who said, "Practise it, and when you learn it let me know," and walked back across the street to The Plantation. Louis and I got so angry, really it was pitiful, so when he got to the door he turned back and waved at us. I looked at Louis and said, "The King got us. What are we going to do?" He said, "We're going to get it." We went on rehearsing down behind the grandstand in the kitchen. We looked at the part and Louis said, "It's easy, but the breath . . . " I said, "Let's take a double breath. Fill our stomachs and our chests up before we get to that place. We'll have to miss a measure to do that. Let's try it." We tried it, and succeeded. The next intermission we went and got Joe Oliver, and told Carroll "Play that number." Carroll said, "Can you wrap it up?" So we played the number, and when we got to the break the trombone, first and second trumpet, we made the break. Oliver said, "At last, you've made it," and he walked away.

Bert Kelly had been after me for a long time, since I was at The Entertainers' Café. He said, "You never can tell what's going to happen. Some day I'll come and tell you I want you to work for me." "Who else have you got?" I asked him. "I've got Gibbs, Charlie Alexander, Johnny Dodds . . . " He mentioned a trombone player, but I've forgotten his name. I told him "OK." Then while I was still working at the Sunset Café a waiter told me, "Did you know a cornet player wants your job?" I said, "He can have it if Carroll wants him." I know why Carroll wanted him: Joe Glaser, the proprietor of the place, really liked my work, the orchestra liked my work, crazy about me. But there's a reason for all things and I dare not say what was told to me. So I told Carroll I was taking a vacation. He said, "Who are you going to send?" I said, "Wilson." That's the man he wanted. I said, "When I know you want a man, I'm going to get you that same man, I don't want you to be disappointed. I won't send no one you don't want." So Wilson took my place. Bert Kelly heard about my vacation. I hadn't had two nights' rest when he sent for me, and said, "Bring your horn down. I want you to sit with that band." Well, Johnny Dodds reads good music, he's a good musician. Charlie Alexander is a good musician, the trombone player was good, Gibbs was a fair drummer, he could read music. I said, "That sounds good to me, I'll come down and play three numbers." He said, "No, you'll play it all the way. I'll pay you for a good night's work." And he did, he paid me very well that night. He said, "Is it possible, can you get away from the orchestra? I've been wanting you since you were at the Entertainers' Café." I said, "According to the rules and regulations of the Union, I have to give two weeks notice." He said, "Is there a possibility that you can get away without giving two weeks notice, because I want you now." "Well," I said, "I'll try." So that Sunday night, during the week I was off, I went over to the Sunset Café. During the intermission I spoke to Louis Armstrong, and said, "I'm leaving." I called Tubby Hall, and Honoré Dutrey, and they called Carroll Dickerson off the bandstand. I told him, "I know you want the young man I sent to you, and I want to know if it's necessary for me to give you two weeks notice, because I want to lay off for a while." He said, "No." I said, "Repeat the words," He said, "You don't have to give two weeks notice," and I had four witnesses. I said, "Very well. I got a job paying me $15 more than I'm making here. I'm going to work tomorrow night." Carroll Dickerson was dumbfounded. He asked me "Where?" I said, "You shouldn't be interested – you weren't interested in my playing." But it looked like it went through Louis, he hated to see me leave, and also the rest of the boys. Louis said, "Where are you going?" I whispered "Kelly's Stables." He said, "Go and take it, Nique." I wasn't away from the Sunset two weeks, when they put Carroll Dickerson out of his own band. Joe Glaser kept asking about me, wondering why I'd quit. I found out the boys told him that Caroll Dickerson had wanted this other cornet player. The whole orchestra was dissatisfied, and didn't want to work under Carroll Dickerson. Jimmie Noone was working at the Apex Club, and I went there after I got through at Bert Kelly's Stables. Jimmie was working there after hours. Carroll Dickerson came by and said, "Hello." He said, "Dominique, from now on I'll be a straight man. You heard they're about to put me out of my own orchestra?" I said, "No, they can't do that." Carroll was a good musician, a good director. He did me a little wrong, but I still liked Carroll. I told him, "The man that you wanted, as I hear it, the brass section is not balanced. The punch is not there."

I went back to Kelly's Stables. This was Bert Kelly's Stables on Rush and Austin, on the north east corner of Rush Street. I think there's a furniture store there now. They had singing entertainers and we worked there five years – Johnny Dodds and I. Then, Baby Dodds, his brother, the greatest drummer and a good musician, was out of a job. I told Johnny, and he said, "Dominique, he's got all those faults." I said, "We all got faults. Get him. He's terrific." When Baby Dodds joined that four-piece orchestra, it was great. Four good musicians, playing all the music that the publishers would bring – swing music, jazz – that joint was packed every night. On Saturday nights we had two shows – top floor and bottom floor. The entertainers would be downstairs, and they had a piano player for them. We'd be playing for the dances upstairs. Bert Kelly's Stables never did advertize. Monday night was Celebrities Night – all these great entertainers from the State Theater, the Chicago Theater, the Oriental Theater, and all the different theaters, come down. It was fixed up like a stable. The first floor you came to, there was a trough with hay in it, harnesses; second floor, all wooden tables. People from the

*Bert Kelly's Stables – 431 Rush Street*

Drake Hotel would come, with all their tuxedos and gowns. When they got there it looked like they was uneasy. Then they throwed off their collars, wing collars, so that they'd be at ease and they'd join the dance. They'd tell Bert Kelly he had a great orchestra. One thing about Bert Kelly – he did not like soft music. He wanted loud music. One night he left to go to New York, he used to go quite often. I said to Johnny, "C'mon, let's get down to New Orleans style." We hit a double forte, and then we come down soft, and Johnny giving that low register on the clarinet, and we were swinging. But one night Bert Kelly came in unbeknown to us. He runs upstairs and shouts, "What's the matter, the band's sick? Where's my orchestra, I don't hear 'em." I took my mute out, I blowed so loud that night, you could hear me on Wentworth Avenue, that's about four blocks away. Johnny Dodds blasts his clarinet. Loud music is more hard to play than soft music. You can relax on soft music. I worked there five years till the Prohibition agents closed the place.

The band consisted of Charlie Alexander on piano, Johnny Dodds on clarinet, myself on cornet and Baby Dodds on drums. That's four of the toughest men you ever put on a bandstand in the United States of America! That's no kidding! Charlie Alexander is in New York now. Albany I think, playing by himself. He's a very good musician and a good pianist. I enjoyed working with them. I've been playing with Baby Dodds ever since. Johnny and Baby Dodds and I worked together for 14 years. Johnny was a great clarinet player. All of the other good clarinet players used to come up there.

One night I was over at the Club 29; Johnny, Jimmie Noone and Barney Bigard was there, all on the stand at one time. Sidney Bechet came in and said, "Hello fellers." We said, "Oh oh, here come the devil!" Bechet said, "We're going to have a little fun tonight." Johnny said, "Now look at that, they broke up my playhouse." Barney looked at him, "Hmm". Johnny said to Sidney, "Alright, pull your stick out, I know you have it with you." So Bechet put his clarinet together and got on the bandstand, and do you know, they all left that bandstand one by one. When I turned around, Bechet was up there by himself. You never heard so much clarinet in all of your life. Bechet worked with Noble Sissle for about 12 or 13 years, and he had a beautiful tone. I haven't heard him play for about 12 or 14 years now. He's playing soprano sax, like Johnny Hodges. Bechet's the only man I ever heard could get a perfect tone out of a soprano sax. That's the hardest instrument to get a perfect tone, I don't know how he does it.

*Johnny Dodds   (photo: Mary Karoley)*

Johnny Dodds and Baby and I stayed together, the big three. When we would get jobs we would hire different guys – we got Leo Montgomery, a good pianist and musician. Sterling Todd played with us one day up in Maywood, and a feller came up to the stand with a piano solo. That's when I found out the musical ability of Sterling Todd. When you opened up that music you couldn't hardly see the white paper the music was on, it was so congested with notes. And Sterling Todd, with no rehearsal, played it from the top to the bottom. He don't like to play with an orchestra. He's more of a teacher, he's a very good teacher.

Now going back to the K-Nine Club – Johnny Dodds, Baby Dodds and myself. We used to have quite a lot of drummers who used to come on that bandstand, and they'd look for the sock cymbal. That's something that I disapprove of. Some of them used to bring their own sock cymbals and I used to get a headache from them. It was really annoying. There's no rhythm in sock cymbal. Great drummers like Baby Dodds, Tubby Hall, Louis Cottrell, never needed them. Take my good friend who's dead and gone, Norman Downs, who played with Ted Weems' orchestra. We had a tough show at the K-Nine Club, and one Saturday night, Norman Downs came in. Baby said, "There's a drummer I want you to hear." I said, "Those drummers got me sick to the stomach." He said, "Just let him play a set, please." So he played. And that's why I love Norman Downs. He's great. An accomplished drummer. He fitted in. I asked him what he wanted to play, he said, "Anything." I asked him if he wanted the music, he said, "If you want to give me the music, I'll play the music." I gave him the parts of the three dances we were going to play. I never heard so much soft and beautiful drums, so much rhythm. That drummer was shooting me, and he do not use a sock cymbal. Lots of drummers talk about press rolls, different corner rolls, that man had rhythm even in his rolls. He played six numbers. I told him, "I'd like you to get down now because we're going to have the show." He said, "Let me look at the show part, maybe I'll be able to play it." He looked at it and said, "I think I'll be able to play it." Of course a good musician will always have his cues on his music sheet. That boy sat there and played that whole show that night without rehearsing. I stood dumbfounded. I've had drummers come up there that didn't know how to read music. I'm not going to mention no names, but you can use your own judgement. Norman Downs, sitting on that bandstand, he knocked so much rhythm in me I was nearly dead. I told him, "Please get off this bandstand, because you're a great drummer, you're killing me. This is Saturday night, pal!" He said, "Oh, just let me sit in." I said, "I've noticed you've been coming here four or five nights a week." He said, "You've got a great band and a great drummer in Baby Dodds. That boy don't know how great he is." Norman Downs and Baby Dodds – they are the only two drummers I admire, because I know their capability of reading music. It's too bad that Ted Weems lost such a great drummer as Norman Downs. There's very few musicians can play a show without rehearsing.

I love a man that can read music like that, and I'd like very much for you boys to put it in your mind to study hard, very hard, and learn everything. Don't give it up when you start, go to it. Get the guts in you. Learn! Learn! Learn! Then you can pick up your instrument and go to Europe if you want, 'cause you're not afraid of that sheet of paper. Learn everything pertaining to music. When I go on a job, the only thing I'm worrying about is if I'm going to get my money. The music don't bother me. That's how I want you youngsters to feel, so please take my advice: don't go halfway; go all the way. Publishers would come to us, with sometimes 25 numbers, and we'd sit there and play all of those numbers. Numbers we didn't like we'd tell them "keep it", but we played all of their numbers to prove we were musicians, capable enough to play their music. Then we'd add to the music – we'd kick it, which is jazz – we'd give them that New Orleans jazz. This consists of intervals, slow triplets, fast triplets, staccato, obbligatos. That's why I preach to you youngsters coming up – no matter what kind of instrument you have – learn it right, 'cause if a man come all the way from New York and he's got a great number, and heard about your great orchestra, he wants you to play his number the way he wrote it. How would you feel if you had to tell that man you cannot play his music? That's very embarrassing.

New Orleans music will always stand out as long as there is jazz music. The New Orleans musician will always play the music as it is. Straight melody first, to get the melody into the public's mind. They'll hum it to themselves. Then, in the third chorus or so, you'll be able to add slow triplets, fast triplets, gliss, staccato . . . because the melody was already there.

Learn everything about drumming, because that's a main instrument in an orchestra. You got to be good to put rhythm on that bass drum. If your teacher corrects you, listen to your teacher.

Coming down to trombone players, you take Honoré Dutrey – I always believed that Dutrey took lessons under Vic Gaspard, 'cause he was a great trombone player. Gaspard could triple-tongue and maybe double-triple-tongue. Dutrey could triple-tongue and had a great tone. He could play soft trombone, regardless of how loud an orchestra played, Dutrey's tone would cut through all that noise. Give your note a value and your tone will stick out. Young men, please learn to sustain your notes. Learn your different 6/4 time, 8/2 time, 3/8 time, 2/4 time – learn everything. So when you go into a band, you can play those 6/8 marches, they're not as complicated as that, 'cause if you learn properly, you can play all that. I know cornet players who play the numbers they know, perfect, but they're slow readers. That's what I call half-learnt. They're afraid they'll be given music they cannot play. On the numbers that they can play, they're terrific. But

*Natty Dominique's Creole Dance Band. (l to r ) Jasper Taylor (dms), Preston Jackson (tbn), Bill Anderson (sbs), Natty Dominique (tpt), Ralph Tervalon (pno), and Odell Rand (clt).*

they'll be playing those same eight numbers for the rest of their lives.

Now, coming to bass players', Oke Gaspard, Piron's brother, and Eddie Jackson, were great musicians. They all knew music from A - Z. Eddie Jackson had more rhythm on the bass than any bass player I heard.

As for my trumpet, I've had every tooth taken out of my mouth. My dentist told me he would have to take out all my teeth but he promised me that when he fitted my new set that I would be able to play just like before. I have no difficulty playing with false teeth. In the old days Oliver had to quit when his teeth went bad, same with my teacher, Manny Perez. Fortunately, I had a good dentist. I was worried, but he said, "Don't worry, Dominique. You'll still play your horn when I get through with you." I've had to build my embouchure all over again to be ready. Nothing is gonna hinder me from playing that horn, because I love that horn.

What kind of trumpet do I have now? I have a Martin and I like it very much. A medium bore. A Martin Committee (De Luxe model) trumpet. Charlie Shavers has the same kind of horn as I have. He was with Tommy Dorsey at the time and he asked how much my horn cost me. I said "$240." He said, "That's what mine cost me." I don't know what bore Charlie Shavers used, but I use a medium bore. I learnt on a medium bore and I've been using it ever since. Louis Armstrong used a medium bore. My mouthpiece is not entirely shallow, it's half shallow. The bore on my mouthpiece is a 22. A lot of trumpet players don't know the size of the bore of their mouthpiece. The bore is what you stick into your horn, and the hole that comes from the cup, that's an addition to your bore. I started learning on an $8 cornet with a lot of lead patches. It was heavy, and Manny Perez said it was a good one to learn on, because when I got a good one I'd be able to play better. I changed to trumpet when I played with Jimmie Noone at the Paradise Café. I got me a Buescher and I liked it. When Louis Armstrong joined us at the Sunset Café we both bought a Buescher. We wore them out in six months. He said, "Well, Nique that's enough of Bueschers. Let's get something else." I said, "Anything you get, Dip, I'll get it." So we bought a Conn apiece, a very good instrument. After that I came back to Martin, and I've been using a Martin ever since. I like the bell of the horn. It rings, it don't go like a piece of tin. When I make my B-natural, it's practically the same when I hit the bell with my mouthpiece – it may be a little flat, but it's nearly a B-natural to your horn. When you got a good bell, you got a good horn. If you got a thin bell, when you go to make them high notes, it flutters. You can feel the vibration. I like a heavy bell. When you got a light bell it vibrates. What I like about the Martin Committee De Luxe, there's a lot of trumpets you can work jazz as well as brass bands, but you can't use that trumpet in orchestra pitch. A trumpet tone is a little distant from you. A cornet tone is nearer to you. But you got to get yourself used to it. Muggsy Spanier always did use a cornet, not a trumpet. A lot of people say you've got to use lung pressure, but you've got to use lip pressure regardless. You just use lung pressure, you got no tone, but you got to have lip pressure. You notice with any cornet player, if there was no pressure on the lip there'd be no mark, you notice the mark on their lip. As for tonguing, the way they teach you, that's how you blow. I get my vibrato from the hand, very slowly.

When I was taking lessons, I was vocalising music, keeping time with my hand, and singing the notes – that's very important to a young man, because when you get a complicated piece of music, you can just hum it inwardly, if there are a few measures that are difficult for you to play. By singing music you get accustomed to it. That's how I learned music, keeping time with my hand. Of course, now I keep time with my foot.

The first record I made was with Jelly Roll Morton here in Chicago, for Okeh. We had two rehearsals: one upstairs at the Local 208, and the other at Jelly's house. Then we recorded *London Blues* and *Someday Sweetheart* in a studio down in the Loop. We had Zue Robertson, a great trombone player, but a very nervous guy. That guy used to lift his pants leg up so high sometimes I'd think he had short pants on. His ability as a musician you can't take away from him. Buster Bailey, a great clarinetist, played with us, and another little fellow, named Shot, a very nice drummer, a good musician, and myself on trumpet. Jelly Roll on piano. We made a pretty good record of *London Blues*, and I was proud because it was the first wax I cut. I went on the road with Jelly Roll Morton, playing at dances, but we never did play here in Chicago. We went all through Iowa, Wisconsin, Michigan, we never got to Detroit, though. I played in Detroit with Bob Crucett, a great violinist and musician. When I left him he nearly had a fit, he was crazy about me and the people liked me. I played three nights with Bob Crucett when I worked at the Westbourn Cigar Factory on Golden and Michigan Avenue in Detroit. My foreman was Morales, a very nice feller; I make cigars by hand, not by mould, Spanish style. They use those hand-made cigars for facing in the cigar box.

I heard Tony Jackson – great. I'll never forget his number, *Pretty Baby*. He sold that number for $50. I don't think he knew what he was doing that night. He composed the music and the words. The man he sold it to made over a million dollars. He played at the Elite Café in the 3400 block near 35th and State Street, on the east side of the street. I used to hear him every night, he was quite an entertainer. He wasn't a great singer, but you understood him pretty well, and *Pretty Baby*, everyone fell for it. A very congenial feller. He had a drummer, a sergeant at arms playing with him, can't remember his name. Teddy Weatherford was another very good piano player, playing at Carroll Dickerson's Entertainers' Café, He played with us at the Sunset, then a group of musicians took him to China, and we haven't seen Teddy Weatherford since. He never wanted to come back to America. He died and they buried him in China.

I composed *Brush Stomp*, *Sweep 'em Clean* and *Lady Love*, both of those came out on a Columbia record, Johnny Dodds and his Footwarmers. My other compositions, *My Little Isabel*, and *Too Tight Blues*, we recorded for Victor. My very latest numbers, *Yalta Jive*, and *You are My Silver Star*, haven't been published yet.

I started to write music when I was playing in Bert Kelly's Stables. Johnny said *Brush Stomp* sounded good, so we recorded it. On *Lady Love*, Dutrey, Johnny and I, got a three-part harmony in there, that's a very sweet number. I think the whole total is nine compositions, and I owe it to Manuel Perez for teaching me music.

# Natty Dominique

*Right:*
Letter from Natty Dominique to
Bill Russell – July 6, 1956. The
"Irene" referred to is Baby
Dodds' wife.

*Below:*
Letter from Johnny Dodds to
Hoyte Kline – March 23, 1939.

6 July 1956

Dear Bill:

I received your letter and was very glad to hear from you. I want to
thank you for advising me about my copy rights. I shall take care of this
before the 9th of July.

Well Bill we sure do miss you, however I am glad that you have a nice job
one that you like. I hope you will be coming back for a visit soon.

Yes, Irene passed May 5th and was buried on the 9th of May. She was put away
very nice.

Baby was going back to New York, but for some reason he changed his mind
and kept the house. He has one of his old-time friends keeping house for him.
He hasn't been too well. However my wife said he is looking so much better.
She was over to see him not too long ago.

Well Bill there isn't any news of importance. We played one job since you
have been away.

The weather here has been hot and cool. Today it is very nice, the nights
have been cool enough to sleep under cover. How is it down there in old
New Orleans? Are you enjoying yourself there? I hope so. I know you can't
help but miss old Chicago. Well Bill I'll say thanks again for all you have
done to help me, I shall never forget you. My wife and my sister-in- law
sends their regards and said to take care of your-self.

I must close now, write when you can, as ever your friend,

Natty
Dominique

---

4919 S. Michigan Ave.,
Cleveland, Ohio.
March 23, 1939.

Dear friend:—
You don't know how glad I was to
hear from you; altho' it took ages for
you to redeem your promise to me;
never-the-less it was a pleasant
surprise.

Yes I am still living at the
same address, you will always find
me here. When are you coming over?
I have not seen your friends since
the night I saw you, probably gone
back to school. Certainly would like
to see you.

I am playing on the far north
side, the name, King Solo Cabaret,
located at Lawn and Western Ave.,
only working two or three nights a
week. It seems Chicago is dead
musically. Only wish I were able
to go to New York, may-be I would
get a break. Should you hear of anything let me know. I am so tired
of fooling around.
My clarinet is still on the
over

---

hum so you can imagine how grate-
ful I am that you found one for
me. It will be more than appreciated.
Tell the music store to release the
stick at once.
The 29 Club has closed and
I hardly think it will open again.
The cats are lucky there to be
able to get a World's Fair en-
gagement. How in the world do you
get one, that would be a good
way for me to get to the Big City.
Love and best wishes,
I am
Yours truly
John Dodds.

# JOHNNY WIGGS

Johnny Wiggs
(originally John Wigginton Hyman)
cornet

Born: New Orleans, Louisiana, July 25, 1899
Died: New Orleans, Louisiana, October 9, 1977

*Johnny started on the mandolin and violin, but was inspired to become a cornetist after hearing King Oliver. He began playing around 1920 with Earl Crumb, then worked with Norman Brownlee (1924-5) and Happy Schilling (1926). In 1927 he toured with a vaudeville show and recorded, as John Hyman's Bayou Stompers. During the 1930s and 1940s Johnny worked as a teacher, but then recommenced playing and, between 1948 and 1973, made several recordings, mostly leading his own band.*

Nobody will ever know what Joe Oliver really sounded like from listening to his records. That was the greatest hot cornet man I ever heard in my life. Louis never did catch all of Joe's style. As great as Louis is, he still misses a lot of the subtlety that Joe had.

I first heard Joe when he played the subscription dances at the Tulane Gymnasium. During term time they worked there most Saturday nights, 8 till 1 a.m. It was so different from any music I'd ever heard. I just stood there with my mouth open. I couldn't imagine any music being played as exciting as that. It was the greatest hot jazz band ever and I've never heard anything since to beat it.

The inspiration came mainly from Joe and the drummer, Happy Bolton. They say a cornet and a drummer will either make or break a band. You've got to have a good lead and a drummer who knows how to drive a band. I couldn't take my eyes off Joe. He could make that cornet talk and he would send the audience wild when he took a chorus.

The band had Joe, Johnny Dodds, Kid Ory, Happy Bolton and Clarence Williams. I don't remember the bass player, but I guess they must have had one. I was so interested in the way Joe Oliver played that I never noticed. People say that Johnny St Cyr was the guitar player. If he was, I don't remember him being there. I'm sure if he had been in the band I'd have remembered him, as I knew Johnny before I even went to Tulane. When I was 16, I was already dating my future wife, and Johnny St. Cyr's mother worked for my wife's mother. In those days negro women would take their children with them when they went to work. I remember once when I was visiting my wife's home, Johnny was there and my wife's mother had a guitar in the room. Johnny got the guitar and took it out on the gallery and played the most beautiful *St Louis Blues* you ever heard. I couldn't get out onto the gallery fast enough to listen to him, and we became good friends. I think Johnny is a little older than me, but that was two years before I started going to Tulane dances, so I'm sure I would have remembered him if he had been there.

They called Joe Oliver's band the "monocle" band. Joe had a cataract over his left eye – a piece of skin growing over that eye, which was cock-eyed and looked towards the left the whole time. He wore a brown derby tilted over his good eye. I believe that's how he got his name, King Oliver. Kid Ory gave him that name because the derby sitting on his head look like a crown. He played a little short silver Conn cornet and held the mute in his hand and worked it in and out of the bell to get some wonderful "blue" sounds.

None of his records show just how good a cornet man he was. He got a hotter sound than Louis ever did. Probably the hottest record I ever heard was Louis' *Cake Walking Babies* that he made with the Blue Five in 1924, but even that was never as hot as Joe sounded at the Tulane Gymnasium. When I first heard those Blue Five records I

*Left to right:
Chink Martin,
"Papa" Jack Laine,
Johnny Wiggs,
Santo Pecoraro,
Doc Souchon –
recording in 1959*

*Happy Schilling's Orchestra (c.1926) Left to right: Johnny Wiggs, Clay Pinner, Monk Hazel, Frank Pinnero, Happy Schilling, Freddie Loyacano, George Schilling and Elery Maser.*

really thought that was Joe. The only record that gives some idea how Joe sounded was the one he made with Butterbeans and Susie – *Construction Gang* and *Kiss Me Sweet.* Joe's playing behind the singers and that gives some idea of how he sounded.

I suppose some would say that Joe was arrogant. If the band played a piece, one of the girls might go up and ask the name of the number. Whatever number they just played, Joe would say "Who struck John!" That was this title he gave everything. Doc Souchon remembers him doing that and he told me when he saw Joe at the Lincoln Gardens in Chicago, he was still telling people "Who Struck John!" if they ever asked what number the band just played.

Later I heard that Duke Ellington brought out a number called *Who Struck John?* Duke took Joe's *Camp Meeting Blues* and put it out as *Creole Love Call.* I believe Lorenzo Tio sold Duke *Mood Indigo.* Lots of New Orleans musicians sold compositions that became famous. Sidney Arodin told me he wrote *Up a Lazy River* and sold it to Hoagy Carmichael. I remember Hoagy once hinted that he really didn't write *Stardust* as it is based on the chorus of *Basin St Blues*, and, of course, Louis always said he really wrote *Sister Kate.*

But coming back to those Tulane dances; the whole band was so wonderful. They played all those New Orleans pieces: *Brownskin, High Society, Tulane Swing* (which later became *Washington and Lee Swing*). They played some old hymns and some real low-down dirty blues and a lot of tunes I didn't know. They played all the latest hits, but in those days they were just local hits. These would be published locally and if one really caught on then maybe a New York publisher might pick it up and publish it nationally. I think in most cities numbers started out by being published locally first. If Piron composed a piece, his band would play it, then he might take it around to some of his friends to see if they liked it. That's the way things became popular. Of course a lot of musicians like Oliver and Keppard were very secretive about their numbers and didn't want other bands to steal their tunes.

At that time I was in a little string band. We called ourselves "The Invincibles". We had Monk Smith, Henry Farrow on piano, Frank Farrow played bass, I played violin and Earl Crumb played drums. We tried to play the same tunes we heard at the Tulane Gym. *Tiger Rag, High Society* and all those numbers. But we never could play them like Joe's band. They had a certain swing and drive that no other band ever had.

I remember they played mostly ensemble and when they all dropped down it was beautiful. I don't remember their passing around too many choruses (solos), but I do remember in the middle of most numbers, Joe would take down to rest his lip and the whole band would pick it up. When Johnny Dodds took a chorus, Kid Ory would be kicking that bass rhythm at the back of him. When the band got going the rhythm was something out of this world.

Happy Bolton, the drummer, was a man you never hear of today. He was like a rubber man. He did all those things that people criticize drummers for today. He played all over the drums and he had six million things attached to his drum set. He played them all, yet his rhythm and his timing was so perfect that he never missed a beat and didn't care what he did. He would sing all those risqué songs and all the boys would ignore the girls and gather round the bandstand to listen. Man, he came out with the dirtiest and funniest things you ever heard. Louis got some of his vocal style from him. Happy was the world's greatest drummer as far as I'm concerned. Paul Barbarin says he got everything he knows from him. Happy was a natural and he was so far ahead of any of the others that I heard. I never did hear a lot of Baby Dodds while he was down here. I might have heard him but he had left town to go on the boats when I started hearing other drummers.

None of the white bands ever had a really good rhythm section. The colored man just seems to have more rhythm in him than the white man. Same with colored dancers; compare Fred Astaire with Bill Robinson. A white dancer may have more technique, but he doesn't have that rhythm. Most white rhythm sections seem too keen on developing technique (a colored rhythm section never does that) and to me, technique has no meaning. Technique is a means to an end and not an end in itself. It's what comes off the drums or out of the end of the horn that counts. Louis Armstrong can fit a whole pile of notes into a break and they all fit perfectly. That's not technique, that's feeling.

The rhythm sections in northern bands love plenty of precision, but they don't swing like a New Orleans rhythm section. And a colored New Orleans rhythm section can out-swing anything. I think the best part of today's colored New Orleans bands is the rhythm sections. This is most noticeable in the street bands. It has just a wonderful soft rhythmic pulse, a round legato feeling, yet it has enough punch and throb in it to drive the band. The bass drum does a few beats and he lets a big gap occur and the rhythm seems to rock right on.

The feeling of the rhythm is tremendous. The beat seems to go on by itself. Anybody that can't play with a rhythm section like that just can't play. That's the only rhythm in the world to play jazz by and the coloured people down here are the only ones who can get it. In a good band everybody contributes to the rhythm and when the band gets going, everybody just floats on top of that rhythm.

A colored New Orleans rhythm section sounds like a great big basket of cotton, so soft and caressing, so liquid, yet it still can whip people into a frenzy. That's the beat I've heard all my life and it's the same beat that I heard from the negro woman bending over a washtub washing clothes, or the bottleman coming down the street. When you hear it, grab it. It makes you want to dance and get out your horn and play.

That's why some of the colored trumpet players could play for hours and hours, because their rhythm sections were so good. They made it easy to play with. I used to enjoy sitting in with George Lewis's band. Slow Drag and Lawrence Marrerro got such a good beat going. It lifted you up and my horn just seemed to play itself. If the rhythm section is wrong it can knock your lip out in fifteen minutes.

If you have a bass, guitar and drums that can stay together, it lifts the front line. If they're good you don't need a piano, as the piano hasn't the sharpness of the beat. But if I have to work with a short rhythm section, I'd lose the guitar first and if I could only use two pieces then I'd just use a piano and drums.

I like the simplest kind of rhythm, just four beats. I've never played in a band that just used two beats. They might accent two of the beats heavier than the others, but they always played four beats to my ears. A drummer might play two beats on the bass drum, but he answers himself with two beats on the snare drum and keeps it going like that. The best beat for me is when they hit one beat on the bass drum followed by a press roll on the snare drum. That sends you forward. They might vary it a little, even four beats on the bass drum for the final chorus, but there's always a carpet under the band of four beats to the measure. The sort of guitar players I like hit the first beat soft, then the second beat hard, the third beat soft and the fourth beat hard. The same with piano players, they must give you that four beats too. I was making a record in New York and I asked the piano player just to give me chords when the band was playing. I showed him just what I meant and he felt insulted. Yet he couldn't get it together with the rhythm section playing all that fancy stuff he wanted to play. He though it was too monotonous just playing chords. That's why most northern rhythm sections are not a success. They're not together, it's like they're all trying to play solos at once. The colored rhythm sections know how to play together instinctively. In New York I played with one bass player once who played more notes than Johnny Guarnieri on piano, but those guys couldn't get a job down here. They don't know how to boot a band. The correct way to pick a bass is with the soft pads at the end of your fingers. But that's no good for New Orleans style, that don't give you any volume or drive. Down here they grab a fist full of notes using the middle part of the fingers and slap the string against the fingerboard to give a double note. That kicks the band along and gives more snap and power to the beat.

Kid Ory used to to make some wonderful bass rhythms behind Johnny Dodds in Joe Oliver's band. Tom Brown and Santo Pecora can do that too, but the best I ever heard do that was Eddie Edwards from the Original Dixieland Band. His playing had more punch than any tailgate trombonist I ever heard. A trombonist like that can give the band a terrific kick and can really drive the band into the final chorus. Trombonists in other cities might be technically better, but they can't kick a band like a good New Orleans trombonist can do.

Most northern musicians play too many notes in the last chorus. As the melody gets more intense, you've got to slow down and not to rush things, but at the same time give it plenty of power. In the final choruses, the cornet should become simpler and simpler, and let the clarinet do all the running. The trombone should push the band to build up the fire and the rhythm should stay steady and hold the tempo. Too many drummers speed up in the final choruses.

I believe that the whole band should get a good attack together right from the first note. That gives a band a good rhythmic start. Now the colored bands won't always start together. Maybe the cornet or the trombone will start something, and the rest of the band will pick it up and come in a few bars later. But I prefer it if the whole band starts together on the first beat.

When I started with Brownlee's Band, I didn't know any better. I hadn't played cornet for some time as I'd been playing violin with the Invincibles. I thought I could just pick up cornet anytime and start blowing. Boy, was I stupid! When I got that job I just took my cornet out of my case on the stand and started blowing right off. After the first set my lip was shot and I couldn't play the rest of the night.

When you start playing you've got to take it easy. It's no good trying to ruin your lip by putting too much strain on it if you're not playing regularly. The most important thing is to get your horn away from your mouth as often as possible. Play as easy as you can. Some nights you're going to have to play hard, if it's a hard driving band. But you'll be surprised at the places where you can relax and get the horn away from your lips. You gotta do this to allow the blood to circulate in your lips. Then you'll develop, in time, a good lip. Of course all this pre-supposes a steady job, you can't get anywhere without a steady job. If you can only play once a week, you're going to find it tough to make any progress. But I know it's hard to practise every night, if you've only got one night a week with a band.

A young cornet player shouldn't try to play too loud at first. Loudness is something you're born with. Just try to get an easy tone and don't strain to play high or loud notes at first. You can ruin your lip trying to play too loud or too high. If you want to play high, take up the piccolo. I usually try to play high on the last chorus in order to get above the band, which is what the cornet is supposed to do, but if you've got the rhythm going right you don't have any trouble hitting those high notes. The rhythm pushes you and there's no strain on the lips. When the rhythm is wrong there's a terrible strain on the lips and it's hard to play.

The only satisfaction you can get out of music is to play professionally and to do that these days you have to be able to read. You can't make any sort of commercial success if you can't read, yet you can't play jazz if you read too much. If you read too much, it slows down your improvisation wits. If you hit a bad note you can't get out of it quick enough. When you're improvising you have to forget about reading and depend on your ear. Practising scales helps if you don't read. It exercises your sub-conscious and makes you a freer thinker than those musicians who depend on reading. You've got to get the scales and chords into your fingering and into your sub-conscious mind, so if you hit a clinker your mind is more flexible and you get out of it quicker.

I have always preferred the cornet to a trumpet. It's more flexible. It's so easy to bend notes on it and slide from one note to another. I think it lends itself to jazz better. I only played trumpet when I worked in big bands, but I always kept a cornet on the stand with me. I've had dozens of cornets; I usually kept them until they were played out. I play an Olds cornet now and it's the best cornet I ever had.

I used to clean out my horn about once every few months. Right after I cleaned it, it sounded great, real easy to blow. Then the next day it was real hard and stayed like that for a week. Cleaning out widened the bore and it took some getting used to. Now I clean it out every day by running water through it and I don't have any trouble.

I use the same kind of Harmon mute that Joe Oliver used. I used to watch Joe using this little bitty mute and the way he kept it in his hand and moved it in and out of the bell. The Harmon mute has got too much of a kick-back if you push it into your bell. Joe used it mainly for high notes as it doesn't respond to low notes too well.

If you're playing a second cornet part in a jazz band, it's a harmony to the lead cornet. You got to keep the melody in your mind, feel the rhythm, and try to get some nice harmonies going. That way you're not going to get in the way of the trombone. Then you can fill in any holes you want. I've not done too much second cornet work, but when I've played I usually find I'm playing a rhythmic part rather than a purely melodic part.

New Orleans musicians have to play any request that comes up, from Grand Opera to the latest hits. If they didn't they'd never get hired again. Jobs are so scarce that if you can't play the request then the next time they're gonna hire a band that can.

Dick Mackie was the cornet player in the Owls. He was 16 when he joined the Owls and he was a great lead man, he had a real dirty tone. He didn't play many notes, but he made every note count. When Dick wanted to quit, Earl Crumb came over and said they had a job for me. I hadn't touched my horn for a couple of years so I said I couldn't do it. Then Earl said it paid $50 a week, so I thought, "Well it's more than I'm making now and if they want me that bad I'll take it." The job was in the basement of the Grunewald Hotel (now the Roosevelt Hotel). Same as when I joined Brownlee's band, I took the job without a lip. No one in the band could read, so I had to learn all the numbers and the arrangements right on the job. Dick stayed in the band a couple of nights while I got my lip in shape and learned the numbers.

I was working at Werlein's when Victor contacted me about a recording they wanted to do with Celestin's band. At that time Celestin had Guy Kelly and another trumpet player in the band. They both sounded a little like Louis and they were always falling out. I wanted the band to work some numbers up so when Victor came down they would be ready. Just across the street from Werlein's, the Rap Truck Company had a warehouse on the second or third floor, so I hired it for the band to rehearse. Guy Kelly was a very mean fellow and the other guy was a very easy-going, good natured fellow. I went up to see Celestin and he pulled out some old march-type negro numbers that I'd never heard before and never heard since. I thought this would be great, but as soon as they started rehearsing there was trouble. They got into a fight and almost broke up the joint. The Rap Truck Company rang up the president of Werlein's and said, "What's going on? That band almost wrecked the place." The President rang down to the head of the department where I was working and complained, so I had to race over there and get them out fast. That was the end of the recording date.

Snoozer Quinn was the greatest guitarist I ever heard and it's too bad that he never made any records to show just how good he was. He was a natural musician. You never saw him without a guitar in his hand. He had a job where he worked 12 hours a day, he just loved to play and he played the most beautiful music you ever heard. I was due to record with Snoozer in a little band I was with, but we had a trombone player who couldn't get his part right when we came to rehearse for the records. We had three rehearsals, going over the same piece over and over again. He never got it right once, so we all got tired and we never did make those records. Except for the trombone player that was a good band. We had Eddie Miller, Siegfried Christensen, Von Gammon on drums, myself and Snoozer. Snoozer also recorded some solos for Victor. A copy of the masters got down here and the guitarist, Joe Capraro, had them for a while. But in the end he lent them out and they disappeared, and then Victor threw out their masters. Columbia did the same thing in Houston, Texas. They recorded Snoozer and lost all the masters before they were released. They figured maybe that he would be way over the people's heads. Snoozer was way ahead of his time. I finally recorded some sides with Snoozer just before he died. He was in hospital and we made some sides – just cornet and guitar – in this little room, about 6 by 10 foot. I was trying to operate the recording machine, keep some of the thread from messing up the needle, keep people out of the room, and play, all at the same time. During one number the telephone started ringing, so I had to throw the phone off the hook. We called that the *Telephone Blues*. I didn't want to tire Snoozer as he was pretty weak then, so I started on a cold lip. By the time my lip had got in shape Snoozer began to get tired and said, "I can't do anymore." He'd been working with an amplified guitar a lot and I had an awful time trying to get him to play without any amplification. Unfortunately there was only a couple of choruses of his picking style, for which he was best known. But at least I got something. The world will never know just how great Snoozer was.

I wish someone would have made a record of the "bottleman" in New Orleans. I never heard anything so "blue" in all my life. The "bottleman" used to come around the neighborhood on a wagon with a cow-bell attached to the horse's neck. He always carried some one cent toys and candy, they called 'em Jaw Breakers. The kids would come out of the houses when they heard him and he would say, "Now, I'll give you this piece of candy or this little chair for so many bottles." He would usually give a toy or a piece of candy for about a dozen bottles, then he would take the bottles to the junk yard and sell them. The "bottleman" had a long tin horn about three feet long with a brass reed at the end. These were Mardi Gras horns that had a wooden mouthpiece to save your mouth from getting cut, but they would take off the mouthpiece and blow directly onto the brass reed. They blew the most hauntingly wonderful "blue" phrases that you ever heard, and all the kids would recognize the sound and come running out of their houses. It was almost like a clarinet, except that it was so much louder than a clarinet.

Without doubt Louis Armstrong is the greatest trumpet player in jazz. Louis has everything, so much physical strength and so much jazz feeling. His tone has the best blues feeling I've ever heard, even today he still has that beautiful blues tone. Everything he plays sounds easy, and that's the way a New Orleans horn should sound, even when playing those high notes in the final chorus. His tone is so big that he cuts through the whole band on those final choruses. Louis will take a popular piece and if there's any chance of playing some blues in there, that will come out of his horn. A lot of people criticize Louis, but it's no fun driving a coal cart. He's been up against strictly commercial people since he left New Orleans and it's remarkable that he's retained what he has. He's still the greatest trumpet player alive, although no one could play more jazz than Joe Oliver did when he was down here. It's difficult for me to say what the New Orleans style is. I only know that I know it when I hear it. I can hear it in Wingy's playing, I can hear it in Louis' playing, but if someone said, "name me one horn man that epitomizes everything about the New Orleans style of playing?" Then I'd have to say. "Joe Oliver." I'm only sorry that people nowadays will never know just how great Joe was. Man, he was really something.

On the way to the graveside, they all walked slowly, following the cornet player. The cornet player was the boss. Sometimes it took them four hours to get them to the cemetery. All the way they just swayed to the music and moaned. At the graveside they chanted questions, such as "Did he ramble?" "Did he gamble?" or "Did he lead a good life until the police shot him down on St James Street?" Then after the body was buried, they'd go back to town and all the way they'd swing. They just pulled the instruments apart. They played the hottest music in the world.

**Wingy Manone**

Joe Oliver had a few numbers that were on sheets of music, but he got away from it as quickly as he could. You see, Joe was no great reader. Joe Oliver was very strong. He was the greatest freak trumpet player I ever knew. He did most of his playing with cups, glasses, buckets, and mutes. He was the best gut-bucket man I ever heard. I called him freak because the sounds he made were not made by valves but through these artificial devices. In contrast, Louis played everything through the horn. **Mutt Carey**

Freddie (Keppard) could play as soft and as loud, as sweet and as rough, as you would want. He loved to play *Pagliacci*, too. Freddie and the other musicians had no idea that the music they were playing was unusual. **Buster Bailey**

My first job was in Billy Phillips' place. We played anything we pleased in that joint; you see, there was no class in those places. All they wanted was continuous music. Man, they had some rough places in Storyville in those days. A guy would see everything in those joints and it was all dirty. It was really a hell of a place to work.

**Mutt Carey**

Mutt Carey, in his day, was equal to Joe Oliver . . . Mutt had a very mellow tone and a terrific swing. The softer the band played, the better Mutt played. The drummer used sandpaper, there being no wire brushes at that time. You could hear every instrument. They seemed to blend better than the average band nowadays. Whenever the band became noisy, Mutt would look back and sideways and say, "Sh,sh," meaning get down softer. That didn't stop them swinging. Some cats can't swing soft. Mutt could make them pretty runs and changes. He was strictly gut-bucket or barrel-house. Nothing technical about his playing. Just swinging all the time, pretty diminished chords. He choked his cornet and made it moan just like Joe Oliver did later. I never will forget Mutt Carey. **Preston Jackson**

If somebody announce you and says you're gonna play *Sister Kate*, well, play *Sister Kate*, play it, let the people understand it. Then after that, you can get off and do what you want, sing or do what you want, long as they know you're playing *Sister Kate*. But if you come out they say play *Sister Kate* and you scat "progressive" style, well, they don't know what you're playing. **Punch Miller**

# New Orleans Style: Trombone

# KID ORY

Edward Ory
trombone

Born: La Place, Louisiana, December 25, 1886
Died: Honolulu, Hawaii, January 23, 1973

*Kid Ory was the most famous of all New Orleans trombonists. He came from a plantation at La Place and settled in New Orleans in 1908, where his band became one of the most popular in the city until he moved to California in 1919. In 1925 he went to Chicago and recorded with Jelly Roll Morton, Johnny Dodds, Louis Armstrong and King Oliver. He returned to Los Angeles in 1929, but left music in 1933 to run a chicken farm with his brother. He guested with Barney Bigard's band in 1942, and then led his own band from 1944 until his retirement in 1966, when he moved to Hawaii.*

I was born in St. John's Parish, LaPlace, Louisiana, on Christmas Day, December 25th, 1886. LaPlace is twenty-nine and three-tenths miles from New Orleans. I travelled it many a time, I should know.

In LaPlace, I used to hear brass bands play all the time, the Pickwick Brass Band and the Onward Brass Band. One was from La Place and the other was from Reserve – just three miles from LaPlace. During the sugar grinding season in the winter time, bands would come up from New Orleans every pay-day. A guy called Peyton, Henry Peyton, he would bring a band there, and sometimes Charlie Galloway. Peyton's band had an accordion and a guitar, it was mostly string music. Galloway's band had horns and played mostly Buddy Bolden's tunes.

Bolden used to pass through La Place on an excursion from New Orleans to Baton Rouge. When the train got to La Place; the band would be set up at the back of the baggage car, and we'd go to the station and listen to them play a number. They was playing right in the doorway, with the horns out there and the bass and drums behind. They'd play at all the stops along the way and the people would board the train. It was a way of advertizing the dance in Baton Rouge. The train would arrive in Baton Rouge about 9 or 9.15, and about 11 o'clock the dance would start, and they'd dance till about 4.30. Then the train would leave about 5, or a little after, and about 8 o'clock that night the train would come back through La Place. They wouldn't play coming back as they were all tired.

I first became interested in music when I was seven years old. I had my own little outfit. We would stand on a bridge at night over the creek and hum different tunes with various harmonies. It was dark and no one could see us, but people could hear us singing and they'd bring us a few ginger cakes and some water. We hummed, and when we knowed the tune itself, the melody, one of us would take the melody and the others would put a three- or four-part harmony to it. Sometimes we couldn't get the correct chord, couldn't get it all the way through, so some would double up. It was good ear training. If we'd hear a brass band playing, say about a block from us, we'd bet to see what key the band was playing in. Boy, I'd win every time.

Then I made some home-made instruments. I made a five-string banjo by cutting a bucket in half, and used thread and fishing chord for strings. But they kept breaking so I started using metal strings. After I made the banjo, well, I had a good idea how other instruments would sound, and I just kept working on them. I made a guitar from a great big cigar box. Then I made a bass from a big soap box, with a handle for the neck, and used different size fishing chord to make the four strings. Then I made a violin from a smaller cigar box and burned out the scroll holes with a red hot iron. Later I made a drum from a big tin tub, and put some cloth inside it to stop it ringing too much. Boom, Boom, you know. Then I made a footpedal. They all sounded pretty good.

I had my own little outfit; it was a kids' band and we all played these home-made instruments. I played all the instruments, but my first regular instrument was banjo. I had the two Matthews boys: Louis "Chif" Matthews and Joe "Stonewall" Matthews and myself. The bass player wasn't doing so good, so I gave him the banjo and I played bass. Then I added another kid named "Bull" White and Eddy Robertson, who we called "Rabbit." I called it the Woodland Band, after the Woodland Plantation.

At first I couldn't get a job, so I started promoting fish fries, so we could play. Our plantation was about 75 feet from the levee, so I used to keep my line in the river all the time. Any time I wanted a fish, I pulled one out and then threw the line back in. At the fish fries we had different kinds of fish: catfish, perch, and we also had potato salad and beer. Five cents a drink and five cents for a fish sandwich. We'd just find an empty house and set up. People would often move to another plantation, and there was often empty houses. We'd bring some candles in and light them up and go to work. Sometimes, we'd get in a pinch; people then didn't have much furniture in the houses, and they'd let us come in the house to have the party, and we'd give them all the food and beer they wanted. Whole families would come to our fish fries and we'd play *Make Me A Pallet On The Floor*, waltzes and schottisches and a lot of old numbers.

I was able to make some money out of it. I was the leader, the promoter, the bookkeeper, treasurer and fish fryer. Then I got some girls to do the fish frying for 50 cents a night, I was a big shot then! We played every weekend and by the time I was ten years old, I'd saved up enough money to promote a big picnic after a baseball game. A New Orleans team came to play the country boys. The owner of the park was my daddy's first cousin and I told him what I wanted to do. I said I wanted to hire the park after the ball game, so we could buy some real instruments. My daddy's cousin and his partner had the grocery store on the plantation, and they gave me everything I needed. Beer and all the foods, all the meats, they gave me everything, free. They were the only ones that had the liquor license around there. During the game I was selling beer and food, then after the game I charged 15 cents to come to the picnic.

You see, after my daddy died, my daddy's first cousin wanted me to work on the plantation with his son. I told him I didn't like plantation work, I just wanted to play music. He accused me of being lazy, but when he heard us play and saw everybody enjoying the music, he said he was sorry, and he said, "You know, everyone is good for something in this world. If there's anything I can help you with, let me know." That's why he was so helpful.

So I made enough money on the picnic to buy the instruments. I bought a valve

trombone, violin, twelve-string guitar, bass, cornet and drum. By that time I had the two Matthews boys; "Chif" took up the cornet and "Stonewall" already knew the guitar. I also had Lawrence Duhé, Alfred Lewis on bass, Eddy Robertson played drums, and myself on valve trombone.

No one taught me how to play. I just taken it up on a Wednesday and on Saturday night I was playing for a dance. I'd come up with music. Sometimes, when brass bands would be playing for a big banquet, the guys would put the horns down and be drinking beer, I'd slip in and get one of the horns and try to blow it. I'd notice how they were putting it into their mouth, and I'd just kept on until I got a tone. When I first started I could only play in one key, but I kept adding and, before long, I could play in all the keys. We were all self-taught.

The people around there would all be looking for a place to go on Saturday night, and they would all flock to where they could get beer and whisky. So I organised a dance every Saturday night and a picnic every Sunday afternoon. We also played up and down the road, from La Place to Baton Rouge. We always dressed the best way we could, but when we got the real instruments, I bought all coats to match, you know, jackets to wear with any kind of pants. Peddlers used to come around the house, and you could get these jackets for 25 cents a week. Some of the boys would wear them out, so I'd take 'em home after the job, so they'd be clean for the next job. They were grey and blue, and we wore white shirts and bow ties.

The first horn I had wasn't real good. I only paid $4 for it and it had a few holes which I filled up with soap. So long as the soap didn't get damp it was all right. If I started blowing bubbles, I'd tell the rest of the guys, "Go ahead, I'll catch up," and I'd have to put more soap in there. When I was eleven I got a better instrument. When I was fourteen I'd saved up enough money to get a better trombone and I went down to New Orleans to buy it. I was staying with my sister on Jackson Avenue and Robertson Street, and I had just bought this valve trombone from Werlein's music store. I was just running over the horn at my sister's, blowing to see how it sounded – I had already tried it in the music store – and Buddy Bolden happened to pass by. He must have stayed out there and heard me play a little. He knocked at the door. "Young man," he said, "Are you blowing the trombone?" "Yeah." He said, "Well, you know who I am?" I said, "I don't really." "I am the King." "King who?" "Bolden." I said' "Glad to know you, Mr. Bolden." He said, "You live here?" "Not exactly. My sister lives here, I live out in the country." He said, "Well, I'd like to have you work with me. You sound very good." And so I said, "Wait a minute," I was so tickled, you know. I thought "Oh man, I'm going to play with King Bolden." I went and got my sister so he could explain to her what he wanted. But she said, "Oh, no, you have to go back home, go to school. You promised your daddy you're going to stay there till you 21." But later I often got down at weekends to sit-in with King Bolden.

At the time when I saw Bolden, he was brown skinned, with reddish-black hair. A round face and plump. Had a sort of Maori look about him. He was well built, but not very tall, about the size of Jim Robinson, but not quite as tall. He never practised in the house; he practised on the box step by the sidewalk. He blew so loud he'd blow everyone out of the house. Bolden got most of his tunes from the "Holy Roller Church", the Baptist church on Jackson Avenue and Franklin. I know he used to go to that church, but not for religion, he went there to get ideas on music. He'd hear these songs and he would change them a little. In those Baptist Churches, they sometimes had drums and a piano while the people sang and clapped their hands. Sometimes they'd have guests and invite a trumpet player or a trombone player to come over and play with them. What we're doing now is about sixty years behind what happened then. That's where Buddy got it from and that's how it all started. Buddy had quite a few of his own compositions too, like *Make Me A Pallet On The Floor* and he also got lots of tunes from the rag man. The rag man used to come around to buy old rags and he'd blow this ten cent toy horn – something like the kids use for Christmas, no valves or keys on it – but he'd play a real tune. Sometimes the notes weren't true notes, but it was enough to give you an idea if you wanted to add to it. Bolden, he stole lots of things from the rag man. You have to give him the credit for starting the ball rolling, but he wasn't really a musician. He didn't study, I mean he was gifted, playing with effect, but no tone. He just played loud.

I went back to La Place and continued playing at weekends around La Place and up as far as Baton Rouge; all the sawmill towns, the society balls, picnics. When I was in Garyville, a small sawmill town, a fellow by the name of Mosby had a slide trombone. He wanted ten dollars for it. I had to borrow some of the money, but I soon had enough to get it.

I'd often go to New Orleans to hear bands. I might be working around Baton Rouge on Sundays and after the job was over, I'd catch the train, it was 90 cents. Sometimes I'd go right through La Place and straight to New Orleans for a dance or a lawn party. I'd hear Edward Clem, Bolden and John Robichaux. Bolden was my favourite band, then Robichaux. I knew Freddie Keppard from the country. He was playing violin then and had a little band. Once we were playing about three miles from them and we sold out; there was no more beer, no more liquor or food to sell. So we got off about an hour early and went to where he was playing. Willie Cornish was playing baritone horn with them. They had no trombone, so I played with them. I said to Cornish, "Why are you playing the baritone?" He said, "That's the best I could do, I didn't have anything else to play on."

The last time I saw King Bolden was at the Masonic Hall. I stayed until the dance was over on a Monday night, and he was having a little money trouble. He had spent all the deposit he'd received on the engagement and when they paid him, he didn't have enough money to finish paying the boys. He said, "Here's your car ride, boys." He looked in his hand and he only had 60 cents left. "This is for Chookie," that was his wife, "ain't anyone going to get this but Chookie," and he walked away. Next time I heard he'd gone crazy and was in Jackson, Mississippi.

I'd always wanted to live in New Orleans. So in 1907, at 4.30 in the morning on Christmas Day, I finally got to be twenty-one. That morning, I walked the three miles to the station and caught the 8 o'clock train to New Orleans. And I been gone ever since.

My brother had a saloon right across from Storyville on Conti and Claiborne. He was married and didn't stay there, but he had a nice room upstairs. He gave me the place to stay. I didn't have to pay any rent. My first job was with George Jones's band at Pete Lala's in Storyville. He had three pieces, himself on bass, a guitar and a piano, then he added me on valve trombone, making four pieces. The bar was in the front and the bandstand was facing it, at the back. The bandstand was raised about four or five feet and you sat down with your back towards Canal Street. All kinds of people came in there. Racehorse people and all. Boy, he had a good spot there. The girls would come in there, after hustling on the street, you know. Down the block was the cribs, you see. They'd make a few dollars, then they'd close up and say, "I'm going cabareting awhile." They'd come in and pick up some guy and then go back. We worked there 8 till 4. A dollar and a half a night and tips, and whatever George didn't steal from us. I stayed there about three weeks, and I got hold of enough money to send for my band.

When they arrived, I rented a furniture wagon and I had two large signs made, saying, "New Band in Town. From La Place, Louisiana, Woodland Band." I put my name down as manager and put my phone number, my brother's phone number and headquarters at Conti and Claiborne. I also had handout cards, you know, throw away cards. The two signs were fastened on the sides and we hitched up two horses and rode around to advertize ourselves. At every corner we stopped to play and people could see the signs. Then the phone started ringing and the first job I got was at the Globe Hall. It was a big place,had a capacity of about 2,000 people, but they tore it down later. Then I started working over in Gretna at weekends, and soon afterwards at the Economy Hall, and Co-operators Hall and up in Milneberg. During Lent, you could get a job any time you wanted in the District. All you did is walk in there with your band, and look and see where there's no band working, and someone would say, "Where you guys going? Do you want to work?" "Yeah. What you paying?" "Dollar and a half a night." Boom! It kept you eating. 'Course you couldn't buy so much with a dollar and a half, but you would probably pick up a dollar and a half in tips, sometimes.

The roughest place I ever worked in was the Funky Butt Hall, an old church on Perdido Street. They hired it for dances, then some jack-leg preacher would come in and put up a big sign, "Reverend So-and So," and it would be a Baptist Church for a while. Then someone would come back and open it as a dance hall again. That was the toughest hall I ever worked in. If you didn't have a razor or a gun, you couldn't get in there. There were fights going on while we were playing, in the hall, on the sidewalk. People would get killed. I only played there once. I said, "No more."

We were still known as the Woodland Band when I started working at Lincoln Park the following summer. It was a big place with an indoor roller skating rink and a big pavilion. The roller skating rink doubled as a dance floor and was about 75 feet from the pavilion. Before I started working there, Buddy Bolden would work at the skating rink and steal Robichaux's customers away. Bolden would begin at 8 o'clock and Robichaux's band had been playing over at the Pavilion since 4 o'clock. Buddy would set up and play a number then pretty soon he would go over to the side window and look out, he'd say, "Well, boys, I guess we'd better call our children home," and he'd start blowing right out of the window. The people would all leave the pavilion and flock around, go in the side gate. When the place would be packed, he'd go back to playing the dance and stay there till four in the morning. Buddy Bartley was the promoter at Lincoln Park, and, as a special attraction, he had a balloon which he'd go up in every Sunday afternoon. But he gave it up when he once came down through a factory chimney. He could have been killed. He just came out full of smut, and said, "Give me a beer," that's all he wanted. He was the one who invented this dance called the Ping Pong. When I started working there Bolden had gone and I followed Robichaux in there, playing in the pavilion. Then all the women started calling me "Kid." We played there there about two Sundays, and on the third Sunday I walked into the place and saw a big sign up on the Boulevard: "Music by Kid Ory." I said, "Say, where did you get this idea of the Kid?" He said, "It's what all the girls call you. You are the Kid from now on." Buddy Bartley was the one that gave me the name.

Then, I taken all Robichaux's work at the Yacht Club, the Country Club and all those society parties up and down St. Charles Avenue, and the Tulane Gymnasium. That was more money, you know. Got away from cheapskates. Then Robichaux come to me and said, "Young man, you play a nice horn. I'd like you to come and work with me." I said, "Thank you, Mr. Robichaux, I'm doing alright." I always called him Mr. Robichaux.

I had a guy named Jake White playing bass with me, he was the worst bass player I ever heard in my life. Then Manuel Perez told me about Eddie Garland, who was playing out at Dixie Park. I told him I needed good bass player. He said, "Yeah, I know a guy, driving a barrel wagon, Eddie Garland. Here's his phone number." So I called him. That was the first time he joined my band.

I first heard Louis Armstrong when I was doing a Labor Day parade in 1912. The band parading behind us was a kids' band from the Waifs' Home. Louis and Kid Rena were in the band, and I heard this trumpet behind me, you know, good solid tone. We stopped for a beer break and a sandwich, and he's still blowing. I said to him, "Come here, I want to tell you something, you're doing a good job." "Thank you, Mr. Ory." I said, "You're going to be all right some day, you keep that up." So I kept him in mind all the time. Well, he got out right after that, got out of the Home. He used to go around to them honky-tonks, go in there and play a little bit.

After "Chif" Matthews left, I got Mutt Carey. Mutt played with me quite a while. Joe Oliver used to come around where we played at Lincoln Park and St. Katherine's Hall and various places. He would say, "Why won't you give me a chance some time?" I said, "Well, when you get good enough." He said "But I'm trying." So finally Papa Mutt dropped out. He had a day job and he felt he couldn't do both jobs, so I told him it would be best for him to try and hold on to one job, if he wanted that job, and I'd have to get someone else. So I got Joe Oliver.

I advertized more than any other band in New Orleans. Sometimes I'd be busy on Sundays, playing out at the Lake, you know, picnics. So if I had a dance on a Monday night, I'd advertize it during the week before. Just did it late in the afternoon. I was the first one to advertize on the back of an automobile truck, so we could catch the other bands, catch the horses. They couldn't get out of the way. It was lots of fun, you know. Most of the bands would just blast and play loud all the way through. We'd get on a corner, play the introduction and come down softly. People would just run out of the house and gang around the truck and start dancing. They couldn't hear it way off, so they'd get close, you see. Bring them to me with sweetness, I guess. Plenty of rhythm. You could hear everything, but it wasn't blasting. They used to tie the wagons together if there was two bands on the street. Black Benny used to do that, rope the wagons together. The other guys were trying to get away from us and they were dragging us along with them to the next corner. One day we met Joe Oliver's band on the street. Got beat so bad he asked me for a job. He didn't have a good tone then, just loud.

All the clubs dressed kind of sporty. Beaver hats, and well, just like the clubs do now. Then some wore blue shirts, straw hats, collars wide open, one suspender down. A lot of the brass bands wore colorful uniforms too. There were a lot of good bands in New Orleans then, a lot of different bands. I liked Freddie Keppard's band better than I did all the rest of them. Freddie was very powerful. He really played a lot of trumpet down there. He was the best until Joe Oliver came up with that different style. Freddie had gone away by then. Joe used lots of mutes, he created a mute to make those "wa-wa" sounds. He used a glass or a bottle, or his hand at the end of his horn, to make the sounds moan higher or lower. I never seen Freddie use a mute. He could get some good effects just with the open horn.

Bunk Johnson played very good; his style of trumpet sounded like he was always behind, but he'd always wind up with the rest. Sometimes you'd think he was going to miss, the way he'd just fall behind. That was characteristic of Bunk's playing

I was playing every place in New Orleans. But, when I found out how much money the guys were making off me, I started promoting my own dances. I rented the Economy Hall and the Co-operators Hall – I tied them up for a whole year – I rented both halls. I sometimes got Buddy Petit to work with me, and I'd put him at the other hall when I couldn't get anybody to play over there. Sometimes, I kept the Co-operators Hall dark, until I couldn't get any more in the Economy Hall, then I opened both halls.

At that time I had Oliver, Manuel Manetta and Johnny Dodds with me. The war was on in Europe. Musicians were being drafted. Oliver was too old to be drafted, but Manetta, Dodds and myself were all eligible. Manetta got his draft papers. I got a job in the shipyards, until they told me, "Everyone knock off, everything's okay, no more work." I was so happy, I jumped on top of a streetcar. I was still expecting to get my draft papers and Johnny Dodds was real worried. The following Tuesday, we were playing for Major Behnman at the Dixie Brewery on Tulane Avenue, and we found out that married men weren't going to be drafted. I was real happy. Me and Johnny Dodds were the only ones who were married.

In 1917, I had an offer to go to Chicago and at that time I was running the two halls. They offered me $50 a week, but I was making $300 and $400 a night off my dances, and working all the rest of those bandstands, so I said "Why go out of business and go and work for someone for nothing, by going to Chicago?" Joe Oliver and Jimmie Noone were with me then. They said, "We'd like to go to Chicago." I said, "You want the job? Here's the telegram." They didn't have the brains to get carfare from the man. They used their own money to get the tickets and didn't have any money left to eat. When I took them down to the station, I gave them ten dollars each so they could buy some food on the journey.

Then after Joe left, Louis started with me around 1917. Some years earlier, Louis used to sit in with my band when we played at the National Park at Third and Willow. Louis was only in short pants and Black Benny Williams would tie him to his wrist, so he wouldn't get lost in the crowd. He'd come in and play *Ole Miss*, and a blues, and *Sister Kate* – he only knew three tunes! Mutt was with me then and he used to borrow Mutt's horn. *Sister Kate* was really his tune, it was called *Get Off Katy's Head* then, but Piron told a different story. Clarence Williams stole my composition, *Do What Ory Say* and called it *Mama's Baby Boy*. We didn't have no copyright on tunes then. Louis sometimes played with us while Joe was with the band. Joe was real good by this time and a big draw. He was in love with Mary Mack, and he got Louis (he used to call him "Dipper") to play in his place from 8 till 11. There were lines of people outside the hall, but they wouldn't come in. About 11 o'clock when Joe came in, the whole place filled up. We called him "chalk-eye", then I named him "King" from the way he wore his derby, tilted over his bad eye, it looked like a crown.

I also had a brass band, Kid Ory's Brass Band. But there was so much work with the dances, that sometimes I was so tired I'd turn the brass band jobs over to some other band. Most of the funerals I used to play for were for the gamblers and the hustlers. They all used to support my dances, and when a friend would die – they wouldn't give him a dollar when he was hungry, but they would all put up five dollars to bury him. The biggest funeral I ever played was for a boy named Kirk. He was the hottest pimp in Storyville. Diamonds in his garters and all over his mouth. So many people came out, you would think it was the President of the United States that was dead. We had three bands out that day. When you had three bands you were in big business.

Louis was with me when Pete Lala and I were running dances together at his place on Claiborne, between Conti and St. Louis Streets. Then Pete Lala got mad when I didn't cut him in on the dances at the Economy Hall and the Co-operators Hall. So he got about fifty cops to go around and run my customers away. I felt I was going to lose my health down there – I didn't like the climate – so I packed up and came to Los Angeles. That was in 1919. I had close on $500 deposit on different jobs. I refunded all the money back to the promoters, told them I was sorry. They told me, "Well, you're an honest man." Told them I was losing my health. That was the only way I could get out of the contracts. I wasn't lying about it.

I planned to go to Chicago, but I thought I'd try Los Angeles first. I got all the boys together to discuss the trip to California. We met at Ben Mulligan's saloon. We had supper and drank a lot of whisky and wine. Louis, Johnny Dodds and Joe Lindsey and myself all got on our knees and swore we were all going to California.

As soon as I got to Los Angeles, some dude called Lee Locking from Galveston, Texas, called me. He was opening a place called the Cadillac on Central Avenue, across the street from Union Station. He asked me to put a band in there. So, after I'd been there about a month, I wired for my band to come out and sent tickets. I sent a telegram to Manetta, who had been playing piano with us, to get the band together. But by that time Louis had taken the job on the boat, so Manetta got Papa Mutt. The porters at the depot told Johnny Dodds that he'd better not go to California, as he would be sent back, like Frankie Duson, 'cause he couldn't read. He wouldn't come. So Manetta got Wade Whaley for clarinet. Papa Mutt and Whaley had been working together at the Bungalow with Walter Decou and Mack Lacey. Mutt and Whaley both wanted to go and Whaley was unhappy about working with Decou. Then Joe Lindsey didn't want to go, he wanted to be a gambler, so, as Lacey had just died, Manetta got Alfred Williams from the Sam Morgan band. We didn't take no bass.

When they got to Los Angeles, I hired a furniture wagon and two mules, just like we used to do in New Orleans, and set up the band on the wagon. The houses in California all had galleries on the second floor, but the doors were blocked off and people didn't sit out on the upstairs porch like they did in New Orleans. When the people heard the music they all come busting down the doors on the galleries. That night the Cadillac was packed with people.

In 1921, my band was working at the Creole Café on Third and Wood in Oakland. One day the Spikes brothers asked me to record for them. They were both saxophone players and they had a music store in Los Angeles. So we took the train down from Oakland and made the records in about three hours. That was the first time I had seen a recording set up. They had big horns, like the ones we used to sing into – megaphones. We each played into a different horn, but the drums and things, they'd just shake along. Some of them came out alright. *Ory's Creole Trombone* came out good the first time, but some of the others we had to go over again. That's the time we had Dink Johnson playing with us. We picked him up in Los Angeles, when Wade wanted to stay in Oakland. Dink patted his feet too loud, so we put a pillow under his feet. But he was still too loud, so we got a mattress off a bed and put that under his feet. He was overpowering the drums and everyone else. The drum didn't record properly. Ben Borders was our drummer. He was a fair drummer, but he didn't have much of a beat on the bass drum.

Henry Martin was the best drummer I ever had in my band. Next, Ed Robertson, the boy that started out with me. Might have to pull a straw between the two of them to figure out which one was better. Henry Martin was like a metronome. You couldn't move him after you thumped your feet. You couldn't make him go faster and you couldn't make him go slower. Any number with funny lyrics to it, like animal noises, he would find a way to imitate the noises. He mainly worked in Storyville with Manuel Perez, but he would work for me too when I needed him. Then he quit drums and took up the guitar for a while, but he starved. I heard he went back to drums later, but he couldn't make it. Joe Lindsey was also a very good drummer.

In 1925 I wanted to see the country. Oliver was waiting for me in Chicago, so I disbanded. I had two bands, I gave one to Papa Mutt and the other to Tudi Garland.

When I arrived in Chicago. it was a Sunday night, and I went to the Entertainers on 35th Street. Carroll Dickerson's band was playing there. Noré Dutrey was in the band, and as soon as I walked in he spied me and said, "There's the Kid." When they had a break they all came over to the table, talking to me, and insisted on me playing a couple of numbers with them. That night, Doc Cook was there and he wanted a trombone player for his number two band at the Municipal Pier out at the Lake. They were going up there for the summer. So I went out there and played from 8 till 12. A

*Kid Ory with his daughter Babette.*

couple of days after, Noré Dutrey was taken ill with asthma, he was so sick I worked both jobs, 8 till 12 with Cook and rushed back and did 1 a.m. till 5 with Dickerson.

Then I started recording with Louis. He wrote to me from New York, he told me he was going to leave Fletcher Henderson. He heard I was coming to Chicago and would I record with them? I worked at the Dreamland with Louis for a while. We were doing real good, so Louis asked for more money. Bill Bottoms, the owner, wouldn't pay it, so we quit. Then I went with Joe Oliver at the Plantation.

We didn't rehearse much on those records with Louis. We rehearsed right in the studio before we started. If we were going to do eight numbers, we'd start about 45 minutes, or, an hour at the most, with the whole numbers. Same with Jelly's records. He had music, but he told me not to worry about my part. He once wrote something out for me and I played it over. "That don't sound like you," he said, "forget it." He told Simmie [Omer Simeon] that too. He told me, "Don't worry about the music. I can't write your music." When I wound up I was recording with eight bands over five years. Once I made $600 in a day recording with two bands. They wanted me to get my own band together to make records, but I figured that if I had my own recording band I'd have to sign a contract. I was making more money freelancing with different bands. I've recorded so many numbers, that I haven't even heard 'em all. I would have recorded more but I just couldn't take it.

I went with Oliver to New York in 1927, but Oliver didn't have any more work, so I came back and worked for Dave Peyton. I left Chicago in late 1929 and came back to California and been here ever since.

I had some good times in New Orleans. Sure missed those picnics they used to have. All kinds of seafood: boiled crabs, shrimps, crawfish, fried fish, fried oysters, gumbo, and barrels of beer. I can sure fix up that kind of food, too. The boys that stayed there never made any money at all. Liked the gumbo down there, I guess. Musicians never made much money in New Orleans, didn't need to. Living was cheap and they could get by.

You've got to know your horn and always try to do better. Even when I was making it big in Chicago, I used to go for lessons. Used to go to a German teacher from the symphony orchestra. I wanted to see if I could get a better tone. You've got to learn to play easy. I smile when I blow.

# ROY PALMER

Roy Palmer
trombone

Born: New Orleans, Louisiana, April 2, 1892
Died: Chicago, Illinois, December 22, 1963

*Roy Palmer, as was the custom in New Orleans, almost certainly played with a number of leaders and in many places during the years 1914 and 1915. After going through two interviews I did with Willie Hightower in Chicago, the only dates he mentioned from his early career were 1908, when he opened his ice cream parlor, and 1915 when he left New Orleans for Chicago. Willie told of a long association with Roy (he even had some music lessons from him) and mentioned engagements everywhere, from the St. Charles Hotel to uptown honky-tonks, without giving any other dates.*

*Since all old-time musicians here played, more or less, the same basic style, they could play with any group without notice or rehearsal. As an example, there was Milneberg, where there were a couple of hundred "camps" (summer cottages built out over the water). On a weekend morning there might be as many as twenty bands going out to the Lake on the Smoky Mary train. If a musician didn't have a job that day he would go down to the foot of Elysian Fields Avenue, the terminal of the train, and bands would be formed right there before boarding the train.*

*There were a few exceptions of New Orleans bands that had a somewhat stable personnel and long engagements, but even today, for the relatively few musicians remaining, a man may work with several bands in different places each month. With the unbelievable quantity of musicians and engagements in the old days practically every musician's business card stated "Music Furnished For All Occasions." So at this date there is no way we'll ever know precisely where and with whom Roy played at any given time.*

*When this interview was done at Roy's home (5123 S. Wells, Chicago) he had quit playing trombone and was working in a steel mill. He said he would have to "soak it in oil" to make the horn work again. His wife, Jessie, was a one-time trombone player and seemed to know almost as much about the personnel of different bands as Roy did.*

*Four years later, after considerable hunting, we found Roy again. He had moved. As usual he seemed busy and tired, but this time he seemed quite bitter and quite definite about not wanting to return to any musical activities. He refused to be interviewed again and talked about being cheated so much in the past, probably on record and composer's royalties. Of the old days he said, "We used to have so much fun playing music."*

I was born in New Orleans in the year of 1892, April 2nd. After learning to play well, I got out with different bunches and I made good. I made a success in music, playing with different bands and being hired out in bands that I didn't belong to. They could give me a break and I did well.

I had an uncle named Charles Henderson, who played trumpet. He was a very good musician. He used to have a band, and I was small and noticed him very much. In fact, that's what caused me to take up music. I didn't know no instrument, couldn't play no instrument at the time but I just listen to the sounds. After I became around 15, I

began to pick up different instruments and took lessons on them and learned to play very well. I came from uptown, around Carrollton. That's way up. We lived on Palmer's Avenue. It was named after a doctor, an old doctor. After my uncle died I got instruction from Jim Humphrey on instruments. There was a fellow named Frank Welch, that I took lessons on arranging and writing from. He taught me different phrases and how to keep out of the other fellow's way. He give me instructions on the chords, how to form a chord and play the melody. Never get into the other fellow's melody. He was a very good teacher. He played trumpet himself. He was a kind fellow, and that way, if you've got a good kind teacher, you can learn more 'cause you're encouraged, see!

First, I played violin and, after I learned scales and different things, I switched around different instruments and finally wound up on the trombone. But how I come to be more familiar with arranging was because I knew many instruments. That's why when you hear me play trombone I never jump into somebody's part.

In the early days in New Orleans we had lots of jobs to play through the week such as funerals and things like that, parties and picnics and other things. We did a lot of lawn parties. We did a lot of that work, giving dances in the open air, generally a large space surrounded by a high fence. There would be usually 100 or 200 people there. Sometimes we played on regular pavements for these things but the people mostly didn't go for those as they would wear out their shoes on the pavement. The people went for dances where canvas was laid, or a wooden floor.

I played with the Onward Band and with the Tuxedo band. The Tuxedo Band was "Sonny" Celestin's band. He was very good. I played lots of parades too. They paid two dollars an hour. They only paraded about two hours and a half, so you only made four or five dollars on a parade, unless it was Carnival; then we made six or eight hours.

Now as to Buddy Bolden. He was a really loud trumpet player, one of the loudest you ever heard. You could hear him clear to the lake, but the numbers he played, you might say, he was used to those numbers and he only played those numbers. Just played the numbers that he was more familiar with. All those musicians played their own tunes, played their own music, their own breaks that they used themselves.

We started an orchestra together, mc and George Foster and his brother Willie, who played violin, Henry Zeno, the drummer, and a couple of others. We got together and had a very nice orchestra. There was so many good musicians, and trombone players. One fellow's name was George Williams. Oh, he was wonderful. He had played with Handy, up in Memphis. I said that he was a better trombone player than I am, but he said that I was better than he was. You can't find those trombone players now. Low positions, make the scales right down in the low positions. Keep down to your seventh position, but they never use that nowadays much. I had a big embouchure. At one time I could hit the highest note and drop down to the lowest note. I used to practise that. Some fellows said, "Well, you can make low notes but you can't make high notes, see." Well, I fought hard to get both. Sometimes I would catch myself, when I'd be playing the melody and make that high note and drop down. Now that's easy to do. You get the embouchure for it and you can do it to look like it's without the least effort. The instruments they use now, trumpets and trombones, they mostly use shallow mouthpieces.

Not so deep. They're made special for high notes. I recommend a medium mouthpiece. Not too deep and not too shallow. Just medium bore. That way you have the ability to make what you wanna make and you don't have to have much help. I used a Conn horn. Later I liked the King. That is a good trombone, one of the best. With a King, you can't blast it. Not those trombones. You never blast because they have a large bore. When you make high notes they come out so sweet and nice. As for the bell, a little bell makes sharp notes, just like the trumpet; a piercing tone. I don't think it's so good. A seven inch bell. That's the best one to get. Just a medium. If you get too big a bell it holds, stays right around the bunch, it don't go out, see. The people sitting out there, they listen to the band. They wanna hear all the instruments.

I think the best way for a trombonist is to hold his trombone straight in front of him and just a little up. Not too high. Just a little up. That makes the sound go right over their heads, the people dancing, I mean. I wash my horn when I get through playing too. I use hot water and soap, and long as I've been playing I go to run it through the system. You just do it to dampen it up 'cause a horn don't sound good too dry. The best way to practise to get a good embouchure is to play the lowest note you can on the horn. Play the lowest note, like the pedal note, see how long you can hold that pedal note then go up in the middle register and go up in the high register and when you get through doing that, you're tough. I used to practise sometimes, two and three hours. That's why I could do anything I wanted with the trombone. Another thing: what kills certain fellows, they use too many mouthpieces. They use a mouthpiece tonight and tomorrow night they got another mouthpiece. The next time you see 'em they got another mouthpiece. You can't get used to one that way. A mouthpiece has to become a part of you. If you lose the mouthpiece you're in bad shape. When I changed a horn, I kept the mouthpiece.

I did most of my teaching up here. Not much in New Orleans. I had around 40 pupils. Some ten white boys from over on the West Side. Maybe 40 in all. I was teaching different instruments. They'd come at night. For a while, I wasn't doing nothing but teaching. I didn't have to work. The only thing was, when I would teach, I'd give too much time. I can't get away from that. I know you're doing good. I wanna see you doing good. Some teachers would hold it to half an hour and then you had to go. My wife used to tell me, "My goodness. You're teaching a fellow that long?" I see him doing good and I just get, you know, I wanna see him still doing better. I never worried about time. I takes too much interest in my scholars. That's the trouble. I used to teach clarinet and violin too. I played a little trumpet, bass fiddle, bass horn and bass drum. I had to know 'em, see, so I just kept on, got 'em all down. Like I say, I never worried about nothin'. If you get to worrying, you gonna get old sooner. I see fellows around my age, I declare, I feel sorry for them. Yeah, all to pieces and it seems they worry a lot. It's no use to worry. You eat plenty, get your food, have a nice meal but to run around and get drunk and all that, laying out in the snow, that's bad.

In New Orleans there was a lot of real good trombone players. There was a fellow by the name of Zue Robertson. He was <u>the</u> man. In fact he was one of the best fellows that would go with me in a band. A brass band. Playing those brass band jobs, you know, we played together all the time. He played first and I played second. He played on one side and I played on the other. Funerals and like that. He was a sweet trombone player, not no whole load of hoarseness, he just played nice and sweet. When he had to play loud, he could play loud. We practised together. I used to go to his house every day and he would come to my house. He must have been six or seven years older than I was. Also there was Jack Carey, Mutt Carey's brother. He's a man that played the trombone and never known music. Never a note. He never worried about notes. He could play but he never worried about notes. He mostly played music by his head. But for music, Zue was the man. Zue was a nice reader. He could play a little bit of piano too. Only thing about him, he learned to play trombone correct and he wouldn't play with a fellow if he didn't play right. A man that came in and played with him, played double with him, and he blasted. Oh! he wouldn't worry with him at all. That's why they say he was kind of funny, you know.

George Filhe was a very nice trombone player. I used to see him play in marches. They played marches and things like that. That's how I learnt. I found out that playing trombone, when you're making those smears, I paid careful attention to him, and watched him closely on a lot of music he played. Then there was Joe Petit with the valve trombone. That's what he used to play. They had a fellow that played with Joe Petit named Yank Johnson, that's Buddy Johnson's brother. They could put out some powerful tones. They didn't think about sweetness. They blasted out, I mean they could blast them tunes. In a parade it's alright but playing a dance, or in a place where a party was, you couldn't do that. You could do it, but the people wouldn't like it so well. A lot of fellows, colored and white, won't do on a trombone. I listened at 'em. They handled an instrument alright, but they don't understand how to take advantage of it. They just blow, blow, blow. They get up

*Roy Palmer*

there and they ain't gonna let you play your part right. They gonna try to go over you and all that stuff. When you play together, then you sound nice. Sometimes the leader has to tell, "Shh, shh," to make 'em go down. A fellow asked me, "How do you know when to get soft?" Well, if you're watching the leader he'll tell you. Or you feel it.

You know Sidney Bechet . . . well, Sidney came right up around me. We played together several times down there. He was a good clarinet player. He used to come around, that's where he got his start, with us. We used to take him and let him play. He had that style too. Big Eye Louis' style. He was glad to sit in 'cause he was catchin' on. A lot of stuff. He had that system like Louis, Big Eye Louis, but he wasn't reading so much. They tell me Big Eye Louis didn't read so much either.

I played a couple of times on the boats. I didn't like it too much. I was afraid of the boat going up and down like that. Just thinking about that boat sinking, I can't swim, see. That's why I wouldn't bother with those jobs.

Around 1918 I moved to Chicago. I came into Chicago with a band, and from that we played on the shows. Different shows, Pantages, the circuits and all that. The band was called "The New Orleans Jazzband," and Louis Keppard was the manager. He was our guitar player. I don't know if he changed to anything else, but that's what he usually featured, guitar. We had a trumpet player by the name of "Sugar" Johnny Smith, and he was one of the most efficient trumpet players that you gonna find. He played nice sweet trumpet and didn't make any records. He died about 1923 or '24. He didn't stay long. The clarinetist was this fellow Duhé, Lawrence Duhé. Now he played a C clarinet and he was very good. We had several other musicians that came along the line too. Then Wellman Braud, he took Eddie Garland's place. We changed so many musicians. We played different theaters. We went from out of here to St. Louis, to Peoria and up around Rock Island. We had an act. A small act. Mamie Elaine was the girl that was on the show. She played a part, you might say. She played a comedienne part and she sang on the show.

We began to build up a nice orchestra around Chicago. We had nice musicians, even a girl playing with us from Chicago. That was Lillian Hardin, the girl that married Louis. We had her playing with us a long time. Afterwards, Joe Oliver came in, and he took over the orchestra. We left The Dreamland, and we came over to the Royal Garden. Lil Hardin was nice, but about the best piano player I heard was Teddy Weatherford. I played with him at the Ritz Carlton and he is about the best piano player I played with. I was with Oliver around 1920 or '22 I think. We used to shift from The Dreamland to the Royal Garden. After awhile some fellows left and Joe had to send home to get the boys he had. I played with Louis a little while, but not no regular job. He was with us over at The Dreamland. Louis used to play a slidin' cornet. Now Joe tried to play one too. He didn't do no good though. I don't know why but he just couldn't do good on the slidin' trumpet.

Paul Barbarin, he played with us for a while. He's a nice little drummer but he didn't stay in Chicago long. But Baby Dodds is just about as good a drummer as a man wants. On strict time, he's as good a drummer as you can want. He can hold the time. He gets a tempo, he's got it. Now all of those boys I played with, I can play with all of them, but it's so easy to play with Baby Dodds.

Freddie Keppard played with us a while at The Dreamland. It was on 35th and State. He was a good, nice trumpet player. He had one style of playing, though. He had a jazz style too but he didn't have so much of it like the other fellows do. He knew his instrument and he put good tones into it. He was so fat. Time he start to playing he was sweating. Louis now, when he sweats he has plenty of handkerchiefs. But Freddie. Oh! Louis puffs his neck out when he's playing. I never did do that. Puffs his jaw out too. I blow from the throat, just right from the throat, I never puff my jaw. Even on the pedal notes I wouldn't puff my jaw. Now take George Brunies. White fellow that come from over in Algiers, he puffs out just one cheek. There is something you can do about all that puffing. Lay off trombone just about two, three months and change your style of playing. I changed that, 'cause I saw it was no good and it prevented me from making quick passages. All that stops the wind you got back in there.

The part the trombone should play in a band, it depends on how the melody runs. If you got a good stomp melody or something like that, the trombone should be played right between the melody and the other part, the harmony. Like the afterbeats and aftercounts. Use a whole note in some places and then use figurations that you know. Jump in the lead sometimes but don't stay in there too long though 'cause you're taking his part. Play the lead if you have to sometimes, then get away from there and go back to your vamping. See, I could balance well. I could balance any orchestra. Trombone plays a rhythm part too. Arpeggios and things like that. It's nice if you can handle them. Lots of fellows try to handle them and they get so mixed up. If I take a solo, I may put all sixteenths in there. I'm going with the melody right on, but I'm putting something in between there, see. There's a lot of little tricks playing in there and it helps the other fellow. Vamping on the trombone is the best thing a man can do. Vamping and playing the off melody, that sweetens a band up. When you're playing a piece, by music or by ear, listen to the guy, what he is doing over there.

This new stuff is alright but they got no foundation, you might say. No foundation. Everybody's jumping up and out and in and up. You can't tell the significance in a piece. You don't know what they're playing. You can't tell the melody. There ain't no lead. The fellow that's playing the lead should be playing the lead. He's jumping from here and different places. You can't tell what they're playing, but you get one band that has a good lead and then the other fellows playing all that other stuff in there, you know it's better. It sounds better.

# Georg Brunis

Georg Brunis
(originally George Clarence Brunies)
trombone

Born: New Orleans, Louisiana, February 6, 1902
Died: Chicago, Illinois, November 19, 1974

*George Brunies was born in New Orleans, in the Irish Channel. On the advice of a numerologist named Garry Moore, he shortened his name. He was told that this would bring him success in the music field, although he was already the most famous member of an unusual musical family. Five of the Brunies brothers were well-known New Orleans musicians.*

*Georg began playing professionally when he was ten years old. In 1920 he went to Chicago, originally to join a drummer named Ragbaby Stevens, from New Orleans. Stevens had sent a cable to Georg and his brother Albert, known as Abbie, to come up and join his band, working at a place called Campbell Gardens, on Campbell and Madison. Both Georg and Abbie were leery of the trip north and they spoke to Paul Mares, their friend, who was also a local trumpet player. Mares took the offer and later sent sixty dollars down to Georg in order that he could make the trip to Chicago.*

*The trip north was a provident one for Georg Brunis, as he became a member of the New Orleans Rhythm Kings, one of the earliest bands from New Orleans to record.*

*About 1924 Brunis began a long association with bandleader Ted Lewis, which lasted, on and off, for seventeen years. Joined later by his friend Muggsy Spanier, he toured extensively and recorded with Lewis.*

*In the 1930s and 1940s Brunis was active in New York. For over ten years he was featured at Nick's, in the Village. After 1950 his activities were again centred on Chicago.*

I was actually raised in the Irish Channel. That's one block from the Mississippi River, Tchoupitoulas Street. We lived at 2135 Rosseau Street. They used to give lawn parties down there. They had oyster shells and bricks comin' out of the ground and they'd get a tarpaulin and put it down and people would dance on that. Then that bunch from Basin Street used to come up in carloads with brickbats. I'd be watchout man and when they'd come out I'd blow through my hands and whistle. That meant for our guys to be ready. Oh! They used to fight like the dickens.

I'm of German descent and part Belgian, I think. Never did know for sure. See, my grandparents were born in Leipzig, Germany and if the Kaiser had won the war, we'd have been wealthy people, which I'm glad he didn't. Their name was Brunias, that's the German way.

Some of the early bands I remember were: they had a colored band they called Buddy Petit. Then there was Papa Laine's; he used to call it the Reliance Band. As for us, we played on a streetcar. Emmet Rogers and my brother Abbie and me. We had a uniform . . . just hats. Abbie had "Leader" on his. I had "Manager" on mine and Emmet, who was a drummer, had "Brunies" on his. We used to play on a sightseeing car and we made good money. These three guys, they'd point out the interesting points of New

Orleans and then we play, like, harmony and stuff, then Rogers would go through with the hat and we'd make fifteen to twenty dollars a day. Later, the Brunies brothers on their job would specialize in harmony. That's pretty stuff. 'Course it's barber shop stuff, but that's what started music. To me, blues come from the Jewish hymns, then they added African bongos and tom toms and they made rhythm to it. That's my opinion of the blues, and to me all blues sound alike. As for my brothers; there was Rudy, the oldest, who played bass fiddle into his seventies. Next comes Richard, the trumpet player, then Henry, trombone, Merritt, Abbie and me. My sister and mother, they played both guitar and piano. My old man would get us all out after dinner and make us all play. We had to. I was playing the upright alto, that was my first instrument. When I saw my brother Henry play trombone, I drooled and I threw away the alto and wanted to play trombone. My sister and mother, they would get in there and we'd play *Mocking Bird* and *When The Maple Leaves Are Falling.* We'd start to playing so nice, with my father playing the violin, then we'd start to jazzing it up and he'd run the hell out of us, throw the violin down and say, "You little jazz damn fools."

My brother Henry, now there was the boy that played trombone. I wish he was living. All the stuff I do is from my brother Henry, playing with the foot and all. Mike Riley and those guys are getting the credit, but my brother was the first one to do that. He could put a trombone in one position and play the national anthem. What control of the lip he had.

In the early days I was still playing that alto horn when Papa Laine used to pick me up to go to work in his Reliance Band. He picked me up and we'd play a dance and get fifty cents an hour. Crescent Park, Owl's Hall, Suburban Park and Alvero Park in Algiers. He'd take me to the job and if it was too far away from my house, then I'd sleep at his house and he'd bring me home next day. He'd give my mother the money and she would give me a dime to get a piece of candy or something.

Well, "Pantsy" Laine, that's Papa Laine's son. His name was Alfred but they

*Henry Brunies*

called him "Pantsy." He played trumpet and his brother-in-law, Leonce Mello, was playing the trombone. I was still with that alto horn.

One time Leonce got under the weather and he didn't show up. We were playing down at the Crescent City Carnival Club, and Pantsy says, "Geez, what we gonna do for a trombone?" "Well I can play the trombone parts on the alto." Pantsy says, "Why don't you try the trombone, Brunies?" So I got to put the trombone together and I liked it. I was thinking all the time of my brother Henry and how I could never be that way. I did a lot of guesswork as it was all new to me. There was never anyone who even showed me the seven positions. Nothing; that just came naturally. I don't think if I'm in the fourth position. I feel it. My heart puts my arm there. I never asked no one about tonguing and breathing, even.

So from then on I played trombone. Of course I played snare drum in parades when I was really young, sometimes. When Tony Sbarbaro had a dixieland band in Biloxi, he used to say, "Brunies, take my drum, I'm tired." Later he played with the Original Dixieland Jazz Band. Drums and kazoo. Tony's a good drummer.

The first trombone I bought for three dollars in a hock shop. This one I got now I had for years. It's about 47 years old. I sent it back to the King people once and they fixed it up good and lacquered it. I would use things for mutes – molasses cans, a bottle, and I've even used a phonograph record. Let it loose and let it vibrate.

I never learned to read music much. Never took a lesson in my life. Well, no, I did take one lesson from Jerry Shermer and he says, "Your ear's too good. You can't learn to read music. I give you something and you'll come in the next day and fake it." Now, my brother Henry, he taught himself to read, then he passed away. I was superstitious, I was afraid to learn to read. I'd advise young kids to get the fundamentals of the horn. Learn the fundamentals through music and after they learn the horn, know the notes, they can listen to records. Listen to those ideas and try to improve the ideas. That's what Ted Lewis always told me, "Brunies, when you go out on your own," he says, "take something somebody else does and try to do it better. When you make a mistake, make a big one and then pull a gag with the audience. You make 'em laugh and they'll forget all about your mistake." He was a great showman and he gave me a great schooling for talking to an audience.

I want to say something about my brother Richie. Most of the time I'd play for Papa Lainc. There was a guy by the name of Benny Mars. He hired all the bands. They used to hire my brother Richie two years in advance. He was the only guy with a little cornet that could hold a 17-piece brass band up with one cornet. They'd stop at City Hall and they'd hear Richie comin', and, "here comes Richie Brunies." They could tell it. Every chorus he'd go up an octave higher. Sometimes a key higher. The boy had an iron lip.

My father died before my mother. He was a hotel maitre d' of all the Mexican Gulf hotels in the southern territory. He supervised them and he was really a hell of a baker. Oh brother! What a baker that man was. That's why we all learned how to cook. Richie was a good cook. I cook fairly well. Abbie's a wonderful cook. Richie was working on the boats, cooking for the crew and they went crazy for his food. Richie's in a bad way now.

Another thing, how I came to get in the union. The union was more stronger then than now. In fact there's no union at all in Biloxi, where my brother Abbie lives. The people in Biloxi didn't want the union and the non-union men are making more than the union guys. Anyway, my uncle had a place called Brunies and Martin. He bought Martin out and then it became Brunies and Brunings. So Bruning wanted me. I had sat in there one time and I wasn't in the union. I was a punk kid. The drummer at the place was the secretary of the union and Bruning says, "I want this boy to work here. I want him in the union." So, he put up 50 dollars and I hadda go down to the union for an examination.

To get in the union: they put up a piano player and he tries you out. I couldn't get in reading for trombone so I went in on cymbals. He played a number I knew backwards. It was, *The Spirit Of Independence.* So I start in, ching, ching, ching. He says, "You're in. That's enough." They thought I was reading it. I was about 16 or 17 then.

Once we got a job in Alexandria, Louisiana. Well, we went in as impostors. We posed as the Original Dixieland Jazz Band. They had a beautiful victrola in the Battle House Hotel, on the porch. These soldiers, and all, sit on the lawn and we had learned *Livery Stable Blues* just note for note. So one guy in the audience, he was a soldier; he says, "Look. I know the Dixieland Band. Those guys are impostors." So the mayor made us get out of town. It was only Alexandria, Louisiana, so I didn't want to send home for

money, so I went to work in a restaurant. I didn't know anybody or anything, so I hadda work 16 hours a day. That's where I learned to holler, "A bowl of chilli, a bowl of hell and oyster stew. A Cemetery Special." I learned all the waitress's things. I was getting $16 a week and all I could eat. I didn't stay long. Just long enough fare to get back to New Orleans.

Back in New Orleans there were some great musicians. On the clarinet, Roppolo and Fazola were, to me, the men. "Rapp," he didn't practise much. Used to run over variations a little bit, you know. For trumpet, Emmett Hardy. If I only got a record of Emmett Hardy on trumpet! The kid was young. He had leakage of the heart and if you ask Louis about him, he said that Emmett was the best. Louis is a changed man now. All his opinions have changed. I played with Emmett Hardy on the boat, but we never had luck enough to get him on record. Bix liked him. He didn't blast much. He'd just play little variations and stuff around. Improvise.

Steve Brown is probably the greatest bass player I ever heard. He was wonderful on the old Goldkette records. As for piano players, some of those early bands we played in didn't even use pianos. "Buzzy," I think his first name was, Williams and Joe Farrell.

*Steve Brown*

*Left to right: Emmet Rogers, Abbie Brunies and George Brunies*

That's about the only ones I know. I know Nick La Rocca's brother; he tried to learn trombone and he played and tried and tried. He got mad and threw it against a wall. It wasn't in him. It's something that's got to be in you. If you haven't got it, you haven't got it.

Tom Brown was terrific too. A guy by the name of Harry James, not the trumpet player, brought them up here to Chicago. That's when Larry Shields and Yellow Nunez switched jobs. Nunez came up with the Original Dixieland Band and they played at the Red Lantern. Tom Brown came up here with the farmers' uniforms and the straw hats. They had these dusters on with straw hats, sun hats. Anyway, so Nunez went with Brown's Band and Shields went with the Dixieland Band. Now, you take them tunes. Nobody knows who wrote 'em. The Dixieland Band came up here and copyrighted them. *Tiger Rag* was called *Number Two* and *Dixieland One Step* was *Mutt and Jeff*. *Sensation* was called, *Meatballs*. The only tune they wrote, I think, was *Clarinet Marmalade*. That wasn't played in New Orleans.

In general, all those New Orleans fellows stick to the slower tempos, where some of the more modern guys try to rush everything. Muggsy's got a tendency to play a lot of fast music. We humor it. We open, say, with a number like *Muskrat* or *Jazz Me Blues* and then the second number, *Someday Sweetheart* or *Squeeze Me*. Then we build a semi-fast number like *Strutters' Ball* or *Georgia Brown*, then we close it with *Rampart*. Give 'em a little variety. I mean, take a piece like *The Saints*. Sometimes they play that so fast you could never march to it. Like, *Panama* and that stuff. Those are march tunes. You can't play them if the beat ain't there. We call that circus music.

The nucleus of good dixieland is a good lead trumpet, unless he's playing a solo. Variations on the clarinet and the contra-melody, they call it, on the trombone. That's the counter melody, and the piano plays a good oompah chord, 'cause dixieland bands nowadays don't use a bass fiddle; they only have five pieces. The drummer can play four beats, or he can play two. Anyway he feels like. Me, I use a lot of variety, soft and sweet. That's what you call shading. Now all the bands are doin' it. Like I play this *South Rampart Street*, I'll stay subdued and all of a sudden I'll holler, "Walk it!" Then we build up and we blast. Right now, I got this thing. I burned my lip. I burnt it with a cigarette. I been suffering the last four nights pressin' that mouthpiece up against it. That's an accident but if you have stomach upsets, you'll start getting cold sores and things. Then these guys put Campo Phenique and all that stuff on there. I just press 'em and break 'em. See, I've got what they call a freak lip. Like Louis. Muggsy calls me Ol' Liver Lip.

The one trombone I got used to now, it's a medium bore. Some people like small bore for high notes, but I specialize in low notes, bass notes. Teagarden cleans his horn out after every set, I clean mine out every month. To me the greatest tone I ever heard on a trombone was Jerry Shermer, he played with Sousa. It sounds like the human voice, to me. The most beautiful thing I heard on the trombone in my whole life.

As for the records I made, they all sound the same to me. I like the New Orleans Rhythm Kings ones. See, I enjoyed working with Paul Mares. He was wonderful, he played wonderful. Paul is like Muggsy, he has what you call a good drive, and if the trumpet is driving, it makes you drive. Now as for the *Tin Roof Blues*, Paul and I used to call it, *The Rusty Rail Blues*, and when we came up here, Walter Melrose, the publisher, why, at the time he was in the real estate business out in Barrington. He came up and he liked the tune, gave us $500.00 advance. He heard the tune at Friars. So he says, "You don't mind if I do anything with it?" He's never been in New Orleans. So, he says, "We're gonna change the title." There's a place in New Orleans, out in Gentilly, called The Suburban Gardens, they used to call it the Tin Roof Café. So Melrose took it and he put lyrics to it. "I have seen the bright lights burning up and down Broadway; there's no lights like my home town," and all that stuff. Well at that time we put Roppolo in there. There was Rapp, Paul and I, then later we put Mel Stitzel and Ben Pollack in, because we didn't figure it was going to do anything.

So, years later; after twenty eight years, you're supposed to copyright a tune. I didn't figure it was nothing, 'cause I was getting twelve to eight dollars on, you know, royalties. So, one day I hear this thing, *Take Me In Your Arms and Never Let Me Go*. I says, "Man, that's *Tin Roof* note for note." So, I call up "Teeny," Paul's wife and I says, "Teeny, have you got a copyright on *Tin Roof?*" She says, "Yes, you can thank me 'cause I just had it renewed." So I said, "Man, you saved the day." Well then we go with this guy, this, ah, Copeland. This kid put the lyrics to it, this is one of the writers. Well, to me, what sold the song is the melody. I used to hear cops on the street whistling it. It's the melody that sold it. So, he's in on it. Melrose got the publishing rights. I get the writer, Paul and Pollack and "Teeny." So we made a few bucks, but it was too many splits.

I guess the trombone solo from that record is the most copied trombone solo. On the date we just played. Rapp took that high chorus and they pointed to me. I just played what felt natural. When first I got in there, I think *Bugle Call Rag* was the first thing we made. And I start blasting in that horn, boy, and the record start jumping all around. So they made me turn around and play to the wall, get the blast in the wall instead of the horn. But you know, a lot of the New Orleans boys had music that others took. You know that thing the late Glenn Miller made, *In The Mood?* That was Wingy's tune. He had to prove that he wrote that. He had a record of *Tar Paper Stomp* he called it. He got a lot of money out of that from Glenn Miller. Wingy is a pretty shrewd boy when it comes to money. He acts illiterate, but he's pretty smart.

For the kids who want to take up instruments – lead a clean life, get a lotta rest, be good and polite to people, and you'll always get by. Stay away from the lush. That's all I tell 'em. Of course, I don't practise what I preach, but for newcomers, it's a good idea. I hear guys say, "What are you trying to prove with that Dixieland two-beat stuff?" To me, Dixieland ain't strictly two-beat. Dixieland is a melody, variations, counter melody, and a beat, whether it's two-beat or four-beat, it's Dixieland.

Yeah, Kid Ory has done a lot of good tromboning and travelling. There's no one that plays like him here now. *(Scats)* That's trombone music, yeah. But now they play it like a trumpet. The trombone sounds like a trumpet now. **Punch Miller**

Music was different in New Orleans because many were too blamed ignorant to read, not like New York or Chicago musicians. Keppard and others practised at the 25 Club, in New Orleans. They would all go down there after they got through with their jobs, late at night. I would play over the new pieces because I could read. Then some other pianist would get up and try to play it; perhaps he could play it a little better. But they would forget it before they got through and would have to fill in with a break and other stuff. That's where the improvisation came from. They had nothing to do all day but play checkers; so they couldn't help learning their instruments. There were no schools; if they wanted to take up an instrument, they had all the time in the world to perfect their playing **Richard M. Jones**

In that Excelsior Band, and Onward band, and Tuxedo Band, they were all readin' bands, strictly music . . . and that Allen band too. You just had to know your stuff, or else you got to have a mighty good head to play if you couldn't read music. 'Course, if you read some, well, you could make out. When they put them heavy marches on you, you had to jump. **Sunny Henry**

*Jim Robinson listening to a band in the carriageway at Preservation Hall:*
Listen, *(during a clarinet solo)*, listen! Where's the trumpet? I don't hear the trumpet playing. There's something wrong with a band when the trumpet isn't playing. It's not right, the band's not right. *(trombone solo starts)*. Where's the trumpet? The trumpet's supposed to be playing. That's bad. That's bad. Same routine. **Jim Robinson**

And Man, we went on that parade [annual Odd Fellows parade] . . . and we start playing that day and they used to make some long parades. They used to start around 8 o'clock, 9 o'clock and play until five or six o'clock in the evening. So we played and played and we'd see musicianers done got burnt out, you know, and settin' out, and the same Sunny Henry say, "Man, I'm gonna quit." Say, "Look at that man over there." One fella dropped dead, you see. **Harrison Barnes**

I enjoy playing for people that are happy. I like to see people happy. If everybody is in a frisky sprit, the spirit gets to me and I can make my trombone sing. If my music makes people happy, I will try to do more. It is a challenge to me. I always want people around me. It gives me a warm heart and that gets into my music. When I play sweet music, I try to give my feelings to the other fellow. That's always in my mind. Everyone in the world should know this. **Jim Robinson**

NEW ORLEANS STYLE:
CLARINET

# OMER SIMEON

Omer Victor Simeon
clarinet/alto, baritone saxes

Born: New Orleans, Louisiana, July 21, 1902
Died: New York City, September 17, 1959

*Omer Simeon was born into a Creole family. His father was a cigar maker and had his own little factory in back of the house. The family moved to Chicago in 1914 and, after graduating from school, Omer started work in the Post Office. He became interested in music and studied clarinet with Lorenzo Tio. He learned fast and within a few years was working with Charles Elgar at the Wisconsin Roof Garden, over the Wisconsin Theater, in Milwaukee. He recorded with Jelly Roll Morton in 1926-27 and became Jelly's favorite clarinetist. Beginning in the 1930s, he played many years in the big bands of Earl Hines and Jimmy Lunceford. He also took up teaching clarinet and gave lessons at Erskine Tate's School of Music, where he had over 25 pupils, most of them white. At times he played with the pit orchestra at the Metropolitan Theater on Chicago's South Parkway. Simeon was able to play a show without a rehearsal, was an excellent reader and was rarely short of work.*

*From 1947 through 1950 he played in the Eddie Wilcox band and from 1951 until his death in 1959, Simeon played in the small group led by Wilbur De Paris.*

I was born in the "back of town" section of New Orleans in 1902. I heard plenty of music during my early years. I heard the bands playing on the wagons and a number of parades, quite a few of 'em mostly downtown around Claiborne and Orleans, close to the neighborhood. The family moved to Chicago in 1914 and a few years later I became interested in music. Particularly, I was interested in the clarinet by going to a little theater at 131st and State and watching the pit orchestra.

Manuel Perez came to Chicago with a jazz band from New Orleans and played at the Arsonia Café. Lorenzo Tio was in the group and my dad knew him from New Orleans. He had been a cigar maker like my dad and they arranged for me to take lessons from him. Every Sunday morning I went over to where Tio lived. He wouldn't take any money for the lessons, so to repay him, my father offered him a box or two of cigars every week. This must have been around 1918, at the close of World War 1. With Tio, I studied the legitimate side of the instrument, tone, holds and such. Tio used an Albert system clarinet and had a music book with pages that had all turned brown. I practised an hour or hour and a half each day, or else had a scolding. My dad had an old nickel-plated cornet, just as a hobby, but cigar making was his trade.

Almost everyone was using Albert system at that time, all through the early twenties. The tone holes are a little farther apart than the Boehm. It's a little farther stretch. The bore seems a little larger too. You can hold an Albert system at the end of the bell and look through it from bell to barrel and notice the difference in the bore of the instrument. I guess that's what makes the tone a little broader. The Boehm has keys that simplify the intricate passages but speaking for myself, the Albert, well I can handle it better. I use a reed between 2½ and 3. Just about a medium reed. All your tones are

better in different registers. You have to find a reed that you can control in all registers. A stiff reed is good for tone in the upper, for your high notes, and a soft reed is good for your low notes.

Tio used to take me on the West Side to play in a brass band. That's where I got that experience, on the West Side of Chicago. It was like a military band. I did a little free dance work around Chicago too. My brother had a little group called, "Al Simeon's Hot Six," and we used to play club dates with about five or six pieces. Preston Jackson and Natty Dominique were in the group. Cliff Jones, the drummer known as "Snags", was also in the group. In 1923 I joined Charlie Elgar's Creole Band in Milwaukee. Then I considered myself a professional, you know. That was about the first big band that I played with.

In those days Johnny Dodds was the well known clarinetist around Chicago. He influenced a lot of youngsters in the early twenties. In fact, I was influenced by Johnny's playing. He was a good blues man and for stomps, as we called them. He had drive and a really good conception of jazz. A good ad lib man. I heard Jimmie Noone at the old Nest Club. Later that name was changed to the Apex Club. It was on 35th Street, on the opposite corner from the Plantation, almost across the street from the old Sunset. As far as the clarinet was concerned Jimmie Noone and Johnny Dodds were the leaders around Chicago. They were two different types as far as style and tone. Jimmie was more relaxed and had a beautiful tone, very smooth execution and a technique very clean. He might not have been the blues man Johnny was, but he was terrific. When I took lessons from Tio, he always had his clarinet alongside of him. Certain passages that I couldn't finger he showed me how to finger them. He used a 13-key clarinet. An Albert System. It might have been a Penzel-Mueller. Anyway, he impressed on me to pat my foot. For a whole note, 4 beats, for a half note, 2 beats. He always impressed on me to keep that foot going while I was playing exercises. Later on, after I started playing with little bands around Chicago, then the drums did that. You got your tempo and the beat from the drums. I mean the drums inspire you to play. A drummer should push soloists. Should give him the drive. It's very important in a jazz band. But Tio played more like Jimmie Noone than Dodds. He had a broad tone. A big broad tone. I never heard him on jobs much because, when I was a youngster, I wasn't allowed to go in the places where he played. I just heard him, you know, in the house.

In 1926 I was recommended to Jelly by a trumpet player. So, Jelly called and we had sort of a little audition. A number Jelly composed called, I think, it was *Mamanita*. I went over to the place where he was staying and he placed some music on the piano and I read over it, you know, sight. So he said, "Well, you're in!" So that's how I got recorded with Jelly. Two of my favorite records with Jelly were *Black Bottom Stomp* and *The Chant*.

I joined Joe Oliver in 1927. We had a recording session, just before we left Chicago. I think that was on the Brunswick label. I remember recording *Willie The Weeper* on which I played the soprano, the clarinet and the alto saxophone. All three instruments on that particular arrangement. Barney Bigard played tenor in that band, Kid Ory was the trombone, Paul Barbarin, drums, Luis Russell on piano and later on, when we reached St Louis, Willie Foster joined the band, Pop Foster's brother. So did

Red Allen, and Paul Barnes on alto. All three joined us in St. Louis. After that we went to New York and stayed about a month, or a couple of months. We played an engagement at the Savoy for two weeks but Joe didn't have a very good booking agent so it was really a struggle to keep the band together. They started leaving one by one, coming back to Chicago. I think Clarence Black was the first to leave, then Ory and eventually Barney and I left. Joe was having trouble with his teeth then. He didn't have a good broad tone.

I played with Tate at the Metropolitan Theater in 1928, '29 and '30. We played legitimate music there besides jazz. Did presentation work in the pit and we played background music for the silent pictures. I got pretty familiar with different overtures and classical numbers.

Keppard and I worked together for a while. He was a terrific drive trumpet player. Had much more drive than Oliver. Big tone he had and could play very sweet on his instrument, very sweet solos. I played with Roy Palmer on a few jobs around Chicago. He had a nice round tone. A very good musician who could transpose and play any part, clarinet part, trumpet part or cello part, almost any part.

Around 1931 I joined Earl Hines at the Grand Terrace Café. It was a night club with a floor show. We had to play dance music and also play music for the show. Anyone that wasn't familiar with reading music, why, there was no place for him in the band. Sometimes we played part of an overture, a dance routine for the chorus, part of an overture like *William Tell* or *Light Cavalier*, in the floor show. So if a musician couldn't read, then he was lost. We played mostly special arrangements which were made by members of the orchestra. Sometimes an outside arranger too. Cecil Irwin was one of the arrangers when I joined the band, then later on Jimmy Mundy; he is quite a famous arranger now. Well, we did mostly one-nighters and theatre engagements up until about 1937 when I left the band.

I played in so many big bands, but in a small band you have a little more liberties. You can play what you want and the way you feel. You get a lot of kicks playing in a small group. Like the type which I'm playing with now, this Wilbur De Paris band. There's six now, the regular New Orleans instrumentation. In a big band you have to stick to the score until it comes to your solo, when you can ad lib. So that's the difference between the two bands. Now this little band I'm with, it's more on the old style jazz. The trumpet carries the melodies. The trombone, his range was below the trumpet, sort of in between the bass or baritone. The clarinet weaves in and out between the trumpet and trombone, variations on the melody or the chords. Numbers like, *High Society*. That's an example. I don't think about the chords when I play. It comes natural. After you're familiar with the tune and the chord progressions, your different changes, you're up and down on the instrument. If the chord holds over to another bar, you have to concentrate on that too.

I never studied harmony, not very much 'cause I never did play piano much. Sometimes I go to the piano to figure out a chord. You get familiar with the chords through the piano and the banjo or the guitar, then it comes natural. I mean, if I play in a trio, I don't change my style. First you introduce the melody, you get the melody established so the people can know what you're playing, then play solos. Improvise, ad lib, whatever you want to, then you probably, in the last chorus, swing the lead. If there's a trumpet in the group, then you don't concentrate on the melody, because the trumpet carries the melody. But with just one wind instrument, you have to play the melody and everything else. Use all your registers but generally in the last, what you call the "out" chorus, when you reach the climax, you have to really drive then on the out-chorus, then you're in your upper register, for the high notes. It depends on the number of choruses you're playing. I very seldom play a whole tune in one register. Usually, I cover the whole instrument. On staccato style, you pronounce the letter T, like T-u or Tut, very short, very quick stroke of the tongue, that's staccato playing. The legato is more like you would pronounce, Dah Dah Dah. That's legato.

I never did any triple tonguing. In jazz it's not necessary for clarinets to double-tongue or triple-tongue. At this type of work that we're doing now, with a small band, I use a reed for about three or four nights. In a pit orchestra maybe a week, or probably longer. I tried a plastic reed. I had one in 1942 and haven't played one since. I got good results out of it, but prefer the cane, as far as tone is concerned.

As for the reed, if a reed is a little too stiff, then you have to take a little penknife or a little piece of fine sandpaper and shave it. I always shave at the heel of the reed. I never shave the tip 'cause that ruins the reed, or the heart of the reed when you shave both sides, that's no good either. I also use what they call single embouchure: teeth resting on the upper part of the mouthpiece. The lay – that's very important too. I use a medium lay. I'm using, now, a Selmer. Improved Selmer. Jimmie Noone used that too. Noone, Barney Bigard and Albert Nicholas. I think, Albert, he changed to a Boehm but Barney still uses an Albert.

If you ask me to advise youngsters on playing New Orleans jazz, I would say, try to develop your own style of playing. Your own tone. It's not necessary to play jazz that you have to copy another man's style, or copy his tone. He probably played 40 or 50 years ago. Most all the clarinetists in New Orleans had different styles. Johnny's style was different from Jimmie's. All of them had their own individual style. So I would advise all youngsters to develop their own style of playing.

# EDMOND HALL

Edmond Hall
clarinet

Born: Reserve, Louisiana, May 15, 1901
Died: Boston, Massachusetts, February 11, 1967

*Ed Hall worked with many of the city's most exciting young trumpet players, but the desire to travel led him to make extensive tours of Texas, Louisiana and Florida. In 1927 he joined Alonzo Ross and travelled with the band to New York. With New York as his base, he worked with Claude Hopkins, Lucky Millinder, Red Allen, Teddy Wilson, Eddie Condon and led his own sextet at the Cafe Society. In 1955 he joined the Louis Armstrong All Stars, and after a visit there with the band, in 1959, moved to Ghana, intending to settle there. After a few months he returned to New York and free-lanced. He also made several solo tours of Europe.*

I was born in Reserve, Louisiana. That's about twenty or twenty-one miles from here, on May 15th 1901. All the family were musical. My father was a clarinet player; he used to play with the famous Onward Band. He went to New York with the band in 1892. Yes, the famous Onward Band, and Jim Humphrey was the leader of the band – Willie Humphrey's grandfather. The whole band used to read. He had all these clarinets. You know in those days a clarinet player in a band had two or three different kinds of clarinets: A-flat, B-flat, C, E-flat; he had all of them. So quite naturally, he just had five boys in the band, and everybody just picked up a clarinet and started playin'. I had an uncle who was a guitar player; practically all the boys could play guitar too. His name was "Chunk", that was a nickname. He just played for his own amusement.

My first instrument was guitar. I used to work with Kid Thomas, playing guitar. Later on I started fooling with the clarinet. My oldest brother was the same way; he started on guitar, then changed to clarinet, so I picked up the guitar and then I changed to clarinet. I just picked it up. My very first job, I think it was with Thomas's band. Just a bunch of kids; we picked up our instruments, then started to play. Thomas Valentine was the trumpet player; we had a drummer by the name of Lionel; I don't know what his last name is now. He used to work with an old-time band around Reserve by the name of Dejan. I remember the bass player's name; he died here, not so very long ago; his name was Sisaint. We had a trombone, too, but can't place his name.

I came to New Orleans, and I joined Bud Rousell's band. I remember the first job I played was with Lee Collins. Bud Rousell played at a place back o' the station up on Rampart Street, they used to call it Function. I remember one Saturday night I got a job playin' with Buddy Rousell, and Lee Collins. I worked with him for quite a while, then it was another band I got with, by the name of Gus Metcalf, a trombone player who used to live uptown. Him and Kid Ory could pass for brothers. The drummer was "Black Happy." Gus Metcalf was the kind of guy, when he'd get a date like that, he'd go around and get different musicians and just pick up a band; tonight you'd be playing with one bunch of guys and the next night with another bunch!

I listened to a lot of clarinet players. I used to like Jimmie Noone, Johnny Dodds,

Big Eye Louis, Picou and Lorenzo Tio. Piron was going to New York. Maison Blanche was the ones who financed the whole trip. Piron was a cripple guy. He played left hand violin, and the last dance they gave, I remember, was at the Knights of Pythian's Hall, out on the old Rampart Street, and I happened to go to the dance that night.

Buddy Petit was the first trumpet player I ever heard spoke about different chords, minor, major, augmented. Bands used to follow his policy. His band was all the go and the rest of the bands used to follow right behind. I remember the time that we played new tunes. Buddy would go down to a music store on Canal Street and he'd go get a piano copy, and play it right off. The rest of the boys would catch it, and that's how we used to get the new tunes, and other bands would pick up the tunes as we played 'em. He's the one started me off, he was my inspiration to start to playing music.

I remember practically all the guys in Buddy Petit's band 'cause we left after I got out there with the band, we left for Covington, Louisiana. That was about 1920 when that picture was taken [See page 221]. I remember that it was taken out in the street in Covington, Louisiana. When I got with Buddy's band, he had this boy, Buddy Manaday, playing banjo, Chester Zardis, bass. "Face-O" (Eddie Woods) was the drummer, George Washington, trombone. When I left, they were the same as in the picture, but the singer there, I don't know who he was. I've never remembered his name. Oh, we played all of those tunes, all of those Dixieland tunes, *High Society*, *Clarinet Marmalade*, and *Tin Roof Blues*. This was Buddy's number, he made up *Tin Roof Blues*. The number had a special name, and the *Tin Roof Blues* was the background to a guy playing a solo. The background was taken and they made a tune out of it. When I heard it, it was *Tin Roof Blues*. We went on tour after we closed in Covington, and we went to Alabama and Mississippi and toured for awhile.

This guy used to hire Buddy. He said Buddy looked like a puff adder when he played. I think he was mixed with Indian; it had to be, his complexion and his hair, he had hair kinda looked like horse meat. I never see a guy with hair with such coarse grain. About that tour, first we left New Orleans and went to Houston, Texas, to play jobs and then another guy came up to us, and say he got a job for us to go to Galveston, Texas. I'll never forget, we took a piano player from New Orleans with us, but after we get to Texas, we found that this piano player wasn't what he supposed to be so we hired another piano player up there by the name of "Lazy Daddy", and he played with us. We was up there for about three or four months. Then we left and went to Lake Charles, Louisiana, and played with a bunch there for a while. That's how Buddy split up when we left Lake Charles, Louisiana. Buddy Petit came home and "Face-O" came home with the trombone player by the name of Ambrose, that's Lawrence Toca's uncle. I stayed with that band when they left me in Lake Charles. Buddy came back. After I came back, we got together again and that's how we happened to go to Pensacola, Florida. Buddy didn't play too high, he was always right there in the staff, he really could play. He had a nice tone, and the way he played, you could tell that he was well schooled. He knew what he was doing and he knew his instrument, there's no question about that. That's the thing that kinda got me interested in music. He played real pretty. Didn't try to get a lot of freak effects and things like that out of a horn, mostly a pretty mellow tone. He didn't play too loud. Buddy was on the order of Bobby Hackett. Nothin' loud, just knew his instrument and he played with a lotta feelin'.

Buddy was a better trumpet player than Chris Kelly. Maybe Chris could hit a lot of higher notes, but he wasn't in Buddy's class. Chris was much more powerful, he could blow loud and everything but for knowing his instrument, I'd say Buddy was the guy.

Kid Rena was another that could do a lot of playing too. He was louder than Buddy. All of them came up just about that same time, Kid Rena, Buddy Petit, Louis Armstrong. Joe Oliver was just before their time. I don't know when Joe Oliver left. When I came to New Orleans, I think Joe Oliver was in Chicago. I don't know too much about Joe Oliver. I heard him several times, because he came out to Reserve when I was a kid and played. He was with Kid Ory, Baby Dodds, Johnny Dodds and that bunch, you know, when I heard 'em.

Our piano player, "Lazy Daddy", was one of them real good ones, at that particular time. He had been in the business for a long time, 'cause he was in Mexico playing for shows and singers. He come from somewhere in Texas.

I worked with Chris Kelly and Jack Carey for awhile. In Jack Carey's band. "Black Happy" was the drummer. Jack played trombone and Lee Collins played with them for awhile. "Punch" Miller was his favorite trumpet player. They usually called *Tiger Rag* "Play Jack Carey." They'd say "Play Jack Carey" and he used to do some kind of triple tonguing in that, and everybody used to go for that.

Al Morgan was in the band too. Al Morgan, Isaiah Morgan and Sam Morgan were brothers and each used to have a band, but Al Morgan never did play with neither one of his brothers. He used to work with Jack Carey and I think he was also with Chris Kelly. He just gigged around with different guys. Jim Robinson worked in Chris Kelly's band. I went to Pensacola with Buddy Petit, "Red Chinee" Foster on drums, Al Morgan on bass, and Earl Humphrey on trombone. A little fellow, I can't think of his last name, his first name was Manny, banjo player. He was a kid, too, we had to get permission from his father to take him along with us.

We stayed there for quite a while, then things got a little tough, so Buddy Petit came back to New Orleans and Earl Humphrey came back, so we got another trumpet player by the name of Mack Thomas, and we also got a piano player, a woman piano player we picked up in Pensacola, Florida. I can't think of her name, but I think Mack Thomas finally did marry her. George Morris was the trombone player in the band, and after Buddy Petit left, George Morris took the band over. He was from New Orleans, too.

After being in Pensacola, we just decided to make a tour of Florida; I met a fellow there by the name of "Eagle Eye" Shields. He like what I was doin', so he ask me, "Anytime things get tough with you, if you want come down to Jacksonville, let me know and we can get together and I'll put you in my band." So, sure enough, we went back to Pensacola, and later when we was in Mobile, Alabama, things got a little tough, so I thought about this Eagle Eye Shields. So I wrote him a letter. I told somebody in the band, "If this guy means business, I'm gonna ask him for some money." So, I asked him for $50; the next day I got the $50. I said, "Well, this guy mean business." So I went on down. He paid my way, train fare and everything, so I went on down to Jacksonville, and

I stayed with his band for quite a long time.  He used to do all his own bookings, there was no booking agent then.  Another fellow in Jacksonville, had a band, by the name of Alonzo Ross.  He was working in Miami, but he was originally from Jacksonville.  He heard me playing and he wanted me to play with his band.

There's a fella by the name of Broadway Jones from New York.  He used to go down to Miami, Florida, as a singer and decided he'd take a band to New York.  He took the trumpet player from "Eagle Eye" Shields' band so he was stuck for a trumpet player.  So, he asked me where he could get a trumpet player, and I recommended "Cootie" Williams.  That's how Cootie Williams left Mobile, Alabama.  He was a kid and I got permission from his father, and we had him come down to Jacksonville to join the band.  Alonzo Ross wanted me to join his band, so I told him, "I got a kid I got to look out for, which is Cootie Williams, so if you can make room for him, we'll join your band."  In the next couple of days I got a letter from Ross saying, "I'll make room for Cootie."  So I say, "Well, this is it."  So, Cootie and I joined Alonzo Ross's band.  Alonzo Ross was making a tour of Florida, so when he came through Jacksonville, we joined his band.  I think he was working nine months out of a year down in Miami.  So when he went to Florida the next time, to Miami, we went with him.  Victor was scouting around for a band and we had some original tunes.  We were touring in Georgia, and there was a band by the name of Blue Steele.  Here's a funny thing, you remember that tune *Girl of My Dreams*?  Well, it was written by one of the guys in that band.  Victor wanted that particular tune.  Well, they wouldn't sell it to him, unless his band would record it.  So they sent a portable set down to Savannah, Georgia, and they recorded the tune.  We was in Savannah, and we also had some original tunes, so the next day, we, Alonzo's band, recorded for Victor.  So, when the record came out, the guy at the Roseland Ballroom he heard it, and sent for the band to come to New York.  That's how we got to New York and I been there ever since.

I didn't practise anything to get my tone on the clarinet.  It just came to me.  I just picked it up.  I got a tendency to get that kind of a harsh tone with certain tunes I play, it just comes to me. But one thing bad about it, if you do it too much, you can't stop it.  So I just do whatever come to my mind, the way I feel. It doesn't come from a type of reed, you sorta use your vocal chords.  It come from your throat, make it sound rash like, you know, like playing blues, that fit in good.  But if you played a nice ballad, that wouldn't do. I'm using a medium hard, La Vase reed.  All your reeds practically now is numbered, but the old days you just have to pick out the reed till you get a good one.  I only used three mouthpieces in my whole life since I been playing.  Never opened the mouthpiece up, just leave it way they are.

I always used an Albert system clarinet.  There's a lot of people come up to me and ask me why I play Albert system clarinet.  I say, "Well, when I started they wasn't making Boehm system clarinet."  Well, I was wrong, I was just guessing because I had never seen a Boehm clarinet before, you see.  So year before last when I went to France, I went through the Selmer Factory and I just happened to be talking to the owner of the factory, and so I say, "I want you to tell me something, people been askin' me why I play Albert system clarinet, and I'm just guessing,  I tell 'em that when I start to playin' they wasn't making the Boehm system clarinet."  He say, "How long you been playin'?"  I told him. He say, "Well, you're mistaken. Boehm clarinet was invented way back in 1852." So he says, "Wait awhile," and he goes in the factory and comes back with a clarinet, and says, "This is the first Boehm clarinet made. My father made it in 1853. This is the first one ever was made." So I said, "Well, how wrong can you get. From now on, when they ask that question, I know the answer to it now."

I've tried the Boehm several times but my fingers are so large, and always so much closer. I didn't fool with it. I get just as much outa my Albert system as you get out of a Boehm. The tone of an Albert is different for a band. Playin' with a combination - a six piece dixieland band, I don't think a Boehm clarinet fits as there. The tone is beautiful and rich and everything, but it hasn't got the Albert big tone, especially when you get in the low register. You get a bigger tone out of the Albert than you do a Boehm.

I have a friend in Hartford, Connecticut, and he's a symphony man in his sixties, and so he wants to know how in the world I can get over that Albert system so fast. I play a solo on *Clarinet Marmalade* and I play it fast, just as fast as they can get. The faster they play it, the better I like it, see, and he wants to know how I can get over it so fast. I say, "Well, I can play *Clarinet Marmalade*. I've been playin' it so much I can play it and think of something that happen twenty years ago. They can't play it too fast. In the old days we didn't play nothing fast. *Tiger Rag* was about the fastest thing they would play. I used an A clarinet when I made the recording with Mutt Carey playing those Joplin rags. I had to use an A clarinet. I had a time finding one but I finally got one. The redbooks belonged to Bunk, you know. Mutt went over and borrowed them.

In the old days they just used two beats. Four beats wasn't introduced. Only some drummers played four beats. Something like on the last chorus, goin' out, they would use four, but everybody was using two beats. Then you get to that last chorus, everybody's shoutin' in there, then he'd go to four beats. I don't remember anybody playing four on slow blues. When I went to New York, everybody was playing tubas in regular dance bands, you know. Here we always did use the string bass. That was a surprise to see. There ain't but one band, I think, that I know was using a string bass. That was Duke Ellington. Braud happened to be playing there and he was playing bass violin, but all the rest of the bands was playing tubas.

When we started we didn't have no piano. We could set up there anywhere in the street 'cause the guitar player or the banjo, he'd have his instrument with him. There was one piano player here that I know that used to play with a dance band, Steve Lewis. He used to play like this, with his two fingers sticking out.

The first place I heard Louis Armstrong was at Tom Anderson's. At that time he was using a piano. I think Zutty was drummin' with him. Now there was a fellow from Baton Rouge used to play clarinet with some band from there. He's the onliest guy that I didn't see use sharp and flat keys. Just used the the six holes C-natural and B-natural and all the rest of the keys he took 'em off and stopped 'em up and played in any key. How he did it, I don't know, but he's the onliest guy. I don't remember his name. I heard him play one night and he could play it, too.

I would advise clarinetists to practise and keep playing. I had to do a lot of practising to make it.

# Raymond Burke

Raymond Burke
(originally Raymond Barrois)
clarinet

Born: New Orleans, Louisiana, June 6,1904
Died: New Orleans, Louisiana, March 21, 1986

*Raymond Burke was often called a New Orleans original. No other clarinet ever sounded like his. He came from the uptown Irish Channel. He started to play harmonies when he was five. When eight he made his own kazoo with "bread paper" and a bobbin from his grandfather's burlap bag shop. Throughout his career Raymond continued to invent and construct unusual wind instruments. Playing his kazoo, he formed a "spasm band" with his neighborhood friend Leo Adde, playing a toy Christmas drum and pot lids. Playing on the streets, outside Irish Channel saloons, they sometimes collected as much as 50 pennies a night.*

*When he was about 13 Ray bought an Albert system clarinet and was on his way. He began playing with "Pansy" Laine, but his first paid job was with Tom Early's Harmony Band. Although influenced at first by Roppolo, Dodds and others, he developed his own style and individual tone. His broad tone, which, on occasion can be pungent, has become famous for its mellow beauty.*

My family were all musical. I was born June 6, 1904 and I just had music in me. I could play from a kid on up, a little bitty kid. The harmonica, kazoo and a home-made bass drum, like the colored kids did. I started playing with Leo Adde. I had a sort of kazoo made from bread paper and a bobbin pin, and Leo, he had a home-made bass drum and a pot cover with little pieces of iron on it. He played this with drum sticks and it had a good tone. We lived up around the Irish Channel, uptown on St. Andrew's Street. I was about 14 when I bought my first clarinet. I got it from a guy who had hoped to learn it but never did. I remember I paid $2.50 for it. I let it lay around the house a pretty good while, then I got to fiddling around with it and got to learn how to play it. I played along with records of the Original Dixieland Band. Played all of Shields' breaks just like the record. The trouble with that horn was that all the bottom keys were out of wack or something. Of course I didn't know how to play it that well. I went to my aunts' one day and they had a clarinet laying around there. I was looking at it and they said I could have it. I played around with Alfred "Pantsy" Laine, but not for money. My first job was with Tom Early's Harmony Band. He was the bass player and leader. See, Charlie Cordilla was playing in that band but I guess he wanted to move on, so he told Tom Early, "There's a kid up in the Irish Channel. I think he'd make a nice clarinet player for your band." Anyway, Tom came up to the house and I was sitting there playing and he asked me if I wanted to make a job. The job was down at Delacroix Island. The Rosenmeyer brothers were in the band. Clifford played drums, Eddie played trombone and the third brother was called Herbie. After the job ended Tom Early gave me $10, and that was really big money.

One fellow who looked like he took an interest in me was Willie Creager. He'd

show me a few things and some things I just learned for myself. I remember hearing Sidney Arodin just around when I started playing. He was a few years older than me and he had already started playing. He played the Albert system too but he had a different tone than me. He never got a heavy tone but he played beautiful clarinet. He worked in a band they called the Sixola Jazzers, with Steve Loyacano and the piano player Al Moranto. Emmett Hardy was their trumpet player and my friend Leo Adde played drums with them.

My uncle Jules Cassard was a trombone player. He played nice chord piano too, and bass fiddle. He must have played half-a-dozen instruments. I used to see him going out to play music all the time. Well, he arranged for me to go to Eddie Cherie for lessons on the clarinet. Eddie Cherie had a barber shop uptown on St Mary's Street, between Magazine and Camp. His barber shop was for colored, but he played with all the white bands. The bands all knew he was colored. Dave Perkins played with all the white bands too. Achille Baquet played with Tom Brown's band and they didn't know he was colored. One day when they had to arrange a job, Tom Brown went by Baquet's house. He knocked on the door and a colored woman came to the door. Tom said, "I'm looking for Achille Baquet. I must have the wrong home." Anyhow, when I went to my first lesson with Eddie Cherie, he took off the mouthpiece and he took my horn. He just wanted me to blow on the mouthpiece. I just couldn't see that way of teaching so I told my step-daddy I wanted to get my horn back. He went over there with me and got the horn back, but I never did get any lessons.

Like I say, I used to play along with the phonograph, learning all Larry Shields' solos. See, you could alter the speed on those things with a little switch, so you could slow the record down till you had it. I learned the *St Louis Blues* solo just that way, then one night the band played it and I tried to play that solo but fluffed it all up. I think I'm better off trying to play my own thing. When I played at Pete Herman's, some of the guys I played with wanted me to play all these solos like Roppolo or somebody. They want me to play Roppolo's solo on *Weary Blues*, or Dodds' solo on *Canal Street*. I used to do all those things but I don't like to do it because I have my own style of playing. I try to get away from playing other people's solos. The only one I held on to, and I even changed that a little bit, is *High Society*.

As for clarinet players, I liked Roppolo very much. I used to play with his brother Nick Roppolo. He played trumpet. Anyway, I used to play with Nick, and Leon would come around. I remember Leon sitting in for me. He played real good. Harry Shields was very good too. He played the ideal way. I think he was right. He played harmonies. I heard Sidney Arodin play many times. He played *Lazy River* around here a lot but he had a different name for it. We were supposed to make a record, Sidney and I, and another clarinet player. I was supposed to play the harmonica too. We rehearsed for it but never did make it. I liked Edmond Hall, Rod Cless and Larry Shields. I guess Johnny Dodds was one of my real favorites, though. If it was blues, I liked Johnny Dodds and Omer Simeon, too.

I think there is so much difference in the style we played here than in other places. It seems that years ago the drummers played a two-beat drum here. That's on the bass drum. Now I can play much better with just the two-beat sound because the drums play behind me, but that 4/4, you got to follow the drum. It looks like the drum got the lead. We used to play for dancing years ago. I find that the bands play much faster now. Then, it was slower and much better. You could improvise. All this wild beating on the cymbals and all that stuff I just don't like. I think they should get rid of the sock cymbals and all that kind of stuff and just have one cymbal up there. I find the drummers today are playing for the public. Every instrument has its role in a band. I think the trumpet should play close to the melody. I don't like for the trumpet player to play a whole lot of stuff. I like it close to the melody, and not a lot of high notes. I believe the leader or trumpet should stomp off every number. Now years ago, a leader like "Pantsy" Laine used to stomp off. He was comical, he'd say all kinds of funny names, like *Who Broke The Lock* for *Panama*. They used to start *Panama* with two accented bass drum beats, but drummers today are lazy. They don't do that any more. Anyway, sometimes Laine would start off without announcing the number. He'd say, "I don't know what I'm going to play, but man, follow me!" We'd just make up some crazy stuff, but he always stomped the tempo off.

In the old days none of the trumpet players took down. Ever. They all played ensembles, but I like solos sometimes. I like harmonies with the trumpet, when the tune calls for harmony. If you can play harmonies, it's almost like singing. Today most of the clarinetists are so busy playing all kinds of stuff, and high notes, that none of them play harmony. I notice the trombone players, they don't play the tailgate. They're playing trombone like a trumpet. When I started playing, the trombone players would fill in all the holes. Men like Brunies and Tom Brown, they would fill all the holes. Just like Jimmy Durante said, "The trombone's playing the trumpet, the trumpet's playing the clarinet and the clarinet's playing the horses."

If I'm playing my clarinet, see, clarinet and cymbals don't work. No. I've heard some of the old time colored musicians play with a little after beat on the cymbal, in the old bands. It would be a sort of after-beat and was very good. Little Abbie Brunies featured that and Monk Hazel would play that. Very nice too. Leo Adde was a very good drummer too. I think there were a lot of colored drummers who were better, like Chinee and all. Paul Barbarin used to play that way. His drum set used bass drum, snare, just one cymbal and maybe a tom tom. See, drummers like that, they back you up, they push you, but that 4/4 beating . . . you just got to follow that. That kills the feeling. It seems like the bass is better in two-beat too.

As for my clarinet, I don't like the Boehm system. I think the Albert has a much better tone. I never did play the Boehm system. I don't know why they make them. Why have all those keys on there, and a half a dozen ways of making a note? I think the less keys and holes you have on a clarinet the better. The 13-hole clarinet is plenty. Sometimes I take the key off a clarinet and stop up the hole. I think the old time New Orleans clarinet players used to like the fake fingering like I do, especially when they played the blues. Roppolo and people like that, they faked the note and that gives you a better feeling in the blues. The note's a little off or something. I wouldn't say it's a quarter tone off. In between like. Johnny Wiggs used to say, "You can bend the notes."

Also, I got a little different mouthpiece, I guess you know, from the average clarinet. I got a Penzel-Mueller mouthpiece and it's opened up, so it gives a big, big fat tone. One time I swapped mouthpieces with someone and it was hard to blow. I kept fooling around with that mouthpiece. I didn't know a lot about opening up the "lay" by facing it or sanding it, but then I started facing it. I liked it and played on it for years, and made quite a few records with it. I finally broke it and sent it to the Penzel-Mueller people so they could make another mouthpiece as close as they could. They wrote to me and said I might have to ream it out a little, but I never did. I just played it. By opening up the mouthpiece and sanding the lay you have a bigger opening. It's harder to blow, but you get a big fat tone. I use about a No. 3 reed. They last until they get weak. This reed has been on my clarinet for about a couple of months. They usually don't last that long. When I get a good reed I hate to put it aside. I like the sound.

When I play a solo I make it up as I go along. The tune I know. Most of the melodies I know, so I guess I keep the tune in my mind. I might get out on a limb sometimes if the piano player messes me up or plays the wrong chord. I generally just make things up right on the spur of the moment. I mean you can tell if things will fit. I don't really think much ahead. I'm almost right on to the head. I don't try to play a chorus ahead. I just think about it when I'm about to start or I just think about it when I'm playing. I'm never thinking about the chords when I'm playing, just the melody, the tune itself. I keep the tune in my mind and amplify it, or make a run on the,chords. I never worry about the chords when I'm playing. I just play by ear.

In a good jazz band the less notes you play, the more tasty notes, the better for the clarinet. A technician who plays a million notes don't mean nothing. But that tone is so important. An Albert, like I said, will give you that better tone. At one time I was so poor, around 1937 when I was out at the Dandy Inn with Tom Brown, that my horn was from two different makes. One part was wood, the other part molded hard rubber. Isn't that something? I heard that Jimmy Dorsey played a clarinet with the top part Albert and the bottom part Boehm.

You know, in playing music, you try to play for the band. I don't try to outshine anyone, or see how many notes I can make. I try to play to match the trumpet. Play the harmonies or something. When I get on my own chorus, maybe I might show off a little bit, but that's what I think a person should do. They shouldn't be showing off all the time. It steals away from the band sound.

# LAWRENCE DUHÉ

Lawrence Duhé
clarinet

Born: La Place, Louisiana, April 30, 1887
Died: Lafayette, Louisiana, 1960

*After starting with his family's band and Kid Ory's band in La Place, Lawrence Duhé also worked with Ory in New Orleans. Then he led his own band at 101 Ranch, Pete Lala's and Tom Anderson's Annex. He left New Orleans for Chicago in 1917 with the New Orleans Jazz Band. When "Sugar" Johnny Smith died of pneumonia in 1918, Duhé engaged Mutt Carey, and then King Oliver, who later took over the band. After a brief vaudeville tour, Duhé returned to New Orleans in 1923. He worked with Jack Carey, and toured with Evan Thomas, Gus Fortinet's Banner Band, and the Rabbit Foot Minstrels. He settled in Layfayette and joined Frank Brown's band, and retired from music in 1945.*

I came from La Place, Louisiana. Born there April 30th, 1887. My first instrument was guitar. My mother was a singer and my father was a violinist. We had a band there with my three brothers, the Duhé Band. When the clarinet player died, I took up the clarinet and been playing it ever since.

I went to New Orleans with Ory but his head got bigger and bigger so we split and each got a band together with other musicians. Johnny Dodds took my place with Ory. I went with the Eagle Band, with Frankie Duson, and played also with Tig Chambers' Band. He had a good tone but mostly played blues. I also heard Buddy Bolden play a whole lot of times. He was a powerful man but more like Bunk than Louis. I went to playing with Piron at the Roof Garden, right across from the Parish Prison.

Now as for the early clarinet players I heard. Willie Warner, Zeb Lenares and "Kaiser" were all top men, but Big Eye Louis was <u>the</u> clarinet man in New Orleans in those times. He played a C clarinet. Played all the violin parts. It looked like two or three of them started that "get off" stuff at the same time. I don't know who was first. Every clarinet player in New Orleans had a different style. I mean every one. One played diminished scales and another would play straight scales. As for trombone players, I guess Earl Humphrey was the most proficient.

Lots of times we had two clarinets in the band. Me and Sidney Bechet worked for a good while together. I would play first, the reading part, and Sidney would be on the hot stuff. Look like he only had to hear the thing once and he was gone with it. He was the best in the business for that stuff.

In April 1917, I went to Chicago with the New Orleans Jazz Band. They had colored bands up there already. Manuel Perez was up there and Freddie Keppard with his "Creole Band". In fact I had Freddie and Joe Oliver in the same band once. They couldn't get along. Never did. See, Freddie wanted more money. But anyhow, Perez and Keppard; all that was up there before I got there. Our band was "Sugar Johnny" on trumpet, Roy Palmer, a nice smooth trombonist, Louis Keppard, Ed Garland and Herbert Lindsey. Later Tubby Hall played drums with us, and we added Lil Hardin. Then Wellman Braud replaced Ed Garland. We went to the Deluxe Cafe, then the Dreamland.

Mitchell Lucalzi and Lee Kraus were our bookers. We raised some sand up there in Chicago. I was there in the 1919 race riots.

You know Louis got his style from Bunk. I played with Bunk in the Eagle Band, but that was before I went to Chicago. When I went back south I got in the Banner Band, out of New Iberia. Gus Fortinet had that band. Later I got Bunk in the band. He played the second under E.T. Thomas. I never heard no trumpet player better than Evan Thomas. We all read music in the Banner Band and played all kinds of music. We had one real hard number called, *The Doll Dance* that we played real good. We killed all the New Orleans bands that would come out there to New Iberia. In fact not many bands came out there when we were there. They were scared of the Banner Band.

Years later I came here to Lafayette and organized a five-piece band. I had got tired of travelling and moving, so I bought here. I have a small family. My wife and I and just one daughter. I teach here now. Reed section stuff and I write a few songs. I have one called, *I Like To Take My Girl To Tea.*

I have always played Albert system. I got a Boehm once but I couldn't do no good with it. I use plastic reeds now. Got tired of them old reeds.

For youngsters I would say, that a fellow who uses his teeth, he don't have good pressure. It all comes from the lips. I advise putting both lips around the clarinet. It all comes from lip control, all your good tones.

*Lawrence Duhé*

216

I think the first ragtime band I ever heard was Bouboul Fortunea. He was the only man at that time who played the slide trombone. It was approximately – well, before 1900. So I was invited down for a rehearsal . . . That particular style of playing without music was very new to me. I think it was impossible to me! It seemed a sort of style of playing without notes. I remember when we got a new piece of music we would get the music and play the tunes with the music, then, after that we didn't need that music no more. We'd go "out of the way" with it. That was ragtime.                                                                              **Alphonse Picou**

Luis and Lorenzo Tio  – they were originally from Mexico. But they migrated to New Orleans when they were in their thirties. Luis was the better known than Lorenzo, and was the older brother and went mostly for teaching. If you look back and compare the playing of all our fine clarinet players such as George Baquet, Charlie McCurdy, Jimmie Noone, Albert Nicholas and Barney Bigard – all of them boys are of the same school. If you compare their style you'll find that they all follow pretty much in the same pattern of technique, which is different from the average clarinet player that you hear these days.                                                                **Charlie Elgar**

As for why New Orleans was such a musical city and had so many bands, I think one reason had to do with the clubs. There were a lot of private  clubs, organizations, in New Orleans. Two or three guys would get together, you know, and make up the club. And it would grow. So, when a member of the club died, they would hire a band for his funeral, and if the club had some part in a parade, they would have a band for that too. All the clubs tried to outdo each other. Like I remember what used to happen when different clubs would go to their camps out on the water by the lake front. There would be one band playing at the camp of one club and another band at the camp of another, and each band would try to outplay the other. You could hear music real well over the water, you know.     **Edmond Hall**

We would play for parades every Sunday during the spring and summer. Each club would hold a parade on its anniversary each year. They still have one or two parades a week in New Orleans, but nothing to what it used to be. There are not enough musicians in the city to play: the younger fellows don't know the time or the tunes. We used to play *Bugle Boy, Gettysburg, Salutation,* etc The leader always carries a little black bag for his music. Now that leader has a cute trick. When he buys the music it has a title printed on the top, but he cuts the name off and puts a number on. So he calls out, "Number nine."   I can't read music, remember, so you see I had to have a sharp ear.                                                                              **George Lewis**

. . . A mellophone and a baritone horn, that's a brass band. But now they got the idea an alto sax and a tenor sax – they gone got mixed up about it. You can't get them fellows to play them alto, "peck horns." That's where all the harmony, all the music is, them "peck horns."                                                                              **John Casimir**

# SEATING OF NEW ORLEANS BANDS

As in classical orchestras, musicians themselves figured out the best positions to sit many years ago. In fact most of the old photos illustrate the positioning of the various instruments. It seems always quite simple . . . they sat in a straight line, or a semi circle, but the drums were always on the far left and the bass violin balanced them out on the far right, looking at the band from the audience. Thus from left to right were placed drums, trombone, trumpet, reeds, chords, bass.

I have never seen New Orleans musicians play standing up out of choice. Sometimes on a concert stage they will, and sometimes in a night club at the request of the proprietor, but, left to their own devices, they will invariably play in a seated position.

Many musicians from other cities in the United States, and especially those in Europe, have been known to criticize this "sit down to play" arrangement. On many occasions I have read in periodicals that this was the practice of old men and should be dispensed with by younger musicians. How so? Are the men in Ory's band old men in the photo below, or the band on the "S.S. Sidney?" Of course not. This was a positioning ordained by the creators of the music many, many years ago. It not only balanced the band's sound, but by sitting they obviously achieved a more relaxed way of playing their instruments.

Even when recording, most of the older New Orleans musicians adhered to the straight line method of seating. Sometimes they were asked to move by the recording

*The Woodland Band at La Place, Louisiana (c.1905). Left to right: Edward Robinson, Kid Ory, "Chif" Matthews, Raymond Brown, "Stonewall" Matthews, Foster Lewis*

engineer, but again, left to their own devices they would play in formation the way they knew best. At the Riverside recordings in 1961 at the Jeunes Amis Hall, each and every band automatically lined up the same way, day after day. There was no deviation whatsoever. Even today at Preservation Hall musicians line up the same way. In this particular case, because of lack of horizontal room they form two lines. This is described as a "front line" and a "rhythm section". With most New Orleans dance bands there is no "front and back line". All the instruments are playing rhythm at the same time. I have heard many of the "old timers" say of a certain horn man, "Yeah' He plays with a great rhythm." This is meant literally. It is unquestioned that rhythm must flow from all the instruments in the orchestra. Without the rhythm, who would want to dance, and this has been the prime function of a New Orleans band for the last 90 years at least.

Talking to the older New Orleans musicians, they are more than willing to alter their natural line up because of lack of space, certain situations, but in general they will retain the same positioning of the instruments. The years have proved they are right. It is simply a matter of "hearing better." By "hearing better" the average musician feels he is able to play better. It is a natural course of events.

Again there is a tendency to "stand up for the out chorus", with most older New Orleans bands. This gives a clear indication that the number is ending. It is so clear and concise, and in fact gives a psychological impetus to the final chorus of each

*S.S. Sidney band in 1918. Left to right: Baby Dodds, Bebé Ridgley, Joe Howard, Louis Armstrong, Fate Marable, David Jones, Johnny Dodds, Johnny St Cyr, Pops Foster.*

Again there is a tendency to "stand up for the out chorus", with most older New Orleans bands. This gives a clear indication that the number is ending. It is so clear and concise, and in fact gives a psychological impetus to the final chorus of each performance. On dances there is a natural system of signals. Usually the trumpet player will give two stomps of his foot. This means, "look out, we're going." Then he will generally give either the tempo of the piece first then two more "half time" beats and "in." Of course this varies from bandleader to bandleader. George Lewis gave the tempo first then his two beats, many give the reverse signal. Percy Humphrey will give just the two beats. Kid Thomas gave nothing, just began to play. Again his "rhythm" was picked up by the band within a very few beats.

Many of the older musicians would not tell the other musicians what was to be played next, they would merely play a few notes of the song and then into the routine previously described.

If the band did not rise for the last chorus the leader would almost always stomp once on the floor at the end of the penultimate chorus. Everyone always knew what this meant and what to do.

The practice of standing up for solos must have arisen in later years, because in the earlier bands there were very few soloists. Of course this is a common sense way to draw attention to the solo player. Sometimes a player would break ranks and move away from the orchestra, as in the case of Mutt Carey with Ory's band, who would invariably go out in the audience to "toot" the drum and bugle corps. section of *Maryland, My Maryland*, or in later years Kid Thomas, who would go as far as the back of the concert hall to play a chorus or two, but generally the musicians never moved their positions.

*The Peerless Orchestra in the City Park (c.1911). Standing, left to right: Vic Gaspard, Andrew Kimball, Oke Gaspard. Seated: John Vigne, Charles McCurdy, Amand Piron, Coochie Martin.*

*Buddy Petit's Jazz Band, Mandeville, Louisiana (1920). Left to right: Leon René, Eddie "Face-O" Woods, George Washington, Buddy Petit, Buddy Manaday, Edmond Hall, Chester Zardis.*

*Superior Orchestra (c.1910). Seated, left to right: Walter Brundy, Peter Bocage, Richard Payne.
Standing: Buddy Johnson, Bunk Johnson, Big Eye Louis Nelson, Billy Marrero.*

# INDEX OF MUSICIANS

224